IS THE
Mormon
MY
Brother?

**Discerning the Differences
Between Mormonism and
Christianity**

BHP Books by James R. White

Grieving: Our Path Back to Peace
The Forgotten Trinity
Is the Mormon My Brother?
The King James Only Controversy
Letters to a Mormon Elder
Mary—Another Redeemer?
The Roman Catholic Controversy
*What's With the Dudes at the Door?**

*with Kevin Johnson

IS THE
Mormon
MY
Brother?

Discerning the Differences Between Mormonism and Christianity

JAMES R. WHITE

BETHANY HOUSE PUBLISHERS
MINNEAPOLIS, MINNESOTA 55438

Published by Bethany House Publishers
A Ministry of Bethany Fellowship, Inc.
11300 Hampshire Avenue South
Minneapolis, Minnesota 55438

Printed in the United States of America by
Bethany Press International, Minneapolis, Minnesota 55438

Library of Congress Cataloging-in-Publication Data

White, James R. (James Robert), 1962–
    Is the Mormon my brother? : discerning the differences between Mormonism and evangelical Christianity / by James R. White.
        p. cm.
    Includes index.
    ISBN 0-7642-2047-0
    1. Church of Jesus Christ of Latter-Day Saints—Doctrines. 2. Mormon Church—Doctrines. 3. Church of Jesus Christ of Latter-Day Saints—Controversial literature. 4. Mormon Church—Controversial literature. 5. Evangelicalism—Doctrines. 6. Church of Jesus Christ of Latter-Day Saints—Relations—Evangelicalism. 7. Mormon Church—Relations—Evangelicalism. 8. Evangelicalism—Relations—Church of Jesus Christ of Latter-Day Saints. 9. Evangelicalism—Relations—Mormon Church. I. Title.
BX8635.2.W52   1997
289.3'32—dc21   97-33881
                                                                           CIP

JAMES WHITE is director of ministries for *Alpha and Omega Ministries*, a Christian apologetics organization based in Phoenix, Arizona, and an adjunct professor with Golden Gate Baptist Theological Seminary's Arizona Campus. He is also professor of Apologetics with Faraston Theological Seminary, and a critical consultant for the Lockman Foundation on the *New American Standard Bible* update.

Do you have comments?
Please address them to:

Alpha and Omega Ministries
P.O. Box 37106
Phoenix, AZ 85069

(602) 973–0318 (fax and message)

For faster response, contact us via the Internet:
http://www.aomin.org

Our web page includes information on
Mormonism, Jehovah's Witnesses, Roman
Catholicism, and General Apologetics. Listing
of debates, tapes, tracts, etc.

E-mail: orthopodeo@aomin.org

The Sage Library CD-ROM, cited extensively in the appendix on
the doctrine of "theosis," is available at www.ageslibrary.com, or by
calling 1–800–297–4307.

ACKNOWLEDGMENTS

For fifteen years now my wife, Kelli, has allowed me to pursue God's call upon my life, and for this I am thankful. My children, Joshua and Summer, have done all they could to help with this project. As a family, my wife and children understand that they are just as much a part of the ministry and, hence, this book, as I am. I could not do it without them. Also, I thank my parents, Ed and Betty White, who so often provide my children with the experience and joy of being at "Grandma and Grandpa's house." Likewise, to Rich Pierce, Larry Vondra, Don Falconer, Dave Amalfitano, and the others who keep Alpha and Omega Ministries moving along when I submerge myself into a work such as this, I say, "Thank you." To the elders and members of the Phoenix Reformed Baptist Church, who again have put up with my strange projects and Bible studies, I am grateful.

Most especially, I wish to acknowledge two men who have believed in me and who have played a very large role in not only this project but others both past and future. Steve Laube has gone to bat for me over and over again, even when the project at first glance didn't seem like it had a future, such as *The King James Only Controversy*. Through Steve I came to know Kevin Johnson, editor, fellow author, fellow bike rider, fellow Fuller grad, fellow thirty-something-type guy, and through all we've gone through over the past few years, friend and confidant. Thank you, Steve and Kevin, for all you've done.

FOREWORD

Some students taking my *Cults of America* course returned from their "hands-on" witnessing assignment perplexed. "We talked to Mormon Elder Bill, and no matter what we said he agreed with us! When we talked about God, he said that he believes in the heavenly Father just as we do. We asked, 'Do you believe that Jesus is the Savior?' Elder Bill replied, 'Sure. Mormons accept Jesus as their Savior just as you do. We are, after all, the Church of *Jesus Christ* of Latter-day Saints.' No matter what we discussed—the Bible, salvation by grace, you name it—Elder Bill believes it too. How can we say Mormonism is a cult if they believe just as we do?"

These students failed to realize two crucial points: (1) Mormonism, like most cults, uses Christian vocabulary but radically redefines it. Their "dictionary," as it were, has the right entries but the wrong definitions. (2) Even if Elder Bill somehow really did believe "just as we do," all it would prove is that Elder Bill rejects official Mormon teaching, "just as we do." My students should have asked Elder Bill, "If you don't believe in Mormonism, why do you think we should?"

Multiply Elder Bill many, many times over and you'll gain some understanding of how Mormons are now positioning themselves as mainstream Christians. And this new spin on Mormonism seems to be working. Even some evangelical Christians are suggesting that we reevaluate Mormonism, since the divide between Mormonism and Christianity is supposedly not as wide as once imagined. Unfortunately, such Christians have not taken into account the Mormon redefinition of terms and are ignorant of who and what speaks *officially* for the LDS Church.

In this lucid book, James White tackles masterfully these and other issues. Drawing on his vast knowledge of authoritative Mormon sources—from Joseph Smith to the modern-day prophets and General Authorities—Professor White skillfully, respectfully, and fairly presents the *official* Mormon teaching on the most central of all issues: Who is God. He demonstrates beyond any doubt who truly speaks for Mormonism, and that these authorities speak with one voice on the nature of the "heavenly father." As White shows, unless we are willing to accept a god who is but one in a pantheon of gods—who was not always god but *became* such through obedience; who is actually an exalted man with a body of flesh and bone; who lives on another planet, procreating spirit children with his goddess wives; and who "sired" Jesus through literal sexual activity with Mary—we cannot in any meaningful way talk about bridging the yawning chasm that divides Mormon polytheism from biblical Christian monotheism.

Contrary to what some anti-evangelical Mormon critics may charge, Prof. White is no "anti-Mormon." He has been truly dialoging with Mormons from all walks of life for over fifteen years, seeking to win them to the God of the Bible. He does so because he cares about their eternal destiny, knowing that faith in a false god—however sincere—cannot save. If White truly were "anti-Mormon" he would let them perish in their error. Thank God that James White loves the Mormons enough to tell them the truth (Eph. 4:15).

> —Alan W. Gomes, Ph.D.
> Associate Professor and Chair
> Department of Christian Thought
> Talbot School of Theology
>   (Biola University)
> Editor, *Zondervan Guide to Cults and Religious Movements* (15 vols.)

CONTENTS

1

WHAT IS A MORMON?

God knew I could never survive rowdy kids, so He gave me two of the best He had on the shelf. My kids do very well in school, and though they show the effects of the fall of Adam from time to time like any others, they have always been tremendously well-behaved. We often spend time in the car or out eating in a restaurant discussing all sorts of important things, like how to know God's will for your life and how to live as a Christian when everyone around you is doing just the opposite. So it was hardly surprising when, only a few years ago, one of my kids asked from the backseat of the car, "Daddy, what is a Mormon?"

My kids knew they could ask me because they know I spend a lot of time talking about "witnessing to Mormons." They know Dad is always gone the first weekend in April and the first weekend in October because he goes to Salt Lake City to "witness to the Mormons." Likewise, they are well aware of the fact that I spend each evening the week before Easter in Mesa, Arizona, passing out tracts to the crowds attending the Mormon Easter pageant. And both had seen my book *Letters to a Mormon Elder*[1] on the bookshelf at home among the other books Dad has written. So I was pretty well prepared for the question. It was what *prompted* the question that concerned me.

I am not the first Christian parent who has noticed that their children are attracted to other kids who are, like them, moral, trustworthy, and good students. And in the case of both my son, Joshua, and my daughter, Summer, their best friends in school have consis-

tently been Mormons. While we do live in a state with a high con-
centration of Latter-day Saints (LDS),[2] that is not the reason my
Christian children have found LDS children to be their most com-
patible companions. Mormon kids tend to be like mine: obedient to
teachers, intent upon doing their schoolwork, unwilling to engage
in the wild behavior of many of their classmates. Consequently, they
run in the same circles and end up being friends.

I had expected the question, and did my best to explain what a
Mormon is when my kids asked. As the years went by, my son began
to accompany me on missions work in Utah and Arizona, to get a
feel for himself about what the real issues are. But that first question
is being asked by many Christian children of parents who do not
have the advantage of having shared the Gospel with thousands of
Latter-day Saints. How, then, are those parents to answer the question, "What is a Mormon?"

Ministerial Fellowship?

Recently I received an e-mail from a minister in another state.
He told me a story about the local ministerial association. Just a few
days earlier he had to resign from that association, though he had
been a member for quite some time. "I had to resign because they
had just elected a Mormon to the next term as president of the association."

Situations like this are arising all over our land. Mormons, who
for many generations had kept aloof from other religious groups, are
now seeking to be included within the broad stream of "Christian"
groups.[3] As a result, ministers are being faced with a simple question: Can I have fellowship with a Mormon as a fellow "Christian"?
Can I lead my church in cooperative efforts with Mormons in, say,
a food drive or a clothing drive? And what of cooperation on moral
issues like abortion or homosexuality?

The Mormon Next Door

The same issue is presenting itself to many Christian laypeople
as they interact with the growing LDS population. Often we find our
Mormon neighbor to be a wonderful person—helpful, kind, gen-
erous. We may strike up a good friendship with him or her, and in

almost all areas of life we can talk—except when it comes to religion. At that point, we become uncomfortable and often simply let the issue pass without serious comment.

In today's culture "tolerance" is a noble cause, and we are strongly encouraged to seek areas of agreement and avoid subjects that are controversial. Thus, many are more than happy to simply "let the Mormons be," even while feeling that some of their beliefs are a little "strange." One may say, "They seem like very nice folks, and they are obviously very sincere. Therefore, I'm sure God will accept them as they are." The relationships that develop often lead to a sliding scale of truth, where we conclude that while they are not quite "right on" with their views, they are "close enough."

How Can Anyone Really Wonder?

There are many others, however, who have no doubts whatsoever about the LDS faith in general and Mormons in particular. "It's a devil-inspired cult" they say, "and that's all there is to it." For many, Mormons are simply polygamous cultists, out to destroy the souls of anyone unwary enough to be caught in their clutches. Yet many who would provide the *strongest* denunciations of LDS theology and practice are the very ones who have done the *least* work in seriously studying LDS writings and interacting with LDS viewpoints. Consequently, a large body of literature exists that is based not so much upon fair, even-handed study of primary source documentation as upon a very large dose of emotion and bias. Such literature normally emphasizes the sensational, seeking to arouse the emotions of the reader *against* the LDS faith. Modern LDS apologists and scholars like to focus on such literature, often treating it as if it is the "norm" for all Christians,[4] and have little difficulty demonstrating inconsistencies and half-truths, thereby dismissing all efforts at refuting LDS claims and evangelizing LDS people. But for those who find in Mormonism the very embodiment of evil itself, there is little reason to ask the question, "Is Mormonism Christian?" And there is even less reason to spend any time at all fairly evaluating the arguments of LDS scholars on the topic.

What Are the Issues?

It should go without saying that we take a very large burden upon ourselves when we say of any group or religion, "This group, though it claims to be Christian, is not, and is, in fact, opposed to the very central teachings of the Christian faith." Such a statement should *never* be made lightly or without proper foundation. This is not to suggest that such a statement should never be made. These days, it is a statement that in many cases needs to be said, and said loudly. But we must be very careful to be fair, honest, and in all things God-honoring in our study before we make such a pronouncement.

The first thing we need to recognize is that the issues we are addressing are crucial. We cannot lightly say of the faith of another, "It is in vain" or "It is in error." Anyone who does so shows great disrespect for the truth itself. On the other hand, there are many who would challenge the idea that we *can* make such a statement, no matter how diligent or fair we have been in our study and consideration of the beliefs of a particular religious group. That is, many today do not feel you can truly define what is and what is not "Christian." For many, the term is either so nebulous as to defy definition, or truth itself is so muddled and subjective that to say, "A is right, but B is wrong" is no longer possible.

Just as the Christian should not speak with bigotry or hatred in the heart and should not revel in casting about condemnations of others, so also the Christian *cannot* embrace the view of a culture around him that makes it impossible to say, "This is truth, and this is error." *Subjectivism about truth is fatal to the Christian faith.* We simply cannot claim to worship Him who is the very embodiment of truth itself, Jesus Christ, and at the same time waffle on whether we can tell the world what the truth is!

Obviously, then, Christians must be able to define what is and what is not fundamental and foundational to the Christian faith itself. Only then can we meaningfully examine the doctrines and beliefs of other groups and say, "This group falls within the boundaries of what can be called Christianity" or "This group, despite its claims, is not Christian."

Next, when it comes to examining Mormonism in particular, a whole new set of questions faces us. First and foremost today would be the question, "How does one define what Mormonism actually teaches?" As surprising as it might be, this will be a *major* question for us. It is not as easy to answer as one might suppose. For those outside Mormonism, it would seem to be an easy quandary to solve:

Just ask the living prophet, right? Doesn't Mormonism claim to have a living prophet and living apostles?

If you wanted to know what Christianity was all about in the days of the apostles of Christ, wouldn't you simply walk up to Paul or Peter or John and ask? Maybe. But we will discover that the answer is not quite that simple when it comes to Mormonism. Mormons have expressed a *wide* variety of views on this topic over the years, and as this cult seeks to find its place among world religions today, a movement is afoot to minimize the weight of the opinions and teachings of a large portion of the former "general authorities" of the Church and to define much more narrowly what is "official LDS teaching" and what is merely a matter of "speculation."

Someone might object to the investment of energy in such a question. Yet we would ask the same favor of anyone who disagreed with our own beliefs. I do not wish to be held accountable for beliefs that are not a part of my own faith. I don't want to have to defend every word that comes out of the mouth of every televangelist these days. So if we seek to be fair and honor the truth, we must allow Mormonism to define Mormonism.

Once we have determined how we can discover what "Mormon orthodoxy" really is, we then need to ask another question: In light of what we find to be absolutely definitional of the Christian faith, what does Mormonism teach on *these* specific issues? That is, we need to try to focus our attention on *what really matters*. We can easily get lost in a veritable forest of doctrines and beliefs that might seem *very* strange to us, but do those doctrines themselves define the most fundamental issues that could separate Christians and Mormons? For example, the large majority of books from a Christian perspective on the topic of Mormonism address a *wide range* of LDS beliefs. My friend Bill McKeever covers topics like the nature of God, Christ, salvation, the *Book of Mormon*, priesthoods, temple works, and baptism for the dead—all in the space of 140 pages in his book *Questions to Ask Your Mormon Friend*.[5] Likewise, I covered all those topics and a number of others in almost 300 pages in *Letters to a Mormon Elder*. There is nothing wrong in covering all these issues, for it was my intention (and Bill's as well) to try to provide a full response to the Mormon who wished to know what I believed about these many issues. But the result can be more than a little confusing to the average Christian who is simply asking one question: Is Mormonism Christian or not? What makes a religion "Christian" or "non-Christian"? Can we define these things? We can, and we must.

Once we have provided a full and accurate portrayal of the LDS beliefs that touch upon the *defining elements* of religious faith, we must then provide a scriptural defense of the historic Christian position so as to provide a "reason"[6] for the hope that is within us, as well as a standard by which we ourselves are willing to be judged.

Then, having done this, we will be in a position to render final judgment on the question, "Is Mormonism Christian?" We will look at the system as a whole, recognizing that individuals may have an incomplete knowledge of what Mormonism teaches or may willingly reject certain elements of it. In either case, to answer the question "Is the Mormon my brother?" we have to first determine whether the religious system known as Mormonism stands within or without the realm of true Christian faith.

The Defining Doctrines

So what, then, *defines* the Christian faith? What is absolutely essential? What, if taken away, leaves us with something *other than* Christianity? Amazingly, this is a question that many have never considered. And on the other hand, others are willing to present a *very* long list of doctrinal beliefs, extending to very minute points that they consider to be "definitional." For them, without these "essentials" there is no Christianity.

It should first be pointed out that even if we decide that a particular doctrine is not *definitional* we are not by so doing saying it is *unimportant*. There is a difference between something *defining* the faith and something being very *important* to the faith. For example, I am Reformed in my beliefs regarding salvation. I believe very strongly that the "doctrines of grace" as they are known are extremely *important* to the Christian faith. But I also recognize that those beliefs are based upon previous beliefs, and hence cannot, *by themselves*, be *definitional* of the Christian faith as a whole. Do I believe these doctrines are dispensable, then, and that we need not even consider them? Of course not. But I also recognize that certain truths come before others in a logical progression of thought. One must, obviously, begin with doctrines about who God *is* before one can speak of what God *does*. My belief in Reformed theology separates me, for example, from persons of the Wesleyan tradition (such as Methodists) on the matter of soteriology (the doctrine of salvation). However, this separation takes place *within* the realm of Christian faith, not outside it. Why? Because as important as my beliefs in the doctrines of grace are, by themselves they do not define what it is to be a Christian. And while some of my brethren in the Reformed tradition may disagree with me, there will indeed be folks in heaven who, while on earth, did not believe in such doctrines as unconditional election.

So upon what basis, then, can we determine that a disagreement on doctrine results in a position being *non-Christian?* Thankfully, when it comes to the subject of Mormonism, the answer is not difficult to find. And despite all the confusion that currently exists over the subject, the situation is really not all that complex. A few moments of thought can provide us with a solid basis upon which to proceed.

What is the most basic element of any religious system? If the system is theistic (i.e., if it actually believes a god exists), the most basic question is, "Is there one God, or many?" This first question (and hence the first place where systems can diverge) involves the difference between *monotheism* (the belief in only one true God) and *polytheism* (the belief in more than one true God). Obviously, if one's religion is monotheistic, one cannot possibly claim adherence to that faith while also being a *polytheist.* This would include all the subcategories of polytheism, such as *henotheism,* the belief in one *main* God with the acceptance of the existence of lesser deities or gods under the major deity.

It is vital that we recognize how fundamental this issue is. Christianity, Judaism, and Islam are all *monotheistic* religions.[7] Each is very zealous to proclaim and defend the fact that there exists only one true God. These religions, because they are monotheistic, assert that God is the Creator of all things in heaven and earth. They can present a system of worship that is based upon the existence of only one divine Being.

Polytheistic religions, on the other hand, are fundamentally separated from monotheistic beliefs. The belief in a plurality of gods introduces tremendous problems into the areas of creation, good and evil, and worship. Polytheism has generally been identified with paganism, and monotheism seen as an enlightened step "upward."

In any case, polytheistic religions cannot provide the focused worship that marks the great monotheistic religions.

Everything else in a religious system is based upon whether you believe there is only one true God or there are many. Worship itself is defined by its object: Is there one true, eternal, omnipotent, omniscient, unchanging God who is worthy of our worship? Or is our adoration to be divided between various deities? To whom does glory belong? Can glory be divided among deities?

The chasm that exists between monotheism and polytheism cannot be bridged. No matter what other "points of contact" that might exist beyond this fundamental level (e.g., a common belief in a need for salvation, common moral concepts, etc.), everything will always come down to this fundamental difference. Monotheism and polytheism are *definitional* to religious faith.

And it is right here that we find *the* issue that defines the Christian/Mormon question. Christianity is unabashedly monotheistic. Christians have *always* believed that there is only one true God who has eternally been God and who created all things, mankind included. What of Mormonism? Does Mormonism agree, or is it separated from Christianity by a different kind of belief? This is the issue that we will focus upon in the rest of this work, for it is the most fundamental issue we can address. While there are certainly many other issues that could be addressed in answering the question "Is Mormonism Christian?" we will direct the reader to other sources of information on those topics as they come up. But to allow for the greatest clarity, and to provide a means of examining *carefully and thoroughly* the actual doctrinal formulations of Mormonism on this *central* issue, we will look only to the doctrine of God as the issue that will provide us the most solid and meaningful basis of asking, "Is the Mormon my brother?"

2

WHAT DO MORMONS BELIEVE?

Every spring the LDS Church puts on its Easter pageant, called *Jesus the Christ*, on the front lawn of the LDS Temple in Mesa, Arizona. Back in 1983 my wife and I jumped on the back of my Kawasaki 440 and drove out to Mesa to "talk to some Mormons." Fifteen years later the only performances I've missed were the ones that were held at the same time as the General Conference in Salt Lake City. Other than that, I've had perfect attendance.

During those years I've noticed something. It's been subtle, but it's plainly there. At first, I didn't have to carry any LDS materials (other than the LDS scriptures) along with me. That is, the people—including the young people—knew what Mormonism taught about such things as the nature of God, the concept of "eternal progression," the "plurality of gods," and the idea that men can become gods. They also knew that God the Father had once been a man and had progressed to godhood. I did not have to explain these things. Instead, I could discuss them and compare these teachings to the Scriptures.

Then things started to change. The younger people especially became more and more liable to ignorance of one or more of these fundamental areas of LDS belief. Over the years I've taken to carrying various works written by LDS General Authorities[1] so that I can explain to Mormons what Mormonism has taught and continues to teach. Such a problem complicates the witnessing situation, to be sure!

It is self-evident that a religious group should have the freedom to define its own beliefs. Nothing bothers anyone more than being misrepresented regarding one's religious beliefs. I certainly tend to take offense when someone blatantly misrepresents what I believe and then, on the basis of the misrepresentation, moves on to attack or ridicule me! Since I don't appreciate that when it happens to me, I do my best not to do it to others. So when discussing Mormonism, how can I be sure I'm talking about the *reality* of what they believe and not my own *perception* of what they believe?

One thing is certain: You won't get far by relying upon "consensus of opinion." That is, you will find as many different versions of Mormonism as you will find Mormons. That's hardly unusual, because you will find all sorts of disagreements and differences among other religious groups as well. There are all sorts of levels of understanding, education, and tradition among believing Latter-day Saints, which results in a pretty wide range of answers to some of the most basic questions. Consequently, we will have to go to the "official sources" to be able to find out what Mormonism really teaches.

Apostles and Prophets

It would *seem* to be an easy task to define Mormon orthodoxy. This is primarily because we have a specific body of LDS scriptures to which we can refer. These works, normally referred to as the Standard Works, include the *Book of Mormon*, which claims to be a record of the inhabitants of North America in ancient times; the *Doctrine and Covenants*, a collection of revelations given primarily to Joseph Smith, the founding prophet of Mormonism; and *The Pearl of Great Price*, a collection of a number of smaller works of differing style and content. The *King James Version* of the Bible is the fourth and final element of the Standard Works of the LDS Church.

It is not our intention here to engage in a critique of these works. Such has been undertaken elsewhere and by others.[2] Instead, we note that the Mormon Church has not only an expanded canon of scripture (as compared to the historical Christian church) but a canon that includes recent (chronologically speaking) scriptures. What is more, Mormonism holds open the door for *additional* scriptures to be added to their canon. How could further revelation be given? This brings us to the concepts of living apostles and prophets and *continuing revelation.*

"God continues speaking to His people" is a statement almost axiomatic among LDS people. When discussing the sufficiency of the Bible as the source of divine truth for Christian people, I have been frequently told that my view means that "God is no longer speaking" and that I "have shut God's mouth." In contrast to the traditional Christian belief, we often hear from Latter-day Saints of how God continues to "guide His Church" and "speak from heaven." The words of LDS Apostle George Q. Cannon are very representative:

> As Latter-day Saints, we need constantly the guidance of Je-hovah. We have the Bible, the *Book of Mormon* and the *Doctrine and Covenants*; but all these books, without the living oracles and a constant stream of revelation from the Lord, would not lead any people into the Celestial Kingdom of God. This may seem a strange declaration to make, but strange as it may sound, it is nevertheless true.[3]

As we shall see below, Mormonism continues to claim that there is a "constant stream of revelation" in the Church. Yet the *form* this revelation takes is a matter of discussion and debate. Only twenty years ago, Mormon Prophet Spencer W. Kimball said,

> Since that momentous day in 1820, additional scripture has continued to come, including the numerous and vital revela-tions flowing in a never-ending stream from God to his prophets on the earth. Many of these revelations are recorded in another scripture called the *Doctrine and Covenants.* Completing our Lat-ter-day scriptures is *The Pearl of Great Price*, another record of revelation and translated writings of both ancient and modern prophets.
>
> There are those who would assume that with the printing and binding of these sacred records, that would be the "end of the prophets." But again we testify to the world that revelation continues and that the vaults and files of the Church contain these revelations, which come month to month and day to day.[4]

It certainly seems, in light of the phrase "revelations, which come month to month and day to day," that Mormonism believes in a con-tinuing, ongoing revelation, and that this authoritative revelation comes through the officials of the LDS Church. This is consistent with the words of another Mormon General Authority, President Joseph Fielding Smith:

> We are blest with revelation; the Church is built upon that foundation. All the revelations given do not have to be written. The inspiration may come as the Lord directs them. It does not have to be printed in a book. We have revelations that have been given that have been written; some of them have been published, some of them have not.[5]

These revelations come to inspired men—apostles and prophets—who make up the hierarchy of the LDS Church. Mormon Apostle Bruce R. McConkie, whose works are cited with regularity in the official publications of the LDS Church, commented about this:

> Further, there is the practical matter of interpretation and of equating and of comparing the written word with the continuing stream of oral utterances that, because the speaking voice has been inspired from on high, are themselves also scripture. Principles revealed in one day must be applied to new situations in another time; the ancient scriptures must tell what the word of God, given anciently, means today.
>
> It takes an inspired man to understand and interpret an inspired utterance. No one but a prophet can envision the true and full meaning of prophetic words. Any person of normal mentality can absorb some of the intended meaning from the scriptures, but no one can plumb the depths unless enlightened by the same power that gave the revealed truths in the first instance.[6]

The titles "apostle" and "prophet" are not meant figuratively in Mormonism. The very same authority that rested upon Paul, Peter, and John is claimed for each of the Twelve Apostles and each of the members of the "First Presidency" of the LDS Church. In light of this, and given the continuing of revelation, one would think that finding out exactly what Mormonism teaches would be as easy as inquiring of the leaders of the Church for a final and infallible answer. Certainly, if the modern LDS apostles function as the apostles of old, this would be the case. Listen to Mormon Apostle George Q. Cannon describe the authority of the leaders of the LDS faith:

The Apostle Paul says that the Apostles were placed in the Church expressly to keep the Saints from being carried away by every wind of doctrine and by the cunning craftiness of men. You watch the men that listen to the Apostles, to the authority that God has placed in His Church, and you will find that they are not carried about by cunning craftiness of men nor by every wind of doctrine. But the people that neglect and deride that authority, they are carried about in that manner. . . . God has placed in His Church the Holy Priesthood and given unto man the keys thereof. It is true that some of His servants who bear the Priesthood may go astray and teach incorrect doctrines, but the authority and power are bestowed by which error can be discarded and truth established and taught in all its plainness and purity. Thus, there being at the head of the Church a man who bears the Holy Priesthood and who holds the keys thereof and others associated with him who bear the Apostleship, they know the truth in its purity and can discern false teachings and expose the false doctrines which they propagate. This is the superiority of the Church of Jesus Christ over all other churches now upon the face of the earth. This is the advantage that the Prophet Joseph and the Prophet Brigham have over wise men of antiquity, the philosophers and teachers and leading men who did not possess the keys of the Holy Priesthood.[7]

But, as anyone who has dealt with this area knows, it isn't that simple. Not only do you have differing opinions expressed by those very leaders on this issue, but many modern LDS apologists and scholars do their very best to disassociate themselves from the binding authority of the statements of many leaders in the early years of Mormonism. We will be able to discern the reason for this below.

Student Manual Religion 333

We need somewhere to start in defining the official teachings of Mormonism, so I will begin with what seems to be a valid assumption. Something that is published *by the LDS Church itself* with the specific intention of being used to teach members of the LDS Church the *doctrine* of that Church is probably a trustworthy source of information. With that in mind, we will often note in the course of our investigation when a source comes to us under the copyright of the

Corporation of the President of the Church of Jesus Christ of Latter-day Saints. Such an indication marks an official publication of the LDS Church and must be taken, logically, as representative of the understanding of the leadership of Mormonism.

One such resource is titled *Teachings of the Living Prophets*, copyright 1982 by Corporation of the President of the Church of Jesus Christ of Latter-day Saints.[8] Here we have a resource that is specifically published by the LDS Church for the purpose of educating its own people regarding LDS beliefs. What does it tell us concerning what is and what is not official LDS teaching? Let us note some important passages. First, this official textbook cites the story of one Elder Orson F. Whitney, which was related in the October 1916 General Conference of the LDS Church. He encountered a "learned prelate of the Greek Catholic Church" who took offense at the use of water in the LDS celebration of the Lord's Supper. The prelate commented that "according to the Bible" this was not right. Whitney then comments,

> My Greek Catholic friend, whether he knew it or not, had hit upon the great distinguishing feature that differentiates God's Church from all other churches under the sun—in this, that while they are founded upon books and traditions and the precepts of men, this Church is built upon the rock of Christ, upon the principle of immediate and continuous revelation. The Latter-day Saints do not do things because they happen to be printed in a book. They do not do things because God told the Jews to do them; nor do they do or leave undone anything because of instructions that Christ gave to the Nephites. Whatever is done by this Church is because God, speaking from heaven in our day, has commanded this Church to do it. No book presides over this Church, and no book lies at its foundation. You cannot pile up books enough to take the place of God's priesthood inspired by the power of the Holy Ghost. That is the constitution of the Church of Christ. If we use water instead of wine in the sacrament of the Lord's Supper, it is because Christ has so commanded. Divine revelation adapts itself to the circumstances and conditions of men, and change upon change ensues as God's progressive work goes on to its destiny. There is no book big enough or good enough to preside over this Church.
>
> In saying this, I speak with all due reverence of the written

word of God, that which is printed in the books, part of which may be obsolete, having fulfilled its purpose and been laid upon the shelf, while the other part is virile, full of life, and applicable to our present state—our present degree of development. But even this part must be interpreted aright. No man ought to contend for what is in the books, in the face of God's mouthpiece who speaks for him and interprets his word. To so contend is to defer to the dead letter in preference to the living oracle, which is always a false position (from Conference Report, October 1916, 55–56).[9]

Here we have one General Authority of the Church (Whitney was an apostle of the LDS Church at the time of his comments in Conference) being cited by an official publication of the LDS Church that is on sale in LDS bookstores across the land today. Therefore, it seems we have a solid basis upon which to accept the idea that "there is no book big enough or good enough to preside over" the LDS Church, and that "no man ought to contend for what is in the books, in the face of God's mouthpiece who speaks for him and interprets his word." The centrality of the living prophet and the relationship of that prophet to the Mormon scriptures seems clear. Indeed, the very next section of this work is subtitled "The Standard Works and Living Prophets Must Be Accepted or Rejected Together." Note the claims of this source:

> We should regard both the standard works and inspired declarations of living prophets as valid and necessary sources of truth. Occasionally misinformed members of the Church will maintain that, although they accept the standard works as divinely inspired, they are reluctant to give equal credence to pronouncements of the living prophet. Such individuals are pursuing an inconsistent course and "err, not knowing the scriptures" (Matthew 22:29), for the scriptures themselves plainly testify of the fact that we must give heed to the living prophets (see D & C 1:14, 38; 21:1, 4–5). Of this, Elder Orson Pratt also testified:
>
> "The very moment that we set aside the living oracles we set aside the revelations of God. Why? Because the revelations of God command us plainly that we shall hearken to the living oracles. Hence, if we undertake to follow the written word, and at the same time do not give heed to the living oracles of God,

the written word will condemn us" (*Journal of Discourses*, 7:373).[10]

The question that further arises is addressed under a section titled "When Are the Words of the Living Prophets to Be Considered Scripture?" This section notes the words of Joseph Smith, often cited by LDS apologists today: "A prophet was a prophet only when he was acting as such."[11] Very importantly, we read,

> Prophets have the right to personal opinions. Not every word they speak should be thought of as an official interpretation or pronouncement. However, their discourses to the Saints and their official writings should be considered products of their prophetic calling and should be heeded.[12]

We note that this official source differentiates between "every word they speak" or their "personal opinions" and "their discourses to the Saints and their official writings." Surely no one would suggest that what a prophet or apostle of the LDS Church says to a friend during a Utah Jazz game should be canonized as scripture. However, it seems quite logical (and very much in line with this Church-published work) to believe that the sermon of the living Mormon Prophet, for example, given during the General Conference of the LDS Church, would at the very least be representative of the *official* position of Mormonism. Such a talk would be a product of "their prophetic calling" and should therefore be heeded.

That we are on the right track is demonstrated by the last section of this next source, which asks the question, "Must a prophet always preface his remarks with 'Thus saith the Lord' for them to be binding upon the Church?" Note the answer:

> Unfortunately, some Church members place limitations on prophetic statements. Some will not accept anything as a genuine prophetic declaration unless it is prefaced by the phrase "Thus saith the Lord." President J. Reuben Clark Jr., demonstrated the fallacy of such a position:
> "There are those who insist that unless the Prophet of the Lord declares, 'Thus saith the Lord,' the message may not be taken as a revelation. This is a false testing standard. For while many of our modern revelations as contained in the *Doctrine and Covenants* do contain these words, there are many that do not"

("When Are Church Leader's Words Entitled to Claim of Scripture?" 10).
"The prophet does not have to say 'Thus saith the Lord' to give us scripture.
"Sometimes there are those who haggle over words. They might say the prophet gave us counsel but that we are not obligated to follow it unless he says it is a commandment. But the Lord says of the Prophet Joseph, 'Thou shalt give heed unto *all his words and commandments* which he shall give unto you'" [*D & C* 21:4; italics added] (Benson, "Fourteen Fundamentals in Following the Living Prophet," 27–28).[13]

Contradictions on Authority?

Sometimes it seems as if some of the same Church leaders contradict themselves by insisting upon the primacy of the Standard Works over the teaching of the living Prophet. Note what Mormon Apostle Joseph Fielding Smith said:

STANDARD WORKS JUDGE TEACHINGS OF ALL MEN. It makes no difference what is written or what anyone has said, if what has been said is in conflict with what the Lord has revealed, we can set it aside. My words, and the teaching of any other member of the Church, high or low, if they do not square with the revelations, we need not accept them. Let us have this matter clear. We have accepted the four standard works as the measuring yardsticks, or balances, by which we measure every man's doctrine.[14]

But even here we may not have to charge the author of these words with full-blown contradiction. We must differentiate between standards by which doctrines are judged, continuing revelation itself, and the power to interpret that revelation. Unfortunately, as some LDS are willing to admit, Mormon theological terminology is not always precise. In fact, it is often anything but precise, and we must be careful before jumping to the conclusion of contradiction. One can indeed find numerous passages that speak of the final authority of the Standard Works when functioning as a *standard* or *arbiter*. For example, Mormon Apostle Harold B. Lee wrote,

All that we teach in this church ought to be couched in the

scriptures. It ought to be found in the scriptures. We ought to choose our texts from the scriptures. If we want to measure truth, we should measure it by the four standard works, regardless of who writes it. If it is not in the standard works, we may well assume that it is speculation, man's own personal opinion; and if it contradicts what is in the scriptures, it is not true. This is the standard by which we measure all truth.[15]

Such a statement would seem to limit us to the Standard Works. Yet such a statement has to be balanced against many others. On the other end of the spectrum, we find yet another *official* publication of the Church, published *by* the Church *for* its own members, titled *Gospel Principles*. This work is found in almost every LDS household and is copyrighted by the Corporation of the President of the Church of Jesus Christ of Latter-day Saints. When discussing sources of authority for Mormons, we read these words:

> In addition to these four books of scripture, the inspired words of our living prophets become scripture to us. Their words come to us through conferences, Church publications, and instructions to local priesthood leaders. "We believe all that God has revealed, all that he does now reveal, and we believe that he will yet reveal many great and important things pertaining to the kingdom of God" (Ninth Article of Faith).[16]

In the study suggestions for group leaders attached to this section, we read:

> Show a copy of a Church publication.
> Have someone read some inspired words of the prophet found there.[17]

We again find ourselves directly facing claims of divine revelatory authority in the persons of the leaders of the LDS Church. This is certainly the position that has been maintained consistently from the beginning of the LDS faith to this day. James Talmage, a Mormon apostle and one of the greatest scholars Mormonism has ever produced, provides a balanced and representative view:

> The Standard Works of the Church constitute the written authority of the Church in doctrine. Nevertheless, the Church holds itself in readiness to receive additional light and knowl-

edge "pertaining to the Kingdom of God" through divine revelation. We believe that God is as willing today as He ever has been to reveal His mind and will to man, and that He does so through His appointed servants—prophets, seers, and revelators—invested through ordination with the authority of the Holy Priesthood. We rely therefore on the teachings of the living oracles of God as of equal validity with the doctrines of the written word. The works adopted by the vote of the Church as authoritative guides in faith and doctrine are four: the Bible, the *Book of Mormon*, the *Doctrine and Covenants*, and *The Pearl of Great Price*.[18]

Note that in two sentences this leading LDS authority can speak of the "living oracles of God as of equal validity with the doctrines of the written word" *and* limit himself to the Standard Works as "authoritative guides." The operative term is *guides*. Guides must be interpreted and applied, and this is done officially and finally only by the General Authorities of the Church, and the President (Prophet) of the Church in particular. One more striking example of this should be examined.

Mormon Apostle Ezra Taft Benson spoke at the General Conference of the LDS Church in October of 1963. Benson would eventually become the thirteenth president of the Church. At one point Benson cites from another of the LDS prophets, Wilford Woodruff. Woodruff had related an incident in LDS history when Brigham Young had been preaching to a congregation in the presence of Joseph Smith. I pick up with Benson's quotation of Woodruff:

"Brother Brigham took the stand, and he took the Bible and laid it down; he took the *Book of Mormon*, and laid it down; and he took the book of *Doctrine and Covenants*, and laid it down before him, and he said, 'There is the written word of God to us, concerning the work of God from the beginning of the world, almost, to our day. And now,' said he, 'when compared with the living oracles, those books are nothing to me; those books do not convey the word of God directly to us now, as do the words of a Prophet or a man bearing the Holy Priesthood in our day and generation. I would rather have the living oracles than all the writing in the books.' That was the course he pursued. When he was through, Brother Joseph said to the congregation: 'Brother Brigham has told you the word of the Lord, and he has told you the truth' . . ." (Conference Report, October 1897, 18–19).[19]

How did Benson understand these words? Note his comments:

> There is only one man on the earth today who speaks for the Church (see *D & C* 132:7; 21:4). That man is President David O. McKay. Because he gives the word of the Lord for us today, his words have an even more immediate importance than those of the dead prophets. When speaking under the influence of the Holy Ghost his words are scripture (see *D & C* 68:4).[20]

The importance of this passage should not be overlooked. Here you have one Mormon apostle (later to be prophet) citing the words of a previous prophet (Woodruff), who himself relates the words of *two* previous prophets of the LDS Church, Brigham Young and Joseph Smith, and *all* come to the same conclusion. If the testimony of *four* prophets of the LDS Church to the continuing validity and authority of Latter-day revelation not found in the Standard Works is not sufficient, nothing else will be.

The Journal of Discourses

What would it be like to have a twenty-six-volume set of the sermons of Paul, John, and Peter? What kind of light could be shed upon the New Testament documents by such a treasure? Would not the entire field of New Testament study and interpretation be revolutionized by the existence of twenty-six volumes of sermons by the early apostles? Surely no person could possibly approach the interpretation of the early church without taking such a source of information into account.

No such set of documents exists for the New Testament. Yet Mormonism *does* have such a set of written records, known as the *Journal of Discourses*. This twenty-six-volume set provides us with the sermons delivered by the president and apostles of the LDS Church in the early days of their stay in Utah, between 1854 and 1886. Here we have thousands of pages of preaching and teaching on the part of Brigham Young, Orson Pratt, Wilford Woodruff, George Q. Cannon, and many others. These individuals knew Joseph Smith personally, and they often relate personal stories and anecdotes that provide invaluable background to the incidents recorded in *Doctrine and Covenants.*

It would seem, in light of the fact that these sermons are given by men who claim to be apostles of Jesus Christ, that the *Journal of Discourses* would function, if not as scripture, at least as a vital and valuable tool in providing an interpretation of the LDS scriptures by the men who knew Joseph Smith best. Imagine how valuable it would be to be able to go to an entire volume of sermons preached by Paul at Ephesus titled "Interpretation of the Doctrine of Justification." In the same way, the *Journal* provides a glimpse into the early days of the LDS Church and supplies us with a tremendous amount of context and background for the LDS scriptures themselves.

However, the *Journal* is not functioning in this way in the modern LDS Church. In fact, many today, as we will see below, would like to marginalize the *Journal of Discourses* as much as possible when it comes to defining what Mormonism does and does not teach. Yet note what the second Prophet and President of the LDS Church, Brigham Young, said regarding the authority of his preaching and teaching:

> Well, brethren and sisters, try and be Saints. I will try; I have tried many years to live according to the law which the Lord reveals unto me. I know just as well what to teach this people and what to say to them and what to do in order to bring them into the celestial kingdom as I know the road to my office. It is just as plain and easy. The Lord is in our midst. He teaches the people continually. I have never yet preached a sermon and sent it out to the children of men, that they may not call Scripture. Let me have the privilege of correcting a sermon, and it is as good Scripture as they deserve. The people have the oracles of God continually. In the days of Joseph, revelation was given and written, and the people were driven from city to city and place to place, until we were led into these mountains. Let this go to the people with "Thus saith the Lord," and if they do not obey it, you will see the chastening hand of the Lord upon them.[21]

Today Young's words are considered "strong," and, as we shall see, many LDS do not accept such a concept of latter-day revelation. Yet there does not seem to be *too much* difference between the thoughts of Young recorded here and those given by Ezra Taft Benson immediately above. Both speak of the living Prophet's words being "scripture." Such claims are found with some regularity in the pages of the *Journal of Discourses*, which may explain why, in fact, many modern LDS scholars and apologists seek to put them off to the side as "noncanonical," hence containing nothing but "commentary" or "speculation." McKeever and Johnson were quite correct when they concluded,

> It is apparent that it is Mormonism's theological evolution and not the *Journal's* inaccuracy that drives LDS Church leaders to downplay their significance. Mormon doctrine has changed drastically since the times of Joseph Smith, Brigham Young, and John Taylor. The *Journal of Discourses* exposes this deviation since it is one set of books that the LDS Church has not doctored up.[22]

The Unmentionable Source

There is another source of authoritative doctrinal teaching in Mormonism that you will *rarely* find any Mormons discussing. At first it does not suggest itself to the student of Mormonism, but upon reflection its importance becomes obvious. I refer to the LDS Temple ceremonies.

Mormons do not speak of the ceremonies to "outsiders." The ceremonies are considered "sacred" and are not to be the subject of discussion with non-LDS. Yet Mormons have, in fact, discussed some of the broad elements of the Temple ceremonies in written form. For those unfamiliar with them, here is the description taken from the LDS-authored *Encyclopedia of Mormonism*:

> The Temple Endowment is spoken of in scripture as an "Endowment," or outpouring, of "power from on high" (*D & C* 84:20–21; 105:11; 109:22, 26; cf. Luke 24:49). Participants in white temple clothing assemble in ordinance rooms to receive this instruction and participate in the unfolding drama of the Plan of Salvation. They are taught of premortal life; the spiritual and temporal creation; the advent of Adam and Eve and their transgression and expulsion into the harsh contrasts of the mortal probation; the laws and ordinances required for reconciliation through the Atonement of Christ; and a return

to the presence of God. The Endowment is a series of symbols of these vast spiritual realities, to be received only by the committed and spiritual-minded (TPJS, 237; see also *Temples: Meanings and Functions of Temples*). "All the ordinances," wrote Heber C. Kimball, "are signs of things in the heavens. Everything we see here is typical of what will be hereafter" ("Address to My Children," unpublished).

The Endowment increases one's spiritual power, based in part "on enlarged knowledge and intelligence—a power from on high, of a quality with God's own power" (Widtsoe, 1921, 55; Widtsoe, 1939, 335; see also Endowment).[23]

The reason I mention the ceremonies is simple: They are considered to convey divine truth. I have had very well-read and informed LDS confirm that the ceremonies are "authoritative" in that the doctrinal content they communicate (as noted in the quote above) is considered to be binding. Even the LDS scriptures themselves bring out this idea. In the 124th section of the *Doctrine and Covenants*, given January 19, 1841, we read the following regarding the building of a temple. Emphasis is added to clarify the point:

> Build a house to my name, for the Most High to dwell therein. For there is not a place found on earth that he may come to and restore again *that which was lost unto you*, or which he hath taken away, even the fulness of the priesthood. . . . And verily I say unto you, let this house be built unto my name, *that I may reveal mine ordinances* therein unto my people (124:27–28, 40).

And Mormon Apostle Bruce R. McConkie said concerning the Temple Ordinances:

> They were given in modern times to the Prophet Joseph Smith by revelation, many things connected with them being translated by the Prophet from the papyrus on which the Book of Abraham was recorded.[24]

The late Mormon Prophet Ezra Taft Benson likewise taught (emphasis added):

> The temple ceremony was given by a wise Heavenly Father to help us become more Christlike. The endowment was *re-*

vealed by revelation and can be understood only by revelation. . . . This temple will be a constant, visible symbol that God has not left man to grope in darkness. *It is a place of revelation.* . . . The laws and ordinances which cause men and women to come out of the world and become sanctified are administered only in these holy places. *They were given by revelation* and are comprehended by revelation.[25]

This will become important when we recognize that the ceremonies communicate a number of important concepts regarding the doctrine of God.

The Minimalists

Before concluding our look at LDS sources of authority, we need to address the movement in the LDS Church toward what I call "minimalism." There are modern Mormons—scholars in some cases, defenders of Mormonism in others—who very much wish to be rid of the legacy of individuals such as Brigham Young or Orson Pratt. They would like to banish to the realm of mere "speculation" some of the more embarrassing elements of LDS theology.

Brigham Young University (BYU) scholar Stephen Robinson has led the way in championing the "minimalist" viewpoint:

> Latter-day Saints are frustrated at the Evangelical use of nonauthoritative LDS sources to define LDS beliefs. . . . The only binding sources of doctrine for Latter-day Saints are the Standard Works of the church. . . . The only official interpretation and applications of these doctrinal sources are those that come to the church over the signatures of the First Presidency or the Quorum of the Twelve Apostles (collectively). All the rest is commentary.[26]

While recognizing that Robinson himself is not a General Authority and hence his words are his own opinion, expressed in a document that is not published by or sanctioned by the LDS Church (making it, by his own definition, mere "commentary"), his views have gained an audience in the LDS Church. Throughout the recent work Robinson wrote in tandem with Christian scholar Craig Blomberg, Robinson beats the drum of minimalism, sometimes coming close to becoming a "*sola scriptura*" Mormon. For example, he writes,

> During my lifetime, and especially during the last decade, the instructions to members have consistently run along these lines: Never mind the *Journal of Discourses*; return to the Scriptures; stick to the Standard Works. . . . Mormonism now seeks to define itself in terms of its own canonized Scriptures rather than the sometimes polemical or speculative sermons of the nineteenth century or the popular theology of the twentieth century. . . . I find it highly revealing that as LDS theology has moved away from late nineteenth-century rhetoric to the specific doctrines of the *Book of Mormon*, it has also been perceived as moving *closer* to Evangelicals.[27]

By relegating anything that is not in the Standard Works or written over the signature of the First Presidency or Quorum of the Twelve to at best "commentary," in the middle "polemical or speculative" materials, or at worst to "late nineteenth-century rhetoric," Robinson and others are able to dismiss entire doctrines, insisting that they will not be held accountable for these things. We will see that this will become very important when discussing such issues as the teaching that God was once a man who lived on another planet and the fact that LDS General Authorities have *consistently* taught that Christ was physically begotten by the Father. When we get to these topics, we will deal with whether these teachings were, in fact, mere speculations or whether they carried the weight of Latter-day revelation.

A Model

What can we conclude from the materials we have examined so far? I would like to suggest a model—a hierarchy of sources, so to speak. I believe the following construction is certainly fair to the official teachings of the Church and cannot possibly be charged with misrepresentation, if, in fact, the LDS concepts of "apostolic authority" and "Latter-day revelation" have any meaning at all.

If we were to put the sources of LDS teaching in order, with the most important at the top left, and then descending in order, I believe we would arrive at the following model:

First Level
- Standard Works
- Living Prophet

Second Level
- Joseph Smith
- First Presidency statements
- Temple ceremonies

Third Level
- Books published under the Authority of the First Presidency
- Statements of General Authorities in Conference

Fourth Level
- Statements of General Authorities elsewhere (books, other talks, etc.)

Consistency from top to bottom, it seems logical to assume, would result in "LDS Orthodoxy." Does a consistency exist between the Standard Works, the living Prophet, Joseph Smith,[28] official statements of the First Presidency, or the Quorum of the Twelve on a particular doctrine? Do the General Authorities interpret these sources in the same way in officially published books and Conference speeches as well as in other statements given outside the confines of official Church publications? If so, it seems logical that such a consistency provides us with the official teaching of the LDS Church.

Apart from the above model, I will not neglect to note other LDS writings as well. I will simply identify them as not having been written by a General Authority, though they may well shed much light upon particular aspects of our inquiry.

In our study of the LDS doctrine of God, we will follow this model in evaluating the weight and value of various sources. We will bend over backward to accurately represent and document the LDS position, for, as we have insisted, we must be fair and honest even with those with whom we disagree. We will place the greatest weight upon those sources that can provide us with the most indisputable authority and less upon those sources that do not. However, when we find "noncanonical" sources speaking in perfect harmony with the Standard Works, the living Prophet, and with *themselves*, we will not hesitate to hold modern Mormon theologians and apologists to the teachings of those they continue to identify as apostles and prophets.

Is Truth Always Truth?

Any person evaluating the claims of the LDS faith must consider a basic fact: Truth is truth no matter when it is given. When God reveals truth "X" about His nature and attributes, "X" will not become "false" tomorrow. While God's *means* of dealing with His people over time may change, His revelation about who He is will not. That is the nature of divine truth. For example, God first revealed to His people the fact that He alone is God, the Creator of all things. His later revelation of His triune nature (Father, Son, and Holy Spirit) is not a contradiction of this earlier truth but an expansion upon it. God's truth will always be God's truth.

In light of this, we point out that if Mormonism is what it claims—a restoration of the true Church of Jesus Christ—then what it taught as God's truth in 1880 will have to be consistent with what it teaches as God's truth today. We must allow for consistent growth in understanding and, in the LDS concept, new revelation, but none of this can provide an excuse for saying that God's truth proclaimed by "apostles and prophets" in 1880 is no longer binding or is no longer literally "true." If authoritative Mormon leaders have taught that God was once a man, that teaching is still binding today. If it isn't, one of two things is possible: (1) The modern Church can deny that the earlier leaders were, in fact, properly ordained authorities in the Church, and were, in fact, in error, or (2) The claim to continued apostolic and priesthood authorities is invalidated by the attempt to cling to conflicting teachings and authorities. I am not aware of any LDS General Authorities who are calling for the denunciation of Joseph Smith or Brigham Young as false teachers. Thus it would seem Mormonism is intent upon holding on to its claims of Latter-day revelation, continuing priesthood authority from the days of Joseph Smith, etc. Supposing this is the case, we can hold Mormonism accountable for her historical teachings, pointing out that if she wishes to free herself from them, she can take the path of the modern Worldwide Church of God, which has denounced her former teachings and embraced orthodox Christian doctrine. If Mormonism is unwilling to denounce those who have taught from her pulpit the doctrines that have historically separated her from orthodox Christianity, she cannot logically do anything other than defend these men as inspired apostles and embrace the doctrines they taught.

I will spend a great deal of time thoroughly documenting the LDS teachings on the subject of the nature of God and the nature of Jesus Christ. Some might well assert the citation of LDS sources as overdone. However, I wish to make sure that any person—whether a minister of the gospel seeking solid and complete documentation or a Mormon truly desiring to honestly dialogue on these issues—will have at their fingertips all of the information they need to decide for themselves regarding these important issues. But before looking at the specific statements of the Mormon faith, let us briefly remind ourselves of the standard against which we would test these statements: the standard of historical Christian orthodoxy regarding God.

3

CHRISTIAN ORTHODOXY

Before we look at Mormon orthodoxy, it would be wise to briefly visit the subject of Christian orthodoxy, since we intend to compare LDS teaching against this standard. When we talk about the nature of God, we can define the basic fundamentals Christians have believed about God over the centuries. We readily admit the controversy that existed in the early church on various points,[1] but the fundamental issues that are at stake with regard to Mormonism were *not* the issues debated in those centuries. This is important to realize, for recent LDS writers have had much success in redefining the real issues at this point. For example, note the following statements by Brigham Young University scholar Stephen Robinson:

> True, we do not interpret the Bible by the Hellenized philosophy of the early church councils (Nicæa, Chalcedon, etc.), but for us the Bible—*without* the councils and creeds—is the word of God. . . . The LDS are troubled by the fact that the God of Christian "orthodoxy" is virtually indistinguishable from the God of the Hellenistic philosophers. . . . The three persons are one God. What is not said in the Bible, but is said at Nicæa and is rejected by Mormons, is that these three persons are ontologically one *being*. . . . While Mormons readily admit that we are not "orthodox" Christians in that we do not accept the councils and creeds, we do accept the Bible without its theological add-ons.[2]

Is it really true that Christian orthodoxy is merely a matter of Hellenized philosophy? Is it true that orthodox Christians who be-

lieve in the doctrine of the Trinity are doing nothing more than adding to the Bible later creedal formulations that function in very much
the same way as the Mormon concept of Latter-day revelation? In a
"joint conclusion" on the subject of Christ and the Trinity, Professor
Blomberg of Denver Seminary and Stephen Robinson wrote,

> Both sides [Evangelicals and Mormons] accept the biblical
> data about Christ and the Trinity, but interpret them by different
> extrabiblical standards (the ancient creeds for Evangelicals, the
> modern revelations of Joseph Smith for Mormons).[3]

Is this true? I cannot more strongly say, "No!" It is a complete error
to think that what separates Mormons and Christians on the issues
of Christ, the Trinity, the nature of God, etc., is a matter of extra-
biblical issues, with the "creeds" functioning as some determinative
factor. The creeds of the first few centuries *came out of the Scriptures*,
and their authority *is based upon their fidelity to the Scriptures*. Hence,
even on issues regarding the highest level of God's revelation, His
triune nature, the creeds take their form and intention *from* the
Scriptures, and have no authority (in Protestant belief) beyond their
conformity to that divine Word.[4]

But it is a grievous error to think that what separates Christians
and Mormons is a matter of the later Christological or Trinitarian
controversies of the third, fourth, and fifth centuries. The main error
made by Robinson in the above statements is this: The issues that
have historically separated Christians and Mormons do not come
from the early church, but from the earliest books of the Old Testament! That is, it is not Hellenistic philosophy that marks the various interpretations of the Bible found in historical Christianity and
Mormonism, but the confession of the people of God made for mil-
lennia: "Hear, O Israel! The LORD is our God, the LORD is one!"
(Deut. 6:4).

Here we have the heart of the Shema, the confession of faith of
the Jewish people. The word "LORD" in the English translations is,
in fact, the Hebrew tetragrammaton *YHWH* or *Yahweh*, the personal
name of God in the Old Testament. Every day the faithful Jew would
confess this faith, that Yahweh (or, as we badly mispronounce it in
English, Jehovah) is our God, Yahweh is one. And the most fundamental revelation of the Old Testament was this: Yahweh is the only
true God. There is no salvation in any other, for there *are* no other

true gods! I will present a biblical defense of this truth in a later chapter.

The key issue upon which Christians have always agreed is this: There is one eternal God, Creator of all things. In the midst of all the disagreements that one can find in the early Christian writings, this is one belief that is found universally. One God, who has eternally been God, is the object of Christian worship and adoration, the object of Christian contemplation and theological study. Not only will one find this confession made over and over again by individual church Fathers but the creeds all begin with the same truth. Long before the Council of Nicæa argued about how the persons of the Trinity, Father, Son, and Spirit, are related to one another, one issue was settled beyond question: absolute, uncompromised, ontological[5] *monotheism*.

The bedrock upon which every one of the early creeds is based is ontological monotheism. It is the starting point in understanding the struggle to deal with the clear fact that the New Testament speaks of the Father as God, the Son as God, and the Spirit as God. This revelation comes to us primarily in the ministry of Christ; that is, the incarnation of Christ is the greatest evidence and example of the Trinity itself. This truth is *always* presented against the background of *absolute monotheism*. If monotheism was not part and parcel of the entire truth of God's revelation, we would see both in the New Testament as well as in the early church repeated mention of gods, a plurality of gods, etc. The logical result of presenting the divine persons, Father, Son, and Spirit, would necessarily be a plurality of gods, *unless* there was another *universally* embraced doctrine that forced us in another direction. And there is: monotheism.

Christian orthodoxy can be summed up fairly easily. When we summarize the main elements of the Nicene Creed, the conclusions of the Council of Chalcedon, etc., and the consistent teachings of the early church, we find that they all emphasized the following *biblical* truths:

- There is only one true God.
- God has eternally been God; that is, God did not "become" God at some point in the past, but has eternally been God.
- God is the Creator of all things. There is nothing that exists in nature that is not the direct creation of the one true God.

- God is not growing, evolving, or changing. He is independent of all other things, owing His existence to no one or anything else.
- God has all power and is not limited by anything outside of His own nature.

These truths *are not derived from Greek philosophy*, but from the plain statements of the Scriptures themselves regarding the true God of Israel. The fact that it is also preeminently *logical* to believe these things about God is not evidence of the *nonbiblical* nature of these beliefs, but simply the confirmation that God's truth is God's truth *for everyone*. God's truth is rational and logical—it is not limited to merely human categories. Man's highest thoughts will find in God's truth the ultimate example of truth.[6]

Once these truths are understood we can then, *and only then*, turn to the doctrine of the Trinity. Briefly expressed, the doctrine states that within the one Being that is God, there exists eternally three coequal and coeternal persons, namely, the Father, the Son, and the Holy Spirit. Even here, the first assertion is that there is only one Being that is God. The Trinity cannot possibly be understood outside of that preeminent assertion. The full deity of Christ depends upon the reality of ontological monotheism, as does the deity of the Spirit. Without monotheism, Christ becomes a secondary god or no god at all, depending on what system you are talking about. And without all the preceding assertions, including the eternality and omnipotence of God, you have no basis upon which to even begin to approach the heights of the doctrine of the Trinity. The early Christians were not simply sitting around splitting hairs when they struggled so hard to embrace in their beliefs *all* that God had revealed concerning himself. They were seeking to honor God's truth and to believe *all of it*. Choosing one aspect of God's truth at the expense of another is not the course of the redeemed. Instead, they seek to embrace and believe all God has revealed.

The Nicene Symbol

How did the Council of Nicæa summarize biblical teachings about Christ so as to exclude those who denied His true deity? As this particular expression of the faith expresses the view of the largest portion of Christianity today, I reproduce it here:

> We believe in one God, the Father Almighty, maker of all things visible and invisible; and in one Lord Jesus Christ, the Son of God, the only-begotten of his Father, of the substance of the Father, God of God, Light of Light, very God of very God, begotten,[7] not made, being of one substance[8] with the Father. By whom all things were made, both which be in heaven and in earth. Who for us men and for our salvation came down [from heaven] and was incarnate and was made man. He suffered and the third day he rose again, and ascended into heaven. And he shall come again to judge both the quick and the dead. And [we believe] in the Holy Spirit. And whosoever shall say that there was a time when the Son of God was not, or that before he was begotten he was not, or that he was made of things that were not [or, "that he came into existence out of nothing,"] or that he is of a different substance or essence [from the Father] or that he is a creature, or subject to change or conversion—all that so say, the Catholic and Apostolic Church anathematizes them.[9]

"We believe in one God." This is probably the most basic thing a Christian can say. Surely, the Christian must say more than this, for a Jew or a Muslim can likewise make this statement. But one thing is for certain: a Christian *must* make this declaration before he can say anything else.

With these brief thoughts concerning the nature of Christian orthodoxy in mind, let us turn to the official statements of Mormonism. Can the LDS faith say, "We believe in one God" *in the same context and with the same meaning* as historical Christianity?

4

THE MORMON DOCTRINE OF GOD: FIRST LEVEL STATEMENTS

Standard Works and Living Prophets

What do the LDS scriptures and the current living Prophet teach concerning the nature of God? What God is proclaimed in the Mormon scriptures? Is there a harmony between the Christian Scriptures (the Bible) and the Mormon scriptures (the Standard Works) when it comes to who God is, how He exists, and how He is related to His creation? Or is there a fundamental difference?

We note first that Mormons would say that the Bible itself teaches their view of God, if even in a veiled way. We cannot go into the discussion of the LDS view of the Bible in full here, but we should note that Mormonism has historically asserted that the Bible has been mistranslated and corrupted over time. The *Book of Mormon* is very plain in its pronouncements. First Nephi 13:27–29, 32, says,

> [27]And after they go forth by the hand of the twelve apostles of the Lamb, from the Jews unto the Gentiles, thou seest the formation of that great and abominable church, which is most abominable above all other churches; for behold, they have taken away from the gospel of the Lamb many parts which are plain and most precious; and also many covenants of the Lord have they taken away.
>
> [28]Wherefore, thou seest that after the book hath gone forth through the hands of the great and abominable church, that

there are many plain and precious things taken away from the book, which is the book of the Lamb of God.

²⁹And after these plain and precious things were taken away it goeth forth unto all the nations of the Gentiles; and after it goeth forth unto all the nations of the Gentiles, yea, even across the many waters which thou hast seen with the Gentiles which have gone forth out of captivity, thou seest—because of the many plain and precious things which have been taken out of the book, which were plain unto the understanding of the children of men, according to the plainness which is in the Lamb of God—because of these things which are taken away out of the gospel of the Lamb, an exceedingly great many do stumble, yea, insomuch that Satan hath great power over them.

³²Neither will the Lord God suffer that the Gentiles shall forever remain in that awful state of blindness, which thou beholdest they are in, because of the plain and most precious parts of the gospel of the Lamb which have been kept back by that abominable church, whose formation thou hast seen.

The extent of the "damage" to the Bible in the LDS view differs from person to person. Some LDS see the Bible as generally trustworthy, while others question almost every other verse. Most often when the topic comes up, one hears the Eighth Article of Faith of the LDS Church quoted:

> We believe the Bible to be the word of God as far as it is translated correctly; we also believe the *Book of Mormon* to be the word of God.

What Joseph Smith meant by "translated correctly" is open to debate. Some LDS feel he meant "transmitted" in the sense of "passed on accurately over time."[1] Others feel he meant "understood," as in "interpreted." Still others take the word literally, indicating the possibility of errors in translation in the English Bible.[2] We need not go into detail here.[3] Suffice it to say that at times the issue of the correct translation of the text comes into play. When this happens, Greek and Hebrew texts will be consulted and the translational issues addressed.[4]

The First Vision

Without question the key "revelation" in Mormon scripture regarding the nature of God is to be found in what is known as the

"First Vision" of Joseph Smith. The vision itself is fundamental to all of LDS theology. Mormon Apostle Bruce R. McConkie described the vision:

> That glorious theophany which took place in the spring of 1820 and which marked the opening of the dispensation of the fullness of times is called the First Vision. It is rated as first both from the standpoint of time and of pre-eminent importance. In it Joseph Smith saw and conversed with the Father and the Son, both of which exalted personages were personally present before him as he lay enwrapped in the Spirit and overshadowed by the Holy Ghost.
>
> This transcendent vision was the beginning of latter-day revelation; it marked the opening of the heavens after the long night of apostate darkness; with it was ushered in the great era of restoration, "the times of restitution of all things, which God hath spoken by the mouth of all his holy prophets since the world began" (Acts 3:21). Through it the creeds of Christendom were shattered to smithereens, and because of it the truth about those Beings whom it is life eternal to know began again to be taught among men (John 17:3). With this vision came the call of that Prophet who, "save Jesus only," was destined to do more "for the salvation of men in this world, than any other man that ever lived in it" (D & C 135:3). This vision was the most important event that had taken place in all world history from the day of Christ's ministry to the glorious hour when it occurred.[5]

And Mormon Prophet Ezra Taft Benson said,

> Joseph Smith, a prophet of God, restored the knowledge of God. Joseph's first vision clearly revealed that the Father and Son are separate personages, having bodies as tangible as man's. Later it was also revealed that the Holy Ghost is a personage of Spirit, separate and distinct from the personalities of the Father and the Son. (See D & C 130:22.) This all-important truth shocked the world even though sustained by the Bible.[6]

How is it that the "creeds of Christendom were shattered to smithereens" and the knowledge of God was "restored" by this one vision? While the story is as familiar to Mormons as John 3:16 is to Christians, we present Joseph Smith's own recounting of the story in full, taken from the LDS scriptures (and hence carrying canonical authority for the Mormon Church). However, we note that the account that appears in the LDS scriptures was written in 1838, eighteen years after the events described:

[14]So, in accordance with this, my determination to ask of God, I retired to the woods to make the attempt. It was on the morning of a beautiful, clear day, early in the spring of eighteen hundred and twenty. It was the first time in my life that I had made such an attempt, for amidst all my anxieties I had never as yet made the attempt to pray vocally.

[15]After I had retired to the place where I had previously designed to go, having looked around me, and finding myself alone, I kneeled down and began to offer up the desires of my heart to God. I had scarcely done so, when immediately I was seized upon by some power which entirely overcame me, and had such an astonishing influence over me as to bind my tongue so that I could not speak. Thick darkness gathered around me, and it seemed to me for a time as if I were doomed to sudden destruction.

[16]But, exerting all my powers to call upon God to deliver me out of the power of this enemy which had seized upon me, and at the very moment when I was ready to sink into despair and abandon myself to destruction—not to an imaginary ruin, but to the power of some actual being from the unseen world, who had such marvelous power as I had never before felt in any being—just at this moment of great alarm, I saw a pillar of light exactly over my head, above the brightness of the sun, which descended gradually until it fell upon me.

[17]It no sooner appeared than I found myself delivered from the enemy which held me bound. When the light rested upon me I saw two Personages, whose brightness and glory defy all description, standing above me in the air. One of them spake unto me, calling me by name and said, pointing to the other— *This is My Beloved Son. Hear Him!*

[18]My object in going to inquire of the Lord was to know which of all the sects was right, that I might know which to join. No sooner, therefore, did I get possession of myself, so as to be able to speak, than I asked the Personages who stood above me in the light, which of all the sects was right (for at this time it had never entered into my heart that all were wrong)—and which I should join.

[19]I was answered that I must join none of them, for they were all wrong;[7] and the Personage who addressed me said that all their creeds were an abomination in his sight; that those professors were all corrupt; that: "they draw near to me with their lips, but their hearts are far from me, they teach for doctrines the commandments of men, having a form of godliness, but they deny the power thereof."

[20]He again forbade me to join with any of them; and many other things did he say unto me, which I cannot write at this time. When I came to myself again, I found myself lying on my back, looking up into heaven. When the light had departed, I had no strength; but soon recovering in some degree, I went home. And as I leaned up to the fireplace, mother inquired what the matter was. I replied, "Never mind, all is well—I am well enough off." I then said to my mother, "I have learned for myself that Presbyterianism is not true." It seems as though the adversary was aware, at a very early period of my life, that I was destined to prove a disturber and an annoyer of his kingdom; else why should the powers of darkness combine against me? Why the opposition and persecution that arose against me, almost in my infancy? (*Joseph Smith History* 1:14–20)

What does this vision, recorded in LDS Scripture, teach concerning God? First and foremost, it presents to us the concept of a *plurality of gods*. This arises from the fact that God the Father is a separate and distinct physical entity from Jesus Christ, His Son. God the Father is possessed of a physical body, as is the Son. This is why McConkie can claim the creeds of Christendom were "smashed to smithereens," for this vision has *always* been interpreted by the LDS leadership to teach that God the Father is a separate and distinct person *and being* from the Son. The unity of Being that is central to Christian theology is completely denied by Joseph Smith in the First Vision. Hence, you have one God, the Father, directing Smith to another God, the Son.

While it is not our intention to critique these teachings at this point, it should be noted that there are a number of problems with the First Vision and with the entire development of the LDS concept of God as well. As we noted, this version of the First Vision was not written until 1838. Previous versions, however, differed in *substantial* details from this final and official account. Most significantly, the presence of both the Father and the Son as separate and distinct gods is not a part of the earlier accounts.[8]

The absence of the concept of a plurality of gods from the earlier accounts of the First Vision leads us to an important point in our examination of LDS doctrinal material: Joseph Smith's development of what is today orthodox LDS belief concerning God. We are again faced with a factor that complicates our task, in that it is almost self-evident that Joseph Smith's theology *evolved* radically between 1829 and his death in 1844. In fact, the reason we can find passage after passage in the earlier writings of Joseph Smith (such as the *Book of Mormon* and the earlier sections of the *Doctrine and Covenants*) that consistently affirm the truth that there is only one true God is that Smith, in those early years, *believed* in only one true God. However, somewhere between 1834 and 1836 his belief changed, and by June of 1844 Smith was saying,

> I will preach on the plurality of Gods. I have selected this text for that express purpose. I wish to declare I have always and in all congregations when I have preached on the subject of the Deity, it has been the plurality of Gods. It has been preached by the Elders for fifteen years.[9]

Yet we find in the *Book of Mormon* statement after statement that does not even begin to fit the mold of preaching a "plurality of gods." The Testimony of the Three Witnesses (Martin Harris, Oliver Cowdery, and David Whitmer) printed in the front of the *Book of Mormon* records them saying, "And the honor be to the Father, and to the Son, and to the Holy Ghost, which is one God. Amen." Here are only a few representative samples from the text of the *Book of Mormon* itself:

> Wherefore they both shall be established in one; for there is one God and one Shepherd over all the earth. (1 Nephi 13:41)
> And now, behold, my beloved brethren, this is the way; and there is none other way nor name given under heaven whereby man can be saved in the kingdom of God. And now, behold, this is the doctrine of Christ, and the only and true doctrine of the Father, and of the Son, and of the Holy Ghost, which is one God, without end. Amen. (2 Nephi 31:21)
> And he hath brought to pass the redemption of the world, whereby he that is found guiltless before him at the judgment

day hath it given unto him to dwell in the presence of God in his kingdom, to sing ceaseless praises with the choirs above, unto the Father, and unto the Son, and unto the Holy Ghost, which are one God, in a state of happiness which hath no end. (Mormon 7:7)

In the same manner, the early revelations of Joseph Smith speak of there being only one true God. The twentieth section of the *Doctrine and Covenants*, given April 1830, speaks often of this fact:

By these things we know that there is a God in heaven, who is infinite and eternal, from everlasting to everlasting the same unchangeable God, the framer of heaven and earth, and all things which are in them. (*D & C* 20:17)

Which Father, Son, and Holy Ghost are one God, infinite and eternal, without end. Amen. (*D & C* 20:28)

In fact, it seems Smith tried to explain God in Trinitarian categories even in the *Book of Mormon*. However, he, like many Christians today, erred, and ended up presenting the ancient error known as *modalism*, the idea that the Father is the Son, the Son is the Spirit, and the Spirit is the Father. Note this section from the *Book of Mormon*, Mosiah 15:1–5:

¹And now Abinadi said unto them: I would that ye should understand that God himself shall come down among the children of men, and shall redeem his people. ²And because he dwelleth in flesh he shall be called the Son of God, and having subjected the flesh to the will of the Father, being the Father and the Son—³The Father, because he was conceived by the power of God; and the Son, because of the flesh; thus becoming the Father and Son—⁴And they are one God, yea, the very Eternal Father of heaven and of earth. ⁵And thus the flesh becoming subject to the Spirit, or the Son to the Father, being one God, suffereth temptation, and yieldeth not to the temptation, but suffereth himself to be mocked, and scourged, and cast out, and disowned by his people.

Studies have been published that address the issue of the development over time of Joseph Smith's concept of God.[10] A clear example of this can be found by accessing the book *Teachings of the Prophet Joseph Smith*, compiled by Joseph Fielding Smith. This work arranges the doctrinal teachings of Smith in a chronological order. The fair investigator cannot help but be struck by the fact that if one starts at the beginning and reads through to the end, the progression and evolution of Smith's thought is clear and striking. What he taught in 1829 is not what he taught in 1844. But a scriptural example is provided by comparing the above cited story of the First Vision with a section from a revelation given in September 1832 in Kirtland, Ohio (*D & C* 84:21–22):

> And without the ordinances thereof, and the authority of the priesthood, the power of godliness is not manifest unto men in the flesh; For without this no man can see the face of God, even the Father, and live.

This section describes the authority of the priesthood[11] and insists that no man can see God the Father without the priesthood and live. According to Mormon theology, Joseph did not receive the priesthood until 1829, while the First Vision story says he saw God the Father in 1820. Why didn't Joseph Smith see a conflict in 1832, when he claimed that no man can see God the Father without the priesthood and live? The answer is simple: He had not claimed to have seen God the Father at that time. The First Vision story had not yet evolved to the point where two separate and distinct gods were presented, so there was no contradiction in the statement he made. Only later, as he developed his concept of a "plurality of gods," does this section require some very intriguing explanation.[12]

The end result of having canonized revelations that span the period of Smith's doctrinal development is simple inconsistency. LDS apologists and theologians normally interpret the *earlier* monotheistic and traditional statements in light of the *later*, more unique statements. The First Vision story becomes the lens through which all else is seen, so that the unity of the Godhead envisioned in various early passages from Joseph Smith is understood to be a unity of purpose only, rather than a unity of being. It is logical, of course, if one believes in ongoing revelation in the LDS fashion, to think that the later pronouncements of a prophet are to be taken as having more authority than the earlier ones, even if those later revelations are contradictory to the prior ones. A prophet has the right, we are often told, to interpret his own messages and "adjust" as necessary.[13]

What do we do with the inconsistencies inherent in the LDS

scriptures? Surely such a fact should be allowed to speak to the question of the inspiration of those scriptures, but for our purposes at the moment, we need to focus upon those passages that have had the greatest impact upon later generations and the teachings of the General Authorities of the LDS Church.

The Testimony of the Book of Abraham

Certainly the most unique section of LDS scripture is found to be the *Book of Abraham*, contained in *The Pearl of Great Price*. This work, "translated from the papyrus by Joseph Smith," is allegedly "a translation of some ancient records that have fallen into our hands from the catacombs of Egypt—the writings of Abraham while he was in Egypt, called the *Book of Abraham*, written by his own hand upon papyrus."[14] The story of the *Book of Abraham* is fascinating but beyond our scope.[15] Its importance to our study lies in the final chapters of the book. Here we find what amounts to a "rewrite" of the opening chapters of the book of Genesis in the Old Testament. Only this time, the fact that Joseph Smith's theology has changed is only too clear.

Joseph worked on the *Book of Abraham* during two major periods, and the second period came later in his life (1842), after he had begun introducing the idea of a plurality of gods into the LDS Church. It is hardly surprising that in "translating" the Egyptian papyri, Joseph "discovered" that Abraham himself had taught a plurality of gods. The reader is directed to chapters four and five of the *Book of Abraham* for a full accounting, but the first few verses are enough to give a flavor of the passage:

¹And then the Lord said: Let us go down. And they went down at the beginning, and they, that is the Gods, organized and formed the heavens and the earth.

²And the earth, after it was formed, was empty and desolate, because they had not formed anything but the earth; and darkness reigned upon the face of the deep, and the Spirit of the Gods was brooding upon the face of the waters.

³And they (the Gods) said: Let there be light; and there was light.

⁴And they (the Gods) comprehended the light, for it was

bright; and they divided the light, or caused it to be divided, from the darkness.

⁵And the Gods called the light Day, and the darkness they called Night. And it came to pass that from the evening until morning they called night; and from the morning until the evening they called day; and this was the first, or the beginning, of that which they called day and night.

⁶And the Gods also said: Let there be an expanse in the midst of the waters, and it shall divide the waters from the waters.

⁷And the Gods ordered the expanse, so that it divided the waters which were under the expanse from the waters which were above the expanse; and it was so, even as they ordered.

⁸And the Gods called the expanse Heaven. And it came to pass that it was from evening until morning that they called night; and it came to pass that it was from morning until evening that they called day; and this was the second time that they called night and day.

By my count, the phrase "the Gods" appears *forty-six times* in only two chapters of text in the *Book of Abraham*, and each time "Gods" is capitalized. Given the obvious dependency upon the text of the book of Genesis, Joseph Smith's point is all too clear and understandable. Only two years later he would claim that the Hebrew term translated "God" in Genesis is mistranslated and should be rendered in the plural. Whatever else we may say about the *Book of Abraham*, one thing is certain: It presents the "plurality of gods" very plainly.

The Doctrine and Covenants

The student of Mormonism is well aware of the fact that the primary source of doctrinal teaching in the LDS scriptures is found in the *Doctrine and Covenants*. While the *Book of Mormon* is widely read, it does not present the vast majority of the unique, definitional doctrines of the LDS faith. Instead, the *D & C* (as it is often abbreviated in LDS sources) is the real source of most modern LDS theology. And it is here we find the clearest presentations regarding the nature of God, especially in reference to God's relationship to man and the concept of deification.

It seems to me that the process that led Joseph Smith to his final statements regarding a plurality of gods and his most prominent statement (which we will examine in a later chapter) that "God himself was once as we are now and is an exalted man," was a process that began with the exaltation of *man*. That is, when you read his statements, including the revelations in the *D & C* in chronological order, you discover that the first steps are with an exalted view of *man*, rather than any particular view of *God* as an exalted man. I present two important passages—one from 1832 and one from 1833—that bear this out. The first is from Section 76 of the *Doctrine and Covenants*, verses 50–60:

> [50]And again we bear record—for we saw and heard, and this is the testimony of the gospel of Christ concerning them who shall come forth in the resurrection of the just—
> [51]They are they who received the testimony of Jesus, and believed on his name and were baptized after the manner of his burial, being buried in the water in his name, and this according to the commandment which he has given—
> [52]That by keeping the commandments they might be washed and cleansed from all their sins, and receive the Holy Spirit by the laying on of the hands of him who is ordained and sealed unto this power;
> [53]And who overcome by faith, and are sealed by the Holy Spirit of promise, which the Father sheds forth upon all those who are just and true.
> [54]They are they who are the church of the Firstborn.
> [55]They are they into whose hands the Father has given all things—
> [56]They are they who are priests and kings, who have received of his fullness, and of his glory;
> [57]And are priests of the Most High, after the order of Melchizedek, which was after the order of Enoch, which was after the order of the Only Begotten Son.
> [58]Wherefore, as it is written, they are gods, even the sons of God—
> [59]Wherefore, all things are theirs, whether life or death, or things present, or things to come, all are theirs and they are Christ's, and Christ is God's.
> [60]And they shall overcome all things.[16]

In discussing the status of the those who have believed and been baptized, Smith goes so far as to describe them as "gods" for the first time (1832). Even though he modifies this with the phrase "sons of God," the movement toward his final theology is clear. From the second passage, found a little over a year later in *D & C* 93, Smith said this about man:

> [29]Man was also in the beginning with God. Intelligence, or the light of truth, was not created or made, neither indeed can be.

Despite these lofty claims for man, we still do not have, at this early stage in his development, the corresponding claims that God was once a man himself. This comes in the latter 1830s and early 1840s. By April of 1843, we find Smith having moved all the way to an assertion that God the Father is *corporeal* in nature, that is, that He has a physical body. In a revelation dated April 2, 1843, Smith provides one of the classic LDS formulations concerning God. From *D & C* 130:22:

> [22]The Father has a body of flesh and bones as tangible as man's; the Son also; but the Holy Ghost has not a body of flesh and bones, but is a personage of Spirit. Were it not so, the Holy Ghost could not dwell in us.[17]

Remember that this passage is contemporaneous with the final form of the First Vision (1838) and the final "translation" of the *Book of Abraham* (1842). Hence, we can see that at this point Smith has joined together the exalted view of man found in his earlier revelations with a corresponding belief that God has a physical form like man (First Vision, *D & C* 130:22). Since both God the Father and Jesus Christ have physical forms, the idea of a *plurality of gods* is easily understandable in the final chapters of the *Book of Abraham*.

But how can men become gods? This is answered in probably the most well-known portion of the *Doctrine and Covenants*, Section 132.[18] This portion, put to paper on July 12, 1843,[19] speaks directly to the issue by introducing the "covenant of eternal marriage." This concept is vitally important to Mormons, and while plural marriage (which was intimately connected with the eternal covenant of marriage) is not currently practiced in official Mormonism (many Mormons look forward to the day when it is reinstituted, honestly believing it is God's highest will for marriage), it is still central to understanding the means by which the LDS Church teaches men can be called "gods." Here is the key passage, verses 19–20:

> [19]And again, verily I say unto you, if a man marry a wife by my word, which is my law, and by the new and everlasting covenant, and it is sealed unto them by the Holy Spirit of promise, by him who is anointed, unto whom I have appointed this power and the keys of this priesthood; and it shall be said unto them—Ye shall come forth in the first resurrection; and if it be after the first resurrection, in the next resurrection; and shall inherit thrones, kingdoms, principalities, and powers, dominions, all heights and depths—then shall it be written in the Lamb's Book of Life, that he shall commit no murder whereby to shed innocent blood, and if ye abide in my covenant, and commit no murder whereby to shed innocent blood, it shall be done unto them in all things whatsoever my servant hath put upon them, in time, and through all eternity; and shall be of full force when they are out of the world; and they shall pass by the angels, and the gods, which are set there, to their exaltation and glory in all things, as hath been sealed upon their heads, which glory shall be a fullness and a continuation of the seeds forever and ever.
>
> [20]Then shall they be gods, because they have no end; therefore shall they be from everlasting to everlasting, because they continue; then shall they be above all, because all things are subject unto them. Then shall they be gods, because they have all power, and the angels are subject unto them.

Later the same passage says, "Abraham received concubines, and they bore him children; and it was accounted unto him for righteousness" (v. 37), and in the same verse, we are told that Abraham, Isaac, and Jacob "have entered into their exaltation, according to the promises, and sit upon thrones, and are not angels but are gods."

Many sermons have been delivered by the General Authorities of the LDS Church on this passage and what it means, but we will have to look at those comments later, as they fall into a different category of authority. For the moment, we note that these scriptural passages assert that men can become gods by abiding in the "covenant," and that as a result they will be "gods," being "from everlasting to everlasting," and that they will have "all power," and that "the angels are subject unto them." When we combine these statements with the previous ones, we can see the general outline of LDS theology today regarding God, the Gods (from the *Book of Abraham*), the idea that God the Father has a physical body, and that man may become a "god" and have "all power."

If these were all the passages we had, we would be hard put to come up with a very clear concept of the Mormon doctrine of God. However, Mormonism is not limited to merely these passages. The concept of continuing revelation, *which gave rise to these passages in the first place*, throws much light on what is meant in these sections. But before we move to "second level" statements, we briefly note the words of the current living Prophet of the LDS Church.

The Living Prophet

At the General Relief Society Meeting held September 23, 1995, in Salt Lake City, President Gordon B. Hinckley, the current LDS Prophet, read the following pronouncement. Since it was read by the Prophet and specifically names the First Presidency and the Quorum of the Twelve as making a "solemn proclamation," we can safely view it as representing the viewpoint and teaching of the current Prophet:

> We, the First Presidency and the Council of the Twelve Apostles of The Church of Jesus Christ of Latter-day Saints, solemnly proclaim that marriage between a man and a woman is ordained of God and that the family is central to the Creator's plan for the eternal destiny of His children.
>
> All human beings—male and female—are created in the image of God. Each is a beloved spirit son or daughter of heavenly parents, and, as such, each has a divine nature and destiny. Gender is an essential characteristic of individual premortal, mortal, and eternal identity and purpose.
>
> In the premortal realm, spirit sons and daughters knew and worshiped God as their Eternal Father and accepted His plan by which His children could obtain a physical body and gain earthly experience to progress toward perfection and ultimately realize his or her divine destiny as an heir of eternal life. The divine plan of happiness enables family relationships to be perpetuated beyond the grave. Sacred ordinances and covenants available in holy temples make it possible for individuals to return to the presence of God and for families to be united eternally.[20]

Note the use of the phrase "heavenly parents" in their assertion that we are all "created in the image of God." This, they say, results in our having a "divine nature and destiny." Such terminology will become more important when we encounter even clearer official explanations of what this involves.

In recent times Gordon Hinckley has been quoted in national media sources making very interesting remarks regarding this topic. But because such sources are anything but official, we will relegate the discussion of these comments to the final section of our investigation of the LDS doctrine of God.[21]

We move now to the "second level" of authoritative pronouncements, those provided by Joseph Smith, the official statements of the First Presidency, and the Temple Ceremonies.

5

THE MORMON DOCTRINE OF GOD: SECOND LEVEL STATEMENTS

Joseph Smith, First Presidency Statements, and Temple Ceremonies

The idea of Latter-day revelation opens up for us a second level of authoritative teachings from which we can glean a great deal of information about the Mormon doctrine of God. We have seen the words of the LDS scriptures and of the living Prophet. We now turn to "second level" statements, those coming from Joseph Smith, the prophet of the restoration itself; from the First Presidency or Quorum of the Twelve Apostles; and from the LDS Temple Ceremonies. We begin with Joseph Smith.

The King Follett Discourse

The King Follett Discourse first appeared in print August 15, 1844, in the Mormon publication *Times and Seasons*. It was reported by a host of qualified sources, including Willard Richards, Wilford Woodruff (who became prophet of the Church later in life), Thomas Bullock, and William Clayton—none of whom had any reason to be unfriendly in their recording of the preaching of Smith that summer morning. It was the Conference of the Church, but it was also combined with the funeral of one Elder King Follett. Prophet Joseph

Smith rose to speak, and what he said has formed the heart of the LDS theology of God.

It has been quoted hundreds of times since by LDS General Authorities in their sermons and books. So often is one section of it cited in Mormon history that even Stephen Robinson, a Mormon scholar who insists that critics of Mormonism stick to a narrow spectrum of "official" teachings of the Church, admits that the authority of a particular statement repeated so often cannot be questioned, even though it has not been canonized.[1] It is quintessential Mormonism.[2]

Let us look extensively at these words of Joseph Smith and pay close attention to his claims in light of what we have already seen. He began by asserting that he was being inspired by the Holy Spirit to dwell on his subject that day:

> Beloved Saints, I will call the attention of this congregation while I address you on the subject of the dead. The decease of our beloved brother, Elder King Follett, who was crushed in a well by the falling of a tub of rock, has more immediately led me to that subject. I have been requested to speak by his friends and relatives, but inasmuch as there are a great many in this congregation who live in this city as well as elsewhere, who have lost friends, I feel disposed to speak on the subject in general, and offer you my ideas, so far as I have ability, and so far as I shall be inspired by the Holy Spirit to dwell on this subject.[3]

The Prophet went on to ask for God's help to speak the truth, and then asserted that he intended to "edify you with the simple truths from heaven." Smith starts at the beginning, so to speak, the very beginning of Creation:

> In the first place, I wish to go back to the beginning—to the morn of creation. There is the starting point for us to look to in order to understand and be fully acquainted with the mind, purposes, and decrees of the Great Elohim, who sits in yonder heavens as he did at the creation of this world. It is necessary for us to have an understanding of God himself in the beginning. If we start right, it is easy to go right all the time; but if we start wrong, we may go wrong, and it will be a hard matter to get right. . . . If men do not comprehend the character of God, they do not comprehend themselves. I want to go back to

the beginning, and so lift your minds into a more lofty sphere and a more exalted understanding than what the human mind generally aspires to.

At this point we can only agree. If we start off in error regarding our understanding of God himself, we will indeed go wrong. And so we see that Smith is intent upon introducing his audience to the very character and nature of God. He goes on to ask his audience to consider "what kind of being is God?" He reminds them of Jesus' words, "This is life eternal that they might know thee, the only true God, and Jesus Christ whom thou hast sent" (John 17:3). He then informs the assembly that his "first object is to find out the character of the only wise and true God and what kind of a being he is." This is encouraging to us, for that is exactly what we wish to know, and there is hardly a better source to turn to for the LDS answer to that question than to the founding Prophet of Mormonism. One can detect some petulance on the part of the Prophet, however, for it seems that there had been many who opposed his doctrine of God:

> And if I am so fortunate as to be the man to comprehend God, and explain or convey the principles to your hearts so that the Spirit seals them upon you, then let every man and woman henceforth sit in silence, put their hands on their mouths, and never lift their hands or voices or say anything against the man of God or the servants of God again.

After this Smith makes some comments concerning freedom of religion and then returns to his main subject:

> I will prove that the world is wrong, by showing what God is. I am going to enquire after God; for I want you all to know him, and to be familiar with him; and if I am bringing you to a knowledge of him, all persecutions against me ought to cease. You will then know that I am his servant; for I speak as one having authority.

There can certainly be no question as to how serious Smith is on this day. These are not offhand remarks. Rather, he is intent upon addressing the very issue that has drawn our interest in this study.

> I will go back to the beginning before the world was, to

show what kind of being God is. What sort of a being was God in the beginning? Open your ears and hear, all ye ends of the earth, for I am going to prove it to you by the Bible, and to tell you the designs of God in relation to the human race, and why He interferes with the affairs of man.

Such claims are indeed sweeping. Here we have the first President and Prophet of the LDS Church telling us what kind of being God is and asserting he will prove this from the Bible! God's designs in relation to mankind and His purposes in this world will be laid out for us. The preliminaries are over. Joseph Smith provides some clear answers.

God Is an Exalted Man

God himself was once as we are now, and is an exalted man, and sits enthroned in yonder heavens! That is the great secret. If the veil were rent today, and the great God who holds this world in its orbit, and who upholds all worlds and all things by his power, was to make himself visible—I say, if you were to see him today, you would see him like a man in form—like yourselves in all the person, image, and very form as a man; for Adam was created in the very fashion, image, and likeness of God, and received instruction from, and walked, talked, and conversed with him, as one man talks and communes with another.[4]

As mentioned earlier, there are few passages of LDS literature cited, quoted, and discussed more often than this one. The foregoing paragraph and the two that follow rank right next to the First Vision in their impact upon LDS theology. The first phrase, "God himself was once as we are now," has become a standard in LDS teaching. This and the statement of Lorenzo Snow that we will examine later— "As man is, God once was; as God is, man may become"—have attained a status in Mormon theology that ranks them as having as much authority as any other statement about God.

The full impact of the statement "God himself was once as we are now" *must* be understood. Here we have a man who is claiming to stand as a prophet of God, as a *Christian prophet,* who is proclaiming that God once existed in a corporeal, human state. God "was once a man like us" (see quote below). If this is true, a number of other things must be true. First, God has not eternally been God. From this progresses the idea of exaltation, a process that God himself has undergone. Secondly, if God has not eternally been God, then it follows that there must have been a God (or gods) before Him (unless one embraces the idea that the universe sprang into existence without divine assistance).[5]

"God is an exalted man." From this assertion we see the coming together of the thought process we observed in the earlier sections of the *Doctrine and Covenants*—the exaltation of man to a high status. God and man are the same species, the same kind of being, differing in level of exaltation. We are not yet exalted; God has undergone this process, and this is why He differs from us. But since He was once where we are, obviously the door is opened for us to undergo the same process and someday become a God as He is.

God has a physical body, for He is an exalted man, just as the 1838 edition of the First Vision asserts. This physical body is not merely an unnecessary *addition* or *accessory*. It is definitional of God himself, just as our body is vital to what it means to be human.

These statements would have been enough, but Joseph Smith was only warming up. He leaves us with no room for misunderstanding his intent.

> In order to understand the subject of the dead, for consolation of those who mourn for the loss of their friends, it is necessary we should understand the character and being of God and how he came to be so; for I am going to tell you how God came to be God. We have imagined and supposed that God was God from all eternity. I will refute that idea, and take away the veil, so that you may see.
>
> These are incomprehensible ideas to some, but they are simple. *It is the first principle of the Gospel to know for a certainty the Character of God, and to know that we may converse with him as one man converses with another, and that he was once a man like us; yea, that God himself, the Father of us all, dwelt on an earth, the same as Jesus Christ himself did; and I will show it from the Bible.*[6]

When speaking of the character of God, Smith insists that God "came to be God." This continues the idea that God was once something other than what He is today. Smith then strikes directly at the heart of Christian orthodoxy—at a belief held by Christians from the very beginning—in saying that he will *refute* the idea that God has been God from all eternity (Psalm 90:2). Obviously, we understand Smith to be saying, without question, that God has not eternally been God.[7] How else could it be? The drive to make it possible for man to become *exalted* must of necessity result in the assertion that God has not always been God. The God of Christian orthodoxy, because He is eternal, unchanging, and exhaustive of every category of perfection, power, and being, simply leaves no room for the kind of future Smith envisioned for man. For this reason, the God of Christian orthodoxy had to be "refuted."

We cannot pass lightly over Smith's assertion that it is "the first principle of the Gospel to know with certainty the character of God and to know . . . that he was once a man like us." I have often heard Mormons say that we shouldn't discuss such "deep issues" as exaltation to godhood, yet Smith says it is the "first principle of the Gospel." It is clear that at this point in his life and teaching, Joseph Smith did not view God's manhood as an optional belief. It is not a side issue upon which we may or may not agree with him. It is doctrine, pure and simple. One cannot disagree on this issue and remain a follower of the Prophet.

Furthermore, we cannot miss his emphasis on the *similarity* of the pre-exaltation existence of God and our own earthly lot. Smith insists that God's existence as a man paralleled the life of Christ on earth. Obviously, Smith meant what he said: that God was a *man* like we are men, a human being going through the same experiences of life that we do.[8] Some modern LDS are uncomfortable with the clarity and force of such statements and would like to pull a veil across the Prophet's teachings so as to not have to defend such doctrine. Nevertheless, this is his teaching.

Learning to Be a God

Smith's attempts to defend this doctrine from the Bible expose his limited abilities as a scriptural exegete, but we will pass over them lightly at this point in order to admit to evidence more material before arriving at an evaluation of these claims.

The Scriptures inform us that Jesus said, As the Father hath power in Himself, even so hath the Son power—to do what? Why, what the Father did.[9] The answer is obvious—in a manner to lay down His body and take it up again. Jesus, what are you going to do? To lay down my life as my Father did, and take it up again. Do we believe it? If you do not believe it, you do not believe the Bible. The Scriptures say it, and I defy all the learning and wisdom and all the combined powers of earth and hell together to refute it.

These statements are followed by another striking proclamation:

> Here, then, is eternal life—to know the only wise and true God; and you have got to learn how to be Gods yourselves, and to be kings and priests to God, the same as all Gods have done before you, namely, by going from one small degree to another, and from a small capacity to a great one; from grace to grace, from exaltation to exaltation, until you attain to the resurrection of the dead, and are able to dwell in everlasting burnings, and to sit in glory, as do those who sit enthroned in everlasting power. And I want you to know that God, in the last days, while certain individuals are proclaiming his name, is not trifling with you or me.

It is certainly difficult to avoid getting Joseph Smith's point loud and clear. "You have got to learn how to be Gods yourselves . . . the same as all Gods have done before you" is an amazing claim. And here we are given a glimpse into the concept of "exaltation," which is defined as "going from one small degree to another, and from a small capacity to a great one." The promised end is to "sit in glory, as do those who sit enthroned in everlasting power." Again we see the driving force: the exaltation of man to the highest category.

I remind the reader that Smith was here preaching a funeral sermon that was combined with the Conference of the Church. He continues on to speak of how these glorious truths are helpful in consoling those who have lost a loved one, for he goes on to say,

> They shall rise again to dwell in everlasting burnings in immortal glory, not to sorrow, suffer, or die any more; but they shall be heirs of God and joint heirs with Jesus Christ. What is it? To inherit the same power, the same glory and the same exaltation, until you arrive at the station of a God, and ascend the throne of eternal power, the same as those who have gone be-

fore. What did Jesus do? Why, I do the things I saw my Father do when worlds came rolling into existence. My Father worked out his kingdom with fear and trembling, and I must do the same; and when I get my kingdom, I shall present it to my Father, so that he may obtain kingdom upon kingdom, and it will exalt him in glory. He will then take a higher exaltation, and I will take his place, and thereby become exalted myself. So that Jesus treads in the tracks of his Father, and inherits what God did before; and God is thus glorified and exalted in the salvation and exaltation of all his children. It is plain beyond disputation, and you thus learn some of the first principles of the Gospel, about which so much hath been said.

The same themes are again struck here, with the emphasis upon the progression, in almost train-track fashion, whereby one person's exaltation adds to those "above" on the ladder, and so forth. We note the words, "To inherit the *same* power, the *same* glory and the *same* exaltation, until you arrive at the station of a God, and ascend the throne of eternal power, the same as those who have gone before." The idea of men becoming gods results in the plain (and necessary) assertion of polytheism,[10] for we hear Smith speaking of those who have "gone before":

> When you climb up a ladder, you must begin at the bottom, and ascend step by step, until you arrive at the top; and so it is with the principles of the Gospel—you must begin with the first, and go on until you learn all the principles of exaltation. But it will be a great while after you have passed through the veil before you will have learned them. It is not all to be comprehended in this world; it will be a great work to learn our salvation and exaltation even beyond the grave.[11]

The Council of the Gods

At this point Smith goes into a fascinating discussion of Genesis 1:1 and how this passage supports his theology,[12] but we move past this to remain focused at this point upon ascertaining the *what* of his theology more than the *how*.

> Oh, ye lawyers, ye doctors, and ye priests, who have persecuted me, I want to let you know that the Holy Ghost knows

something as well as you do. The head God called together the Gods and sat in grand council to bring forth the world. The grand councilors sat at the head in yonder heavens and contemplated the creation of the worlds which were created at the time. . . .[13] In the beginning, the head of the Gods called a council of the Gods; and they came together and concocted a plan to create the world and people it. When we begin to learn this way, we begin to learn the only true God, and what kind of a being we have got to worship. Having a knowledge of God, we begin to know how to approach him, and how to ask so as to receive an answer. When we understand the character of God, and how to come to him, he begins to unfold the heavens to us, and to tell us all about it.

Every LDS person who embraces these words as true must realize how they sound to the ears of an orthodox Christian. God calling a council of the gods? Concocting a plan to create the world and people it? Such words are so far removed from historical Christian belief that many struggle to react properly to them. We must remember that it is claimed by Mormons today that this is also what was believed by the apostles of Jesus Christ, such as Paul, John, and Peter, yet their testimony to these things has been muted by time and by the corruption of the Scriptures.

Man's Spirit—Eternal and Uncreated

Smith goes on to lay the foundation of the LDS denial of *creatio ex nihilo*, "creation out of nothing," the historical Christian belief that God did not create the universe out of preexisting matter but solely by His creative power and will.

Now, I ask all who hear me, why the learned men who are preaching salvation, say that God created the heavens and the earth out of nothing? The reason is, that they are unlearned in the things of God, and have not the gift of the Holy Ghost; they account it blasphemy in anyone to contradict their idea. If you tell them that God made the world out of something, they will call you a fool. But I am learned, and know more than all the world put together. The Holy Ghost does, anyhow, and He is within me, and comprehends more than all the world: and I will associate myself with Him.

How does Smith deal with the assertion that God *created* the heavens and the earth, as well as man himself?

> You ask the learned doctors why they say the world was made out of nothing; and they will answer, "Doesn't the Bible say He *created* the world?" And they infer, from the word create, that it must have been made out of nothing. Now, the word create came from the *baurau* which does not mean to create out of nothing; it means to organize;[14] the same as a man would organize materials and build a ship. Hence, we infer that God had materials to organize the world out of chaos—chaotic matter, which is element, and in which dwells all the glory. Element had an existence from the time he had. The pure principles of element are principles which can never be destroyed; they may be organized and reorganized, but not destroyed. They had no beginning, and can have no end.

Here Joseph Smith clearly teaches the eternality of matter and the idea that God does not *create* but *organizes*. It should be noted that while Smith has said that God has not eternally been God, matter has eternally existed. Hence, matter preexists God in that God has not always been God!

At this point Smith moves to the spirit of man. Note well what he says:

> We say that God himself is a self-existent being. Who told you so? It is correct enough; but how did it get into your heads? Who told you that man did not exist in like manner upon the same principles? Man does exist upon the same principles. God made a tabernacle and put a spirit into it, and it became a living soul. [Refers to the old Bible.] How does it read in the Hebrew? It does not say in the Hebrew that God created the spirit of man. It says "God made man out of the earth and put into him Adam's spirit, and so became a living body."
>
> The mind or the intelligence which man possesses is coequal[15] with God himself. . . . I am dwelling on the immortality of the spirit of man. Is it logical to say that the intelligence of spirits is immortal, and yet that it had a beginning? The intelligence of spirits had not beginning, neither will it have an end. That is good logic. That which has a beginning may have an end. There never was a time when there were not spirits; for they are coequal [coeternal] with our Father in heaven. . . . But

if I am right, I might with boldness proclaim from the house-
tops that God never had the power to create the spirit of man
at all. God himself could not create himself (bracketed mine).

Especially note the assertion "God never had the power to create
the spirit of man at all." This flows from the idea that "the intelligence of spirits is immortal" and without beginning, and that God
himself is to be numbered among the intelligences that are coeternal
with Him. This is what Smith means when he says "God . . . could
not create himself." The equation is complete in that God and man
are one species and one kind along the divine continuum, separated
by time and exaltation but not by *being*.

The Principles of Eternal Life

The first principles of man are self-existent with God. God
himself, finding he was in the midst of spirits and glory, because
he was more intelligent, saw proper to institute laws whereby
the rest could have a privilege to advance like himself. The relationship we have with God places us in a situation to advance
in knowledge. He has power to institute laws to instruct the
weaker intelligences, that they may be exalted with himself, so
that they might have one glory upon another, and all that
knowledge, power, glory, and intelligence, which is requisite in
order to save them in the world of spirits.

This is good doctrine. It tastes good. I can taste the principles of eternal life, and so can you. They are given to me by the
revelations of Jesus Christ; and I know that when I tell you these
words of eternal life as they are given to me, you taste them, and
I know that you believe them. You say honey is sweet, and so
do I. I can also taste the spirit of eternal life. I know it is good;
and when I tell you of these things which were given me by
inspiration of the Holy Spirit, you are bound to receive them as
sweet, and rejoice more and more.

With these words we close our examination of Smith's King Follett Discourse. One might wish to reread the citations, or even read
the entirety of the discourse as found in numerous LDS sources, to
fully grasp the breadth of the doctrines that are so plainly announced
therein. This sermon "fleshes out" the passages we examined in the

LDS scriptures and will shed much light on the many other passages we have yet to examine. But to close this section, we note a vital truth: For Mormonism, this concept of God—including exaltation, progression, and the plurality of gods—is *intimately associated with the Gospel itself.* Smith speaks of the "principles of eternal life," and when Mormon leaders so speak, they are referring to the concepts found in the King Follett Discourse. An understanding of this fact has tremendous ramifications with reference to our overall inquiry regarding the nature of Mormon teaching and the relationship between Mormonism and Christianity.

More From Joseph Smith

While the preceding discourse is certainly the longest extant presentation of the LDS doctrine of God and man from the Mormon Prophet, it is certainly not *all* he said on the subject. Indeed, in the few years before his death in 1844, Smith spoke often of this concept. He encountered a good bit of opposition on this, even from within his own movement. This would seem to indicate that it was, indeed, a development that took place over time and that had been absent from the earlier forms of the Mormon faith. Note his words from June 16, 1844, a scant eleven days prior to his death:[16]

> It is altogether correct in the translation. Now, you know that of late some malicious and corrupt men have sprung up and apostatized from the Church of Jesus Christ of Latter-day Saints, and they declare that the Prophet believes in a plurality of Gods, and, lo and behold! we have discovered a very great secret, they cry—"The Prophet says there are many Gods, and this proves that he has fallen."

The passage of Scripture to which Smith makes reference is Revelation 1:6 in the *King James Version* of the Bible, which reads, "And hath made us kings and priests unto God and his Father; to him be glory and dominion for ever and ever. Amen." From this passage Smith will derive the concept of the plurality of gods,[17] as he himself declares,

> I will preach on the plurality of Gods. I have selected this text for that express purpose. I wish to declare I have always

and in all congregations when I have preached on the subject of the Deity, it has been the plurality of Gods. It has been preached by the Elders for fifteen years.

I have always declared God to be a distinct personage, Jesus Christ a separate and distinct personage from God the Father, and the Holy Ghost was a distinct personage and a Spirit: and these three constitute three distinct personages and three Gods. If this is in accordance with the New Testament, lo and behold! we have three Gods anyhow, and they are plural; and who can contradict it?[18]

Smith goes on to insist that he had "taught all the stronger doctrines publicly, and always teach stronger doctrines in public than in private." Unabashedly, he is *preaching* the *doctrine* of a plurality of gods. This is not mere conjecture or opinion—it is doctrine.

John was one of the men, and apostles declare they were made kings and priests unto God, the Father of our Lord Jesus Christ. It reads just so in the Revelation, hence the doctrine of a plurality of Gods is as prominent in the Bible as any other doctrine. It is all over the face of the Bible. It stands beyond the power of controversy. A wayfaring man, though a fool, need not err therein.

Smith then calls upon Paul's testimony to the Corinthians (1 Corinthians 8:4–6) and says,

Paul says there are Gods many and Lords many. I want to set it forth in a plain and simple manner; but to us there is but one God—that is *pertaining to us*; and he is in all and through all. But if Joseph Smith says there are Gods many and Lords many, they cry, "Away with him! Crucify him! Crucify him!"

Mankind verily say that the Scriptures are with them. Search the Scriptures, for they testify of things that these apostates would gravely pronounce blasphemy. Paul, if Joseph Smith is a blasphemer, you are. I say there are Gods many and Lords many, but to us only one, and we are to be in subjection to that one, and no man can limit the bounds or the eternal existence of eternal time. Hath he beheld the eternal world, and is he authorized to say that there is only one God? He makes himself a fool if he thinks or says so, and there is an end of his career or progress in knowledge. He cannot obtain all knowledge, for he has sealed up the gate to it.

Some say I do not interpret the Scripture the same as they do. They say it means the heathen's gods. Paul says there are Gods many and Lords many; and that makes a plurality of Gods, in spite of the whims of all men. Without a revelation, I am not going to give them the knowledge of the God of heaven. You know and I testify that Paul had no allusion to the heathen gods.[19] I have it from God, and get over it if you can. I have a witness of the Holy Ghost, and a testimony that Paul had no allusion to the heathen gods in the text.[20]

How, then, does Joseph Smith, here at the very end of his life, view those whose viewpoint he once held regarding the Godhead? He tells us in this sermon,

Many men say there is one God; the Father, the Son and the Holy Ghost are only one God. I say that is a strange God any-how—three in one, and one in three! It is a curious organiza-tion. "Father, I pray not for the world, but I pray for them which thou hast given me. Holy Father, keep through Thine own name those whom thou has given me, that they may be one as we are." All are to be crammed into one God, according to sectarianism. It would make the biggest God in all the world. He would be a wonderfully big God—he would be a giant or a monster.[21]

I noted in the preceding chapter that even when attempting to express Trinitarian concepts in the *Book of Mormon*, Smith demon-strated a misunderstanding of the doctrine, and fourteen years or more did nothing to disabuse him of his misconceptions. He did not understand the Trinity even in his last days.

Can There Be a Doubt?

The strength of the preceding statements may cause the reader to wonder why it is necessary even to continue the study, let alone multiply citations! How can anyone question the teaching that is plainly presented by the founding Prophet of the LDS Church? But we must indeed document that Smith's doctrine then became the official doctrine of the Church in his day, that it has been believed and taught in the days since then, and that it *remains* the teaching of the LDS Church at the end of the twentieth century. What is more, the teaching of later General Authorities expands upon and explains these seminal sermons from the Mormon Prophet.

More Official Pronouncements

Another form of official teaching of the LDS Church is found in the statements of the First Presidency and the Quorum of the Twelve Apostles. There are very few declarations to examine, but most of them are directly relevant to the subject at hand. By these statements that are meant to define with measured accuracy and certainty what the Church of Jesus Christ of Latter-day Saints believes, we are truly left with little doubt as to the key issues of Mormon orthodoxy regarding the doctrine of God.

The first statement comes from the First Presidency in 1909. Responding to the controversy concerning Darwin's evolutionary theory, the leaders of the LDS Church spoke of the nature of man and, in the process, the nature of God as well. The statement is titled *The Origin of Man* and reads in part,

> The Father of Jesus is our Father also. Jesus Himself taught this truth, when He instructed His disciples how to pray: "Our Father which art in heaven," etc. Jesus, however, is the firstborn among all the sons of God—the first begotten in the spirit, and the only begotten in the flesh. He is our elder brother, and we, like Him, are in the image of God. All men and women are in the similitude of the universal Father and Mother, and are literally the sons and daughters of Deity. . . . What more is needed to convince us that man, both in spirit and in body, is the image and likeness of God, and that God Himself is in the form of man?
>
> The Church of Jesus Christ of Latter-day Saints, basing its belief on divine revelation, ancient and modern, proclaims man to be the direct and lineal offspring of Deity. God Himself is an exalted man, perfected, enthroned, and supreme. By His almighty power He organized the earth, and all that it contains, from spirit and element, which exist coeternally with Himself. Man is the child of God, formed in the divine image and endowed with divine attributes, and even as the infant son of an earthly father and mother is capable in due time of becoming a

man, so the undeveloped offspring of celestial parentage is capable, by experience through ages and aeons, of evolving into a God.[22]

We need to note a few important teachings in this official pronouncement. First, the passage specifically makes mention of our heavenly "Mother." Many find such a phrase most strange. And yet this is exactly what the Church teaches.[23] Such is hardly surprising, given the centrality of the concept of the family, coupled with the belief that God is an exalted man. Second, we are told that God himself "is in the form of man." Is this not exactly what Joseph Smith taught sixty-five years earlier in the King Follett Discourse? Then we can show a consistency between the teachings of the LDS Prophet on this topic and his followers half a century later.

Next, the First Presidency claims it bases itself upon divine revelation in saying that God "is an exalted man, perfected, enthroned, and supreme." This, again, is perfectly in line with what has come before. Finally, it is directly asserted that man has the capacity, as "the undeveloped offspring of celestial parentage," of "evolving into a God."

The final paragraph cited above appeared in another such official pronouncement, this one dated 1925 and titled *"Mormon" View of Evolution*. This statement, too, is signed by the members of the First Presidency. Consequently, the assertion that men are capable of "evolving into a god" carries the weight of the signatures of *six* General Authorities, including two LDS Prophets.

The longest statement from the First Presidency that is relevant to our study comes from 1916 and is titled *The Father and the Son: A Doctrinal Exposition by the First Presidency and the Twelve*.[24] This document appears as an appendix in a very popular work by James Talmage entitled *Articles of Faith*. There is much in this statement that would be worthy of examination, especially as it relates to Christ, but we will focus again primarily upon those statements dealing with God and exaltation:

> Those who have been born unto God through obedience to the Gospel may by valiant devotion to righteousness obtain exaltation and even reach the status of godhood. Of such we read: "Wherefore, as it is written, they are gods, even the sons of God" (*D & C* 76:58; compare 132:20, and contrast paragraph 17 in

same section; see also paragraph 37). Yet, though they be gods they are still subject to Jesus Christ as their Father in this exalted relationship; and so we read in the paragraph following the above quotation: "and they are Christ's, and Christ is God's" (76:59).

Some light is shed on what it means to be "exalted," and on the nature of "celestial parentage," by the following:

> Jesus Christ is not the Father of the spirits who have taken or yet shall take bodies upon this earth, for He is one of them. He is The Son, as they are sons and daughters of Elohim. So far as the stages of eternal progression and attainment have been made known through divine revelation, we are to understand that only resurrected and glorified beings can become parents of spirit offspring. Only such exalted souls have reached maturity in the appointed course of eternal life; and the spirits born to them in the eternal worlds will pass in due sequence through the several stages or estates by which the glorified parents have attained exaltation.

We are told here that Jesus is one of the "spirits who have taken . . . bodies upon this earth." Further, only those who have gone through the period of mortal probation (life on earth) and have been resurrected and glorified "can become parents of spirit offspring." These celestial parents have spiritual offspring who themselves go through the process (this all being known as the Eternal Law of Progression) that their "glorified parents" have gone through so as to attain "exaltation." This is, again, completely in line with Smith's comments that began this chapter.

The LDS Temple Ceremonies

Recognizing that Mormons find discussion of their ceremonies offensive, we present only that information which is vital to determining the *theological teaching* of those ceremonies. We have already established the fact that these ceremonies are believed to be revelatory, and thus *must* be allowed to speak with reference to the *official* LDS doctrine of God.

What do the LDS Temple ceremonies teach concerning the na-

ture of God and Christ? At one point during the Endowment ceremony,[25] the temple patrons hear the following words:

> Brethren and sisters, as you sit here, you will hear the voices
> of three persons who represent Elohim, Jehovah, and Michael.
> Elohim will command Jehovah and Michael to go down and or-
> ganize a world. The work of the six creative periods will be rep-
> resented. They will also organize man in their own likeness and
> image, male and female.
>
> *Elohim*: Jehovah, Michael, see: yonder is matter unorganized.
> Go ye down and organize it into a world like unto the other
> worlds we have heretofore formed. Call your labors the First
> Day, and bring me word.
> *Jehovah*: It shall be done, Elohim. Come, Michael, let us go
> down.
> *Michael*: We will go down, Jehovah.
> *Jehovah*: Michael, see: here is matter unorganized. We will or-
> ganize it into a world like unto the other worlds we have
> heretofore formed. We will call our labors the First Day, and
> return and report.
> *Michael*: We will return and report our labors of the First Day,
> Jehovah.
> *Jehovah*: Elohim, we have done as thou hast commanded, and
> have called our labors the First Day.
> *Elohim*: It is well.[26]

Here we have very clearly presented the concept that we have
seen already, specifically, the plurality of gods. Here Elohim (the Father) is seen as one personage; Jehovah, the Son, is another—a separate god. The role of Michael is a fascinating one in LDS history,
but beyond our scope here.[27] Elohim directs the "creation" (in reality,
the "organization" of preexisting matter), and Jehovah does Elohim's
bidding.

The LDS Temple ceremonies have undergone a good deal of evolution and development over time. In fact, a major change was
made in the Endowment ceremonies in April of 1990. The ceremonies, which had been ninety minutes in length, were radically
altered and now last only sixty minutes. The scene recorded above
is from the current (1990) edition of the Endowment. However,
many LDS today have gone through both the pre–1990 version as
well as the post–1990. Prior to 1990, and for the vast majority of

the history of the LDS Church, a "sectarian minister" was presented (and mocked) in the LDS endowment ceremonies. What is significant for our purposes is the fact that specific doctrinal information was presented in the words of this sectarian minister. In this case, however, it was *doctrinal error* or, more specifically, the very doctrines *of Satan himself* that were presented. We pick up with Lucifer encountering the Preacher:

> *Lucifer*: Good morning, sir!
> *Sectarian Minister*: Good morning!
>> (The Preacher turns and looks into the camera.)
>> A fine congregation!
> *Lucifer*: Yes, they are very good people. They are concerned about religion. Are you a preacher?
> *Sectarian Minister*: I am.
> *Lucifer*: Have you been to college and received training for the ministry?
> *Sectarian Minister*: Certainly! A man cannot preach unless he has been trained for the ministry.
> *Lucifer*: Do you preach the orthodox religion?
> *Sectarian Minister*: Yes, that is what I preach.
> *Lucifer*: If you will preach your orthodox religion to these people, and convert them, I will pay you well.
> *Sectarian Minister*: I will do my best.

At this point Lucifer leads the minister to Adam and Eve, and a conversation ensues:

> *Sectarian Minister*: I understand you are inquiring after religion.
> *Adam*: I was calling upon Father.
> *Sectarian Minister*: I am glad to know you were calling upon Father. Do you believe in a God who is without body, parts, and passions; who sits on the top of a topless throne; whose center is everywhere and whose circumference is nowhere; who fills the universe and yet is so small that he can dwell in your heart; who is surrounded by myriads of beings who have been saved by grace, not for any act of theirs, but by His good pleasure? Do you believe in this great Being?
> *Adam*: I do not. I cannot comprehend such a being.
> *Sectarian Minister*: That is the beauty of it. Perhaps you do not believe in the devil, and in that great hell, the bottomless pit, where there is a lake of fire and brimstone into which

the wicked are cast, and where they are continually burning but are never consumed?

Adam: I do not believe in any such place.

Sectarian Minister: My dear friend, I am sorry for you.[28]

I emphasize that this material is not a part of the *current* LDS Temple ceremonies. However, it *was* a part of the ceremonies for *at least a century*, and it *does* communicate a fair amount of information about how the LDS leadership views God. In light of the claims that the LDS ceremonies were given by *revelation*, many even in Mormonism have questioned how the Church could so radically alter the ceremonies. But that issue aside, the LDS Church taught, as revealed doctrine, that to believe in the Christian concept of God is to believe, in reality, in the very teachings of Satan himself. One does not have to look too hard to see the influence of the Westminster Confession of Faith in the preaching of the "Minister," and the phrase "without body, parts, and passions" comes directly from that Confession (2:1):

> There is but one only living and true God, who is infinite in being and perfection, a most pure spirit, invisible, without body, parts, or passions; immutable, immense, eternal, incomprehensible, almighty, most wise, most holy, most free, most absolute, working all things according to the counsel of His own immutable and most righteous will, for His own glory; most loving, gracious, merciful, long-suffering, abundant in goodness and truth, forgiving iniquity, transgression, and sin, the rewarder of them that diligently seek Him; and withal, most just, and terrible in His judgments; hating all sin, and who will by no means clear the guilty.[29]

One might well recall that Joseph Smith claimed upon his returning home after the First Vision that he told his mother, "I have learned for myself that Presbyterianism is not true" (*Joseph Smith History* 1:20).

Conclusions

We are seeking to establish, as fairly as possible, the *official* LDS position based upon their own scriptures, statements, and teachings.

We have come a long way in looking at these "second level" statements from Joseph Smith, the First Presidency, and the Temple ceremonies. The outlines we were able to see in the LDS scriptures and in the words of the living Prophet have been greatly expanded by these teachings. We find a strong consistency here, for the concepts of a plurality of gods, God once having been a man, and the possibility of exaltation to godhood have been affirmed over and over again all across the spectrum of evidence.

The next level of statements are likewise very important, for they take us to another level: What does the Church teach its people in its own publications? When a young Mormon person approaches the Church seeking doctrinal instruction, what is he or she taught? What does the Church teach in its own curriculum of courses? And when a faithful Latter-day Saint attends the General Conference in Salt Lake City, or joins hundreds of thousands of others in watching the Conference via satellite, what is he or she taught? When the apostles and prophets gather at Conference to instruct the Church, what theology underlies their teachings? We turn now to the "third level" statements, those found in books published under the authority of the Church itself (mainly those printed with the copyright of the Corporation of the President of the Church of Jesus Christ of Latter-day Saints) and those provided by the General Authorities of the Church during their General Conference.

6

THE MORMON DOCTRINE OF GOD: THIRD LEVEL STATEMENTS

Material Published Under Authority of First Presidency and Statements of General Authorities in Conference

The Church of Jesus Christ of Latter-day Saints provides a tremendous amount of literature to its people. This body of printed material can hardly be surveyed here. However, we can focus upon those publications that are specifically meant to communicate *doctrinal truth* to the members of the Mormon Church. Because the vast majority of this material appears in *Church-published documents*, we feel quite confident that we are being fair in allowing it to speak and bear testimony to the LDS position. As many of these beliefs have already been explained in the two previous chapters, I will keep commentary to a minimum.

Melchizedek Priesthood Study Guide

The Melchizedek Priesthood, or the Holy Priesthood after the Order of the Son of God, as some Mormons refer to it, is central to the LDS concept of authority. The Church has published a book titled *Search These Commandments*, subtitled "Melchizedek Priesthood Personal Study Guide."[1] In Lesson 21, pages 151–158, there is a study based upon *D & C* 132:20. The first section of the lesson is titled "God Was Once a Man As We Are Now." The topic of Lorenzo

Snow is brought up in these words:

> When he was a young man, Lorenzo Snow was promised by the Lord through the Patriarch to the Church that through obedience to the gospel he could become as great as God, "and you cannot wish to be greater" (Eliza R. Snow Smith, *Biography and Family Record of Lorenzo Snow*, 9–10).

> President Lorenzo Snow recorded this experience that occurred when he was still a young elder: "The Spirit of the Lord rested mightily upon me—the eyes of my understanding were opened and I saw as clear as the sun at noonday, with wonder and astonishment, the pathway of God and man." Elder Snow expressed this newfound understanding in these words: "As man now is, God once was: As God now is, man may be." Later the Prophet Joseph Smith assured him: "Brother Snow, that is true gospel doctrine, and it is a revelation from God to you" (quoted by LeRoi C. Snow, in "Devotion to Divine Inspiration," *Improvement Era* [June 1919]: 651–56).

I believe the significance of this is clear: The Church has no qualms about promoting Snow's couplet in modern times and even citing a very secondary source regarding Joseph Smith's confirmation of the verity of Snow's ideas. Not surprisingly, the next citation is very familiar to us:

The Prophet Joseph Smith said,

> *It is the first principle of the Gospel to know for a certainty the Character of God, and to know that we may converse with him as one man converses with another, and that he was once a man like us; yea, that God himself, the Father of us all, dwelt on an earth* (*Teachings*, 345–46; italics in original).

The continued relevance and authority of Smith's teaching are here plainly demonstrated. So, too, is the weight of a General Authority speaking in Conference, as the next citation provided shows:

> President Brigham Young elaborated on this concept: "It must be that God knows something about temporal things, and has had a body and been on an earth; were it not so He would not know how to judge men righteously, according to the temptations and sins they have had to contend with" (as cited by Harold B. Lee in Conference Report, April 1969, 130; or *Im-*

provement Era [June 1969]: 104).

Are modern Mormons taught that God was once a man and *progressed* to Godhood? Most definitely. The second section of this lesson is titled "Our Father Advanced and Progressed Until He Became God." What sources are provided to the Melchizedek priest to substantiate this claim?

> President Joseph Fielding Smith said: *"Our Father in heaven, according to the Prophet, had a Father*, and since there has been a condition of this kind through all eternity, each Father had a Father" (*Doctrines of Salvation* 2:47).

> President Joseph F. Smith taught: "I know that God is a being with body, parts, and passions. . . . Man was born of woman; Christ, the Savior was born of woman; and God, the Father was born of woman" (*Church News* [September 19, 1936]: 2).

> President Wilford Woodruff explained: "[God] has had his endowments a great many years ago. He has ascended to his thrones, principalities and powers in the eternities. We are his children. . . . We are here to fill a probation and receive an education" (*Deseret News Weekly* [September 28, 1881]: 546).

Aside from demonstrating how deeply embedded in LDS thought is the idea of eternal progression, the use of all of these "noncanonical" sources *by* the Church *to* its own members should be noted. The Church is not merely providing "private speculation" from these leaders to her members. By citing these sources the Church is demonstrating that her truth can be found not only in the Standard Works but in a wider body of literature.

Next we find that the Church specifically says that the mortal life of God the Father, prior to His exaltation, was basically the *same* as our life today:

> How does it help us to know that the basic elements of God's life in a mortal world were the same as ours? President Brigham Young explained:
>
> "He is our Father—the Father of our spirits—and was once a man in mortal flesh as we are.
>
> "There never was a time when there were not Gods and worlds and when men were not passing through the same or-

deals that we are now passing through. . . .

"It appears ridiculous to the world, under their darkened and erroneous traditions, that God has once been a finite being" (*Deseret News* [November 16, 1859]: 290).

The next section is titled "Through Obedience to the Gospel, Man May Become Like God." To illustrate this, they quote from a devotional speech in which Elder S. Dilworth Young attributes words to the Father in heaven "as He revealed His plan to us in our premortal home."

> My children all: You see in me
> Exalted man, of flesh and bone
> And spirit pure. One time, long,
> Long ago, I was as you, a spirit son
> Of an exalted Father. [See *HC*, 6:302–317]
> You may become as now I have become
> But you must do as I have done."

Take special notice that the Father's *Father* is here mentioned. That is, the God of God, the God that the heavenly Father worshiped when He was a man is here affirmed to exist. Some modern LDS refuse to speculate beyond what "pertains to this earth," but the Church, in teaching its own people, is willing to discuss such matters. The centrality of Smith's King Follett Discourse is seen again: The reference *HC* 6:302–317 is to the *History of the Church* by Joseph Smith, and the King Follett Sermon is found in volume 6, page 302 and following. The lesson returns to the idea that God's mortal existence was very much like ours by quoting an LDS Prophet:

> President Joseph F. Smith said, "We are precisely in the same condition and under the same circumstances that God our heavenly Father was when he was passing through this or a similar ordeal" (*Gospel Doctrine*, 64).

Following these quotes, the student is asked some questions. One is "What can a child grow up to be?" which is immediately followed by "What can a son of God grow up to be?" There is only one answer: a God. The student is then told that God "does not jealously guard his position and power."[2] The King Follett Discourse is cited again, this time the section that says, "You have got to learn how to be Gods yourselves, and to be kings and priests to God, the same as all Gods have done before you."

After more discussion the lesson concludes with a most interesting note: "Be careful in presenting this material that you don't bring God down to man's level. Our objective is to perfect ourselves and *raise* our level to his exalted place."

This is the LDS Church teaching her members her theology and, in so doing, being quite open about the ramifications of believing that God was once a man. Even here, one hundred and forty years after Joseph Smith stood to deliver his sermon at Conference on the character of God, the emphasis remains upon the *exaltation* of man to the position of the divine.

Student Manual

The LDS Church also offers various courses in religion and doctrine and publishes manuals to go along with these courses. One such manual, *Doctrines of the Gospel*,[3] is meant for the Religion 231 and 232 classes. In chapter 3 of the manual the nature of God is addressed from the LDS viewpoint. It is no surprise that as soon as the topic is broached, Joseph Smith's King Follett Discourse is cited as authoritative by this official Church publication. But then there is an interesting quotation from Spencer W. Kimball:

> "God made man in his own image and certainly he made woman in the image of his wife-partner" (Spencer W. Kimball, *The Teachings of Spencer W. Kimball*, 25).

Here we encounter the concept of the heavenly Mother, God's wife in heaven, and have the interesting assertion that women are made not in the image of God but in the image of God's "wife-partner."

The discussion goes on,[4] eventually coming to the topic "The Father Presides Over the Godhead." Mormon Apostle Bruce R. McConkie is cited defining what the "godhead" is:

> Three glorified, exalted, and perfected personages comprise the Godhead or supreme presidency of the universe. . . . They are God the Father; God the Son; God the Holy Ghost.
>
> Though each God in the Godhead is a personage, separate and distinct from each of the others, yet they are "one God" . . .

meaning that they are united as one in the attributes of perfection. For instance, each has the fullness of truth, knowledge, charity, power, justice, judgment, mercy, and faith. Accordingly they all think, act, speak, and are alike in all things; and yet they are three separate and distinct entities. Each occupies space and is and can be in but one place at one time, but each has power and influence that is everywhere present (McConkie, *Mormon Doctrine*, 319).

We see that the unity of the "godhead" is not an *ontological* unity but a unity of *agreement* between three "separate and distinct entities." These "entities" occupy space and "can be in but one place at one time." So in essence the unity of the godhead in Mormon theology would be akin to saying that Congress is "one in agreeing on a bill" while consisting of multiple separate entities or persons.

Achieving a Celestial Marriage

A "celestial marriage," that is, one wherein the couple is sealed in the Mormon Temple, is the "key to exaltation" according to a publication produced by the Church of Jesus Christ of Latter-day Saints. *Achieving a Celestial Marriage* is another student manual, copyrighted 1992 by the Corporation of the President of the Church of Jesus Christ of Latter-day Saints. What it says about God is especially relevant because it does so in the context of guiding couples into the very relationship that makes exaltation to godhood possible! On pages 129–132 of this official publication we encounter the plain and clear words regarding the means by which men are exalted to the status of a god. As usual, the source begins with the idea of man's capacity for progress and exaltation and from this moves to the idea that God himself went through a similar process.

> The gospel of Jesus Christ teaches that man is an eternal being, made in the image and likeness of God. It also holds that man is a literal child of God and has the potential, if faithful to divine laws and ordinances, of becoming like his heavenly parent. These truths are generally well understood by Latter-day Saints.

The reader has surely noted the repeated emphasis, throughout the literature surveyed so far, on the absolute necessity of faithfulness "to divine laws and ordinances" if one is to gain exaltation. Here these concepts are said to be definitive *of the Gospel of Jesus Christ itself*. We cannot emphasize too strongly that in Mormonism the idea of advancement to godhood *is the gospel of the Church*. If we fail to understand this, we risk seeing the doctrine as a mere side issue rather than the defining concept that it is. The necessity of obedience to such "laws" comes out in the next section as well:

> Less well understood, however, is the fact that God is an exalted man who once lived on an earth and underwent experiences of mortality. The Prophet Joseph Smith refers to this as "the great secret" (*Times and Seasons* 5:613 [August 15, 1844]. See also Joseph Smith, *Teachings of the Prophet Joseph Smith*, 345.) The progression of our Father in heaven to godhood or exaltation was strictly in accordance with eternal principles, "for he who is not able to abide the law of a celestial kingdom cannot abide a celestial glory" (*D & C* 88:22).

One of the concepts that is especially troubling to the Christian reviewer of these beliefs is that part and parcel of the idea of "exaltation" and the power of God is the concept of procreation. It is not as if there is something wrong with human sexuality. It is the projection of creaturely means of propagation onto the Creator himself that causes the orthodox Christian to read the following words with abhorrence:

> By definition, exaltation includes the ability to procreate the family unit throughout eternity. This our Father in heaven has power to do. His marriage partner is our Mother in heaven. We are their spirit children, born to them in the bonds of celestial marriage.
>
> The Lord would have all his children attain exaltation, but men must have their agency. Only those who subscribe by ordinance and by faithful adherence to covenant are worthy of "a continuation of the seeds forever and ever" (*D & C* 132:19).

When making the decision concerning the magnitude of difference between the LDS view of God and the historical Christian view, the idea that God has a "continuation of the seeds forever and ever," and that this is made a part of His *deity*, should be kept in mind.

This section is followed by one titled "God Was Once a Mortal Man," and again we find the LDS Church falling back, not upon her scriptures to teach her people, but upon the King Follett Discourse. Subtitles include "He Lived on an Earth Like Our Own" and "He Experienced Conditions Similar to Our Own and Advanced Step by Step." This is followed by another section, "God is Now an Exalted Man With Powers of Eternal Increase," with a subtitle, "Our Father in Heaven Lives in an Exalted Marriage Relationship." Under this section, Melvin J. Ballard is quoted:

> No matter to what heights God has attained or may attain, he does not stand alone: for side by side with him, in all her glory, a glory like unto his, stands a companion, the Mother of his children. For as we have a Father in heaven, so also we have a Mother there, a glorified, exalted, ennobled Mother" (Melvin J. Ballard, as quoted in Bryant S. Hinckley, *Sermons and Missionary Services of Melvin J. Ballard*, 205–206).

The repetition of the same theme concerning the heavenly "Mother" should also play a large role in comparing LDS teaching to historical Christian theology. The literal parent-child relationship of God and humans is then emphasized with subtitles including "We Are Literal Children of God" and "We Lived With Our Heavenly Parents Prior to Coming to Earth."

Men Are Gods in Embryo

At times LDS representatives have complained that Christian writers use Mormon terminology that Mormons would never use. Sometimes there is truth to this complaint, but in the case of the Mormon doctrine of God, one will find some of the strangest terms used in LDS literature. It might seem to some that saying Mormons believe men are "gods in embryo" is to engage in sensationalism, but in reality this is the title of the next section of this LDS Church-published student manual. To introduce a citation from the First Presidency's statement *The Origin of Man*, quoted in the previous chapter, the LDS Church chose the title "Men Are Gods in Embryo." Under this title they quote,

> Man is the child of God, formed in the divine image and

endowed with divine attributes, and even as the infant son of our earthly father and mother is capable in due time of becoming a man, so the undeveloped offspring of celestial parentage is capable, by experience through ages of aeons, of evolving into a God (The First Presidency [Joseph F. Smith, John R. Winder, Anthon H. Lund], "The Origin of Man," *Improvement Era* [November 1909]: 81).

This divine potential, we are told, was transmitted to us through our spiritual birth in the preexistence. Lorenzo Snow is cited to explain,

> We were born in the image of God our Father, he begot us like unto himself. There is the nature of deity in the composition of our spiritual organization: in our spiritual birth, our Father transmitted to us the capabilities, powers and faculties which he himself possessed, as much so as the child on its mother's bosom possesses, although in an undeveloped state, the faculties, powers and susceptibilities of its parent (Lorenzo Snow, *Deseret Weekly News*, 20:597).

The King Follett Discourse is again cited to substantiate the statement that exaltation is attained "by going from one small degree to another." This section is followed by another that discusses the importance of the family units and the sealing of the priesthood authority that keeps families together for eternity. The student manual then teaches the faithful Mormon that "Only Through Celestial Marriage Can a Person Become Like God." The centrality of the Temple and celestial marriage is explained by Joseph Fielding Smith:

> If you want salvation in the fullest, that is, exaltation in the kingdom of God, so that you may become his sons and his daughters, you have got to go into the temple of the Lord and receive these holy ordinances which belong to that house, which cannot be had elsewhere. *No man shall receive the fullness of eternity, of exaltation, alone; no woman shall receive that blessing alone; but man and wife, when they receive the sealing power in the temple of the Lord, if they thereafter keep all the commandments, shall pass on to exaltation and become like the Lord.* And that is the destiny of men; that is what the Lord desires for his children" (Smith, *Doctrines of Salvation* 2:43–44).

So if a person is married in the eternal marriage ceremony, and endures to the end, what is the result? Smith again explains,

> But if we are married for time and for all eternity and it is sealed upon our heads by those who have the authority so to seal, and *if we then keep our covenants and are faithful to the end*, we shall come forth in the resurrection from the dead and receive the following promised blessings:
> *Then shall they be gods. . . .*
> So if you want to enter into exaltation and become as God, that is, a son of God or a daughter of God, and receive *fullness* of the kingdom, then you have got to abide in his law—not merely the law of marriage but *all* that pertains to the new and everlasting covenant—and then you have the "continuation of the lives" forever, for the Lord says:
> "This is *eternal life*—to know the only wise and true God, and Jesus Christ, whom he hath sent. I am he. Receive ye, therefore, my law" (*D & C* 132:24 [Smith, *Doctrines of Salvation* 2:62–63]).

If you are a resurrected and glorified being, you have the capacity to become parents of spirit offspring and begin the process all over again, just as the heavenly Father (Elohim) did on this planet.

> So far as the stages of eternal progression and attainment have been made known through divine revelation, we are to understand that only resurrected and glorified beings can become parents of spirit offspring. Only such exalted souls have reached maturity in the appointed course of eternal life; and the spirits born to them in the eternal worlds will pass in due sequence through the several stages or estates by which the glorified parents have attained exaltation (A Doctrinal Exposition by the First Presidency [Joseph F. Smith, Anthon H. Lund, Charles W. Penrose I], and the Twelve, "The Father and the Son," *Improvement Era* [June 1916]: 942).

This pronouncement is followed by the assertion that "Celestial Marriage Makes Women Queens and Priestesses unto Their Husbands." Remember, this is what the faithful LDS couple will read as the teaching of their Church prior to entering into a Temple marriage. McConkie is then cited as saying,

> If righteous men have power through the gospel and its

crowning ordinance of celestial marriage to become kings and priests to rule in exaltation forever, it follows that the women by their side (without whom they cannot attain exaltation) will be *queens* and priestesses (Rev. 1:6; 5:10). Exaltation grows out of the eternal union of a man and his wife. Of those whose marriage endures in eternity, the Lord says, "Then shall *they* be gods" (*D & C* 132:20); that is, each of them, the man and the woman, will be a god. As such they will rule over their dominions forever" (McConkie, *Mormon Doctrine*, 613).

The discussion ends with the continuation of the cycle of eternal progression. The subtitle reads, "Celestial Marriage Makes It Possible for Us to Claim Our Mortal Children in Eternity As Well As to Propagate Ourselves Throughout Eternity."

> Parents will have eternal claim upon their posterity and will have the gift of eternal increase, if they obtain the exaltation. This is the crowning glory in the kingdom of God, and they will have no end. When the Lord says they will have no end, he means that all who attain to this glory will have the blessing of the continuation of the 'seeds' forever. Those who fail to obtain this blessing come to the 'deaths,' which means that they will have no increase, forever. *All who obtain this exaltation will have the privilege of completing the full measure of their existence, and they will have a posterity that will be as innumerable as the stars of heaven. . . .*
>
> The Father has promised us that through our faithfulness we shall be blessed with *the fullness of his kingdom.* In other words, we will have the privilege of becoming *like him. To become like him we must have all the powers of godhood; thus a man and his wife when glorified will have spirit children* who eventually will go on an earth like this one we are on and pass through the same kind of experiences, being subject to mortal conditions, and if faithful, then they also will receive the fullness of exaltation and partake of the same blessings. There is no end to this development; it will go on forever. *We will become gods and have jurisdiction over worlds, and these worlds will be peopled by our own offspring.* We will have an endless eternity for this (Smith, *Doctrines of Salvation* 2:43–44, 48).

This ends the discussion of celestial marriage and the nature of God in the student manual used by the LDS Church to instruct its own people concerning the nature of God. The reality of the Eternal Law of Progression could not be more clearly pronounced. The goal of the Mormon gospel of exaltation to godhood is plainly stated: "We will become gods and have jurisdiction over worlds, and these worlds will be peopled by our own offspring."

Before turning to the statements of the General Authorities as they speak in Conference, I wish to reiterate the importance of this section of materials taken directly from the publications of the LDS Church. What is said "in house" is always more revealing and more honest than what is said to those "outside." We well know that when speaking among our own friends and compatriots we speak more frankly than we might to others. When we look at the statements of the LDS scriptures or leading authorities, we may take a word or phrase another way than it was intended. But when we read the plain statements of the Church *to her own people*, there is little doubt regarding the doctrines of the Church concerning God as an exalted man and men as gods in embryo. I also point out that while some modern Mormons would like to be free of the weight of the teachings of Bruce McConkie or Joseph Fielding Smith, *the Church itself cites from these sources as authoritative, accurate, and correct.* How can anyone say that such sources are merely "speculative" when cited by non-Mormons, when they are authoritative when cited by the LDS hierarchy?

Statements of General Authorities in Conference

The semiannual General Conference of the Church of Jesus Christ of Latter-day Saints provides a forum for the leaders of the Church to give constant, up-to-date guidance to the LDS Church. Here the Apostles gather with the Prophet and instruct the Church on issues both doctrinal and moral. The LDS Church has diligently recorded the sermons and talks delivered at the Conferences over the years, providing us with yet another solid source of reference material upon which to determine the teachings of the LDS Church. If one cannot accept as authoritative and accurate the sermons of the leaders of the Church when preaching in Conference, when *can* such leadership be expected? I also note that the talks given in modern times are *very closely scrutinized* prior to their being delivered. Consequently, the chances of encountering some errant, nonconformist speech during Conference is very small indeed.

I will present a representative sample going back to the turn of the century and then move toward modern times. As the main outlines of LDS doctrine are already in place, I will only note the specific claims that are often disputed.

From the April 1898 Conference, Mormon Apostle Franklin D. Richards said,

> The three great patriarchs, Abraham, Isaac, and Jacob, started with a small beginning, and revelation tells us that they have become Gods, and the promise was given to them that their seed should be as numerous as the sands upon the seashore. We are their children, and are not the blessings of Abraham, Isaac, and Jacob our blessings?[5]

Note the continued emphasis upon "faithfulness and diligence in keeping the commandments of God" in the following statement by LDS Apostle John W. Taylor:

> Here is set forth in inspired language, what it is possible for the children of men to attain to in the eternal worlds, through their faithfulness and diligence in keeping the commandments of God while they live upon the earth. Just imagine for a moment the idea that through the principle of eternal progression we can ultimately become like our Father and God!
>
> This revelation was given to President Lorenzo Snow in his early manhood, and the principle of revelation was his guiding star to the hour of his death.[6]

Anthon Lund commented upon John 10:34 in these words:

> Now, we are not ashamed of the glorious doctrine of eternal progression, that man may attain the position of those to whom came the word of God, that is, gods.[7]

Elder Charles Callis fully connects the Gospel of Christ with the law of eternal progression and exaltation to godhood:

> My brethren and sisters, I desire to say unto you, for I believe it with all my heart, that the road to exaltation and eternal progression lies through sacrifice and work. Jesus said, "Be ye perfect, even as your Father which is in heaven is perfect." He

did not limit the attainment of perfection to time, degree, or state. Eternal progression wilt be along the lines of orderly knowledge, and of law, because the Gospel will be in force in eternity as it is here. It is impossible for a being, mortal or immortal, to progress without a due regard for law and without obeying the mandates of the Almighty.[8]

In this sermon by Elder Thomas Rees the full extent of the LDS doctrine of God is seen in the use of the term "creators" (in the plural) of exalted human beings. Note especially the claim that out of their hands "will roll systems of worlds":

The I AM within us teaches us that we existed before we came here, that we exist now, and it seems impossible with the feeling that we have within us to ever cease to exist. Then we should teach our boys and girls the lessons of obedience, virtue, honesty, and truth, that they may walk before their heavenly Father as he would have them walk, and before their fellow men in dignity and in the power of the holy priesthood. We are claiming the greatest blessing that can be given to the children of men—these boys and girls—for they will be with us throughout all eternity. In the eternities they can be perfected with us. Think of the possibilities, what they mean to us, the little children whom God gives to our arms to teach. Think of the minds of these children and the power inherent in them to be creators in the hereafter! Do they not mean more to our lives than our lands and our chattels? For our children will have the power of eternal progression, until out of their hands will roll systems of worlds, with all the wealth necessary to their creation. Far greater are these blessings to us than the things of this life.[9]

Do Mormons use Lorenzo Snow's couplet among themselves? Indeed they do, and that in Conference:

We have in the Church a saying that we very frequently repeat: "As God now is, man may become," a beautiful statement of the great law of eternal progression. I believe that in this matter of faith we can appeal to the intelligence as well as to the emotions, and I believe that if we are going to have our faith firmly established on an enduring rock, it must be based upon the agreement of our intelligence with our emotions.[10]

A *most* interesting section is found in the comments of Elder

Kenneth R. Stevens, who had served as Mission President of the LDS work in Tahiti. During the Conference of October 1941, Elder Stevens said,

> I rejoice that while being in the midst of that people I came to learn through their legends that there was a time when they believed in the Gods of heaven as we do, even a plurality of Gods, and that they believed in the creation of this earth even as our doctrine teaches. This, however, has been explained away and replaced by modern Christian doctrine which teaches of a God who is everywhere present, and so small He dwells in the human heart, but who has no parts nor passions, and by a different story of the creation. And so, it thrilled me when our missionaries preached Mormonism to have those people nod their heads and say, "It sounds like the old doctrine which was common to our people."[11]

For many, it would be highly significant that natives in Tahiti would find LDS theology, especially with reference to a plurality of gods, similar to their own native beliefs. LDS writers often criticize Christian apologists for identifying Mormonism as a polytheistic religion, yet would they likewise criticize us for identifying the pagan religions found among the natives of Tahiti as polytheistic?

Mormon Apostle Stephen L. Richards gave an important insight into the Mormon concept of exaltation and its relationship to the Gospel in the following talk, also from 1941. Note how Richards identifies this as a "new interpretation of the Gospel of Christ":

> On the basis of such statements the doctrine of eternal progression was deduced and taught. Men were given to understand that through obedience to the laws of the Gospel they might continue to grow and develop in knowledge and power until in eternity they would come to divinity itself; that the highest order of intelligence is that intelligence which comprehends the things of God and eternity; that, "It is the glory of God to bring to pass the immortality and eternal life of man," and that "men are that they might have joy." The place of good and evil in the world and their necessity for the exercise of man's free agency were all set forth in this new interpretation of the Gospel of Christ.[12]

Milton R. Hunter, a General Authority of the LDS Church, referred to the nature of God a number of times in his sermons and writings. Here, in referring to the means of progression to godhood, Hunter speaks the importance of education:

> I am convinced that the educational program is completely in line with the gospel as revealed to the Prophet Joseph Smith—that man "cannot be saved in ignorance"; that "we are saved no faster than we gain knowledge"; that "the glory of God is intelligence. . . ." We are a group of people who know that we must gain knowledge of truth in order that we may progress on to godhood.[13]

A few years later Hunter referred again to the topic of exaltation:

> We believe that God is a personal being. By a personal being, we mean that he is a man—an exalted man. Approximately one hundred years ago, soon after Lorenzo Snow became a member of the true Church of Jesus Christ, he formulated a remarkable couplet which has since that time become famous. He said: "As man is, God once was; as God is, man may become" (Lorenzo Snow, *The Millennial Star*, 54:404). Time and time again during the period of the restoration of the gospel of Jesus Christ to the Prophet Joseph Smith, various evidences were given to him sustaining, amplifying, and explaining the personality of God. If time would permit, many excellent quotations could be cited from the *D & C* which would help to describe the personality of our Eternal Father. However, I would like on this occasion to quote a statement taken from a great sermon which was given by the Prophet Joseph shortly before his death. This quotation is a continuation of the statement I have already quoted from the Prophet.[14]

Again, citation of the King Follett Discourse followed. I emphasize the continuing validity of that foundational sermon by Joseph Smith, as seen in its consistent appearance *throughout* the writings, teachings, and sermons of the General Authorities of the LDS Church.[15] The simple repetition of citation is more than sufficient to establish the authority of the sermon in Mormonism.

Elder Heber J. Meeks is representative of the continuing emphasis upon the exalted nature of man as a god in embryo, here in a talk from the Conference of April 1951:

I rejoice in the Gospel of Jesus Christ, and the glorious message which it has brought to me, for it tells me that I do not have a common origin nor a common destiny with the beasts of the field, that birth into this life was not the beginning of my soul, and that death is not its oblivion. But it tells me that I am a son of God, an eternal being; that as a son of God, there is within me all the qualities, all the powers of my Father which is in Heaven, that there is within me the power to rise to Godhood, that I may share with God, my Father in Heaven, forever and ever, all His power and glory and dominion, through Jesus Christ, our Savior, Amen.[16]

Spencer W. Kimball, prior to his being made Prophet of the Church, spoke in Conference concerning the possibility of rising to Godhood:

When one realizes the vastness, the richness, the glory of that "all" which the Lord promises to bestow upon his faithful, it is worth all it costs in patience, faith, sacrifice, sweat, and tears. The blessings of eternity contemplated in this "all" bring to men immortality and everlasting life, eternal growth, divine leadership, eternal increase, perfection, and with it all—Godhood.[17]

The immutability of God—that awesome truth that God does not change, evolve, or undergo alteration—is anathema to the Mormon view of God. Here, LDS Apostle Hugh B. Brown identifies it as "stagnation" and "damnation":

We believe that in his infinite and eternal development toward a Godlike status, man moves toward and through a turnstile called death; that there is no interruption of life at this portal, for eternity is indefinitely prolonged time. We believe that man, after passing through this turnstile, will continue his eternal journey from the point where his actions in this life have brought him. "Whatever principle of intelligence we attain unto in this life, it will rise with us in the resurrection" (D & C 130:18). To deny the possibility of eternal progression is to accept the awful alternative of eventual stagnation which would be damnation.[18]

The relationship of the priesthood, celestial marriage, and exaltation to godhood all appear together in this comment by Antoine R. Ivins, one of the Seventy:

> All that our Father hath shall be given to him who magnifies that calling, and that means that he shall take his wife to the temple, because we are told also that men who succeed in fully living up to all of the privileges and responsibilities of the Melchizedek Priesthood shall become gods with the power of eternal increase. That is the pearl of great price, brethren and sisters.[19]

The following last five examples come from men who either advanced to the First Presidency (Marion G. Romney also served as President of the Quorum of the Twelve) or became the President of the Church (Smith, Kimball, Hinckley). These statements come from the past few decades, from the lips of the highest leaders of the Church. If there has been a doctrinal "change" in the Church on the subjects of God being an exalted man or men becoming gods, such change should appear in the writings and sermons of these men. I begin with Spencer W. Kimball in the October Conference of 1964:

> How conclusive! How bounded! How limiting! And we come to realize again as it bears heavily upon us that this time, this life, this mortality is the time to prepare to meet God. How lonely and barren will be the so-called single blessedness throughout eternity! How sad to be separate and single and apart through countless ages when one could by meeting requirements, have happy marriage for eternity in the temple by proper authority and continue on in ever-increasing joy and happiness, growth and development toward Godhood.[20]

By now the reader recognizes plainly the repeated emphasis upon the priesthood, eternal marriage, and exaltation toward godhood. These seemed to be strong elements of the October 1964 Conference, for Marion Romney likewise addressed the topics at that time:

> This knowledge of God opened up to Joseph Smith, as it does to all of us, a vision with infinite promise. We all know that like begets like and that for the offspring to grow to the stature of his parent is a process infinitely repeated in nature.

We can therefore understand that for a son of God to grow to the likeness of his Father in heaven is in harmony with natural law. We see this law demonstrated every few years in our own experience. Sons born to mortal fathers grow up to be like their fathers in the flesh. This is the way it will be with spirit sons of God. They will grow up to be like their Father in heaven. Joseph taught this obvious truth. As a matter of fact, he taught that through this process God himself attained perfection. From President Snow's understanding of the teachings of the Prophet on this doctrinal point, he coined the familiar couplet: "As man is, God once was; as God is, man may become." This teaching is peculiar to the restored gospel of Jesus Christ.[21]

Romney says this teaching—exaltation to godhood—is "peculiar to the restored gospel of Jesus Christ," which is a specific LDS phrase referring to the gospel as restored to the earth by Joseph Smith, but lost for nearly 1,700 years before that. I again point out that this gospel itself, by the testimony of the leaders of the LDS Church, has as its goal the exaltation of men to the status of gods. Likewise, Joseph Fielding Smith, who became the Prophet in 1970, said this just a few years earlier:

> We are in the mortal life to get an experience, a training, that we couldn't get any other way. And in order to become gods, it is necessary for us to know something about pain, about sickness, and about the other things that we partake of in this school of mortality.[22]

Spencer W. Kimball said the following in a priesthood meeting held during Conference:

> Brethren, 225,000 of you are here tonight. I suppose 225,000 of you may become gods. There seems to be plenty of space out there in the universe. And the Lord has proved that He knows how to do it.[23]

And it seems fitting to close our survey of *some* of the statements from Conference talks with the current Prophet, Gordon Hinckley, who was then First Counselor in the Presidency, October 8, 1994:

> On the other hand, the whole design of the gospel is to lead us onward and upward to greater achievement, even eventually

to Godhood. . . . Our enemies have criticized us for believing in this. Our reply is that this lofty concept in no way diminishes God the Eternal Father. . . . But just as any earthly father wishes for his sons and daughters every success in life, so I believe our Father in Heaven wishes for His children that they might approach Him in stature and stand beside him resplendent in Godly strength and wisdom.[24]

Hinckley's words tie together some of the main threads in the LDS doctrine of God: the idea that the goal of the Gospel is exaltation to godhood and the idea that men can "approach Him in stature" and hence become gods. And it also shows us how the leadership of the LDS Church is still preaching the same doctrine of God that Joseph Smith propounded so clearly and forcefully in 1844. Surely the modern Mormon Church has learned to be more circumspect and to couch its teachings in a little more palatable form. But the doctrine is still the same.

We have looked at three levels of representative doctrinal statements, all from LDS General Authorities, including Prophets and Apostles. We have looked at official publications and seen sections of sermons from the General Conference of the Church.

Now we will cover the final level of statements, those found outside official LDS publications, yet still from the leaders of the Church. We will briefly survey these statements, discover if the consistency we have charted through the first three levels is to be found here, and if so, we will then be in a position to respond to the LDS doctrine of God and answer the question, "Is the Mormon my brother?"

7

THE MORMON DOCTRINE OF GOD: FOURTH LEVEL STATEMENTS

General Authorities

I remember well the first LDS Book and Supply I visited. It was a small store in the Phoenix area, located in a strip mall, conveniently close to the main road I took back and forth to college. When I began my study of Mormonism I became a regular at the store. The clerk's name was Mary. It became a bit of a joke each time I would approach the counter carrying something like McConkie's *Mormon Doctrine* or Joseph Fielding Smith's *Doctrines of Salvation*. As I would write out my check, Mary would ask, "What ward?"

"I'm not LDS" I would reply.

"Oh, keep reading these books, and you will be soon!"

I'm not sure Mary would be too happy about the use to which all those books have been put, but at least I was open with her about the fact that I was an outsider, doing my best to learn Mormon belief.

The rapid growth of the Mormon religion has spawned a correspondingly rapid growth of LDS literature. The General Authorities are constantly producing books, which are dutifully stocked on the shelves of LDS bookstores around the nation. I try to keep abreast of what is new in the world of LDS publications, and one of the regular stops for me and my volunteers during each General Conference (after spending the day passing out tracts outside the

Temple gates) is our obligatory visit to the Deseret Book in down-town Salt Lake City.

One will, admittedly, find a *wide* variety of viewpoints in the broad spectrum of "LDS literature." However, if we stick to the writings of the LDS leaders and scholars, we will find the same beliefs we have charted in the previous chapters.

We shall look first at the sermons and writings of notable Mormons throughout the history of the Church, and then note some statements from the relatively recent volume, *The Encyclopedia of Mormonism*, a monumental work produced by a wide range of LDS scholars and writers.

Lorenzo Snow

We have already had reason to note the couplet of Lorenzo Snow regarding the relationship of God and man:

> Lorenzo Snow is remembered for his couplet "As man now is, God once was; as God now is, man may be." These words came by revelation to Lorenzo when he was a young man in Nauvoo. Their truthfulness was reaffirmed when he heard the Prophet Joseph Smith teach the very same concept. Over the years this simple yet profound statement has stirred the minds of many individuals and caused them to further investigate The Church of Jesus Christ of Latter-day Saints.[1]

Orson Pratt

One of the most flamboyant of the early Mormon leaders was Apostle Orson Pratt. His book *The Seer* is one of the most interesting early LDS publications. He also provided many sermons that appear in the *Journal of Discourses*. While he had several viewpoints that an orthodox Christian would find unusual and very troubling (especially with regard to his view of the Bible), we are here concerned only with his statements concerning the doctrine of God.

One of the passages that Christians turn to in response to LDS theology is Isaiah 43:10. Orson Pratt addressed this passage in a sermon delivered February 18, 1855:

> "But" inquires one, "how are you going to get along with the

passage in Isaiah, where the Lord declared that, 'There is no God before me, nor shall there be any after me?' " How can we believe this, when we believe in the revelation given through Joseph Smith, which says there are many Gods, and that Abraham, Isaac, and Jacob are Gods, and that all good men in this Church shall become Gods? Paul also speaks of the only wise God. Perhaps some may suppose that it is translated improperly. But you will find the same thing in the *Book of Mormon*, translated by the Urim and Thummim; the same things are also contained in the new translation of the book of Genesis, given to Moses, where the Lord declares that, "There is no God beside me." In these expressions, God has reference to the great principles of light and truth, or knowledge, and not to the tabernacles in which this knowledge may dwell; the tabernacles are many and without number, but the truth or knowledge which is often personified and called God, is one, being the same in all; God is one, being a unity, when represented by light, truth, wisdom, or knowledge; but when reference is made to the temples in which this knowledge dwells, the number of Gods is infinite.

This explains the mystery. If we should take a million worlds like this and number their particles, we should find that there are more Gods than there are particles of matter in those worlds.[2]

By depersonalizing the term "God" and making it refer to "truth or knowledge," Pratt thinks to find a way around the repeated assertion that there is but one true God. Yet when it comes to *individuals* who can be called "gods," his assertion that there are literally *billions* of such gods is as blatant a teaching of polytheism as any religious system I have ever encountered. Orson Pratt's writings are no less clear on the same point:

The Gods who dwell in the Heaven from which our spirits came, are beings who have been redeemed from the grave in a world which existed before the foundations of this earth were laid. They and the Heavenly body which they now inhabit were once in a fallen state. Their terrestrial world was redeemed, and glorified, and made a Heaven: their terrestrial bodies, after suffering death, were redeemed and glorified and made Gods. And thus, as their world was exalted from a temporal to an eternal state, they were exalted also, from fallen man to Celestial Gods to inhabit their Heaven forever and ever.[3]

One of the points that is here often disputed by modern LDS (and possibly even by LDS at the time of the writing of Pratt's work) was the idea that God was "once in a fallen state." Some LDS prefer to believe that God the Father was like Jesus for another world: a sinless Savior. Of course, if the entire scheme of eternal progression is true, the worthy Mormon male today, who confesses to being a sinner and being redeemed, if he should someday become a god, would have at some time in the past been in a fallen state himself. Among the billions and billions of gods in the cosmos, the vast majority would have to have been fallen beings at one time, for the number of "savior gods" would have to be very small in comparison with the "redeemed gods."

Parley P. Pratt

Orson's older brother was named Parley, and he, too, was one of the original Apostles of the LDS Church. He wrote the work *Key to the Science of Theology*, in which he made the following comments:

> Gods, angels, and men are all of one species, one race, one great family, widely diffused among the planetary systems, as colonies, kingdoms, nations, etc. . . . Each of these Gods, including Jesus Christ and His Father, being in possession of not merely an organized spirit, but a glorious immortal body of flesh and bones, is subject to the laws which govern, of necessity, even the most refined order of physical existence.[4]

We will see the assertion again that God and man are "all of one species" in a modern LDS source.

George Q. Cannon

Mormon Apostle George Q. Cannon served in the First Presidency of the LDS Church for many years. His work *Gospel Truth* is an invaluable testimony to early LDS beliefs. He was certainly unashamed of his belief in a plurality of gods and the idea that men could become gods. For example, note his words regarding the theory of evolution:

We hear considerable about evolution. Who is there that believes more in true evolution than the Latter-day Saints?—the evolution of man until he shall become a god, until he shall sit at the right hand of the Father, until he shall be a joint heir with Jesus! That is the Gospel of Jesus Christ, believed in by the Latter-day Saints. That is the kind of evolution we believe in, but not the evolution of man from some low type of animal life.[5]

This is not the only place where Cannon spoke of "evolution" and applied it to eternal progression and exaltation to godhood:

Men talk about evolution. This is the true evolution—being such as we are and developing and advancing and progressing in that upward and onward career until we shall become like Him, in truth, until we shall possess the powers that He possesses and exercise the dominion that He now exercises. This is the promise that is held out to us.[6]

The following is significant for its straightforward attitude in telling us all what "the Mormons believe."

The Mormons believe that all men were born in the spirit world of the union of the sexes, having a literal father and a literal mother before coming to this world, that the spirits are just the same in appearance as the body, that God is a married Being, has a wife at least, as Jeremiah said the angels were offering incense to the queen of heaven. The Latter-day Saints believe that God is an exalted Man, and that we are the offspring of Him and His wife (April 15, 1884, *Salt Lake Herald*).[7]

How literally do Mormons understand the term "Father"? One cannot get much more literal than Cannon:

The "Mormons" believe that God is the Father of our spirits—that we are His offspring; and we think it just as consistent and reasonable to believe that He has a partner or partners as to think that He sits, isolated and solitary in lonely grandeur, in a state of bachelorship, and yet a Parent of so innumerable a progeny (March 29, 1856, *WS*, 47).[8]

The biblical use of the term "Father" to mean "Creator" is not enough for Cannon:

There are many people who imagine that we are the children of God because He is our Creator. But we differ from all other people in this respect. We believe that we are the literal descendants of our Eternal Father, that we are the offspring of Deity, that those aspirations which man has and which cause Him to perform the mighty works that we see on every hand as we travel throughout the earth are inherited from our Eternal Father. They come to us by descent; or, to use another phrase, they are hereditary. The doctrine of heredity is manifested in the works of man. We descend from this great Father who formed the earth and who governs this universe.

Cannon certainly stands firmly in the tradition of Joseph Smith in proclaiming the concept of eternal progression:

Among the Latter-day Saints there is a knowledge concerning the Personage of God. We have some conception of Him. We know that He is a Being of tabernacle. Among the Latter-day Saints there is a knowledge concerning the Personage of God. A remark suggests itself to my mind which I heard a few days ago from one of our Apostles—Brother Lorenzo Snow. It was something to this effect: That as God now is, we will be; as man is, God was. It is very comprehensive. And we descend from this Father. We are His offspring. We possess His attributes. It is true they are not developed, but we possess them; and He desires to lead us forward until we shall be like Him. This is the object of the Gospel.[9]

I cannot overemphasize the *consistency* that exists throughout these sources not only on the doctrine of God (i.e., that God was once a man, that man can become gods just as God is a god, etc.) but as well on this idea: that the *Gospel of Jesus Christ* as proclaimed by the LDS Church and the plan of *eternal progression* are one and the same. The Gospel is that men can become gods, according to Mormonism.

Wilford Woodruff

Wilford Woodruff became the fourth President of the LDS Church in 1889. While known to history more as the Prophet through which the Manifesto ending polygamy came to the LDS

Church, he also spoke to the topic of our study in the years prior to his elevation to the Presidency, here from 1857:

> If there was a point where man in his progression could not proceed any further, the very idea would throw a gloom over every intelligent and reflecting mind. God himself is increasing and progressing in knowledge, power, and dominion, and will do so, worlds without end.[10]

Woodruff's statement, while perfectly in line with what Joseph Smith said in the King Follett Discourse, is controversial today, for many LDS wish to say that God has completed His progression. This can be seen in a statement by Mormon Apostle Bruce R. McConkie:

> It should be realized that God is not progressing in knowledge, truth, virtue, wisdom, or any of the attributes of godliness.[11]

B. H. Roberts

Brigham Henry Roberts is one of the two greatest scholars Mormonism has produced since its inception (I would include James Talmage as the other). Here we encounter a great mind that attempts to provide some consistency to the system created by Joseph Smith. His book *The Mormon Doctrine of Deity* is one of the first examples of LDS apologetic literature. He knew the vocabulary of Christian theology and hence struggled to express LDS beliefs in that language. For example, with regard to how the term "omniscient" (having all knowledge) could be applied to the LDS God, he wrote,

> So with the All-knowing attribute, Omniscience: that must be understood somewhat in the same light as the other attributes considered: not that God is Omniscient up to the point that further progress in knowledge is impossible to him; but that all knowledge that is, all that exists, God knows. He is Universal Consciousness, and Mind—he is the All-knowing One because he knows all that is known.[12]

True omniscience becomes *potential* omniscience or *relative* omniscience. This kind of redefinition of terms is absolutely necessary in attempting to fit the anthropomorphic God (or, as some put it, the theomorphic man) of Mormonism into classical terminology. The same is true regarding omnipresence:

> So the attribute "Omnipresence"—the Everywhere Present attribute. This must be so far limited as to be ascribed to God's Spirit, or Influence, or Power: but not of God as a Person or Individual: for in these latter respects even God is limited by the law that one body cannot occupy two places at one and the same time. But radiating from his presence, as beams of light and warmth radiate from our sun, is God's Spirit, penetrating and permeating space, making space and all worlds in space vibrate with his life and thought and presence: holding all forces—dynamic and static—under control, making them to subserve his will and purposes.[13]

Omnipresence becomes a matter of God's Spirit radiating throughout creation, though we are left to wonder if *all* of creation is meant or only those worlds under this particular god's control. In either case, there was a time when this God wasn't a god, so whose influence was then felt throughout "creation"? These are difficult questions for the LDS position to answer. Despite Roberts's interaction with historical, orthodox Christian belief, he still maintained the full LDS viewpoint regarding the plurality of gods:

> A Plurality of Divine Intelligences: We have already shown that the Father, the Son, and the Holy Ghost are three separate and distinct persons, and, so far as personality is concerned, are three Gods. Their "oneness" consists in being possessed of the same mind; they are one, too, in wisdom, in knowledge, in will and purpose; but as individuals they are three, each separate and distinct from the other, and three is plural. Now, that is a long way on the road towards proving the plurality of Gods.[14]

Roberts's classic work on the subject is titled *The Mormon Doctrine of Deity*. This work, which contains a dialogue and debate on the nature of God with a Catholic clergyman, Van Der Donckt, is a must-read for the person looking into not only the definition of LDS theology but the means used to defend it. But a single citation will be enough to include Roberts among all the others we have examined regarding the nature of the LDS God:

> But since the premises themselves have been shown to be

utterly untenable, as relating to God, as revealed in the scriptures, and in the person and nature of Jesus Christ, the conclusions are wrong; and the facts established are that while God in mind, faculties and in power is doubtless infinite, in person he is finite; and as his spirit is united to a body, he is composite, not simple; and as Jesus Christ was God manifested in the flesh, the express image of God the Father's person, the counterpart of his nature, and yet at the same time was a man—it is neither unscriptural nor unphilosophical to hold that God, even the Father, is also a perfected, exalted man.[15]

James Talmage

Another leading scholar (and General Authority) of Mormonism was James Talmage. His books *Articles of Faith* and *Jesus the Christ* have been read so widely that they are almost quasi-canonical. Indeed, both have been published by the LDS Church itself, sometimes in leather-bound editions! They are often included in the books given to Mormon missionaries as they prepare for their mission work. I quote from *Articles of Faith* regarding godhood:

> Those who have been born unto God through obedience to the Gospel may by valiant devotion to righteousness obtain exaltation and even reach the status of godhood. Of such we read: "Wherefore, as it is written, they are gods, even the sons of God" (*D & C* 76:58; compare 132:20, and contrast paragraph 17 in same section; see also paragraph 37). Yet, though they be gods they are still subject to Jesus Christ as their Father in this exalted relationship; and so we read in the paragraph following the above quotation: "and they are Christ's, and Christ is God's" (76:59).[16]

And in another of his works, *The Vitality of Mormonism*, Talmage commented,

> If man be the spirit offspring of God, and if the possibilities of individual progression be endless, to both of which sublime truths the Scriptures bear definite testimony, then we have to admit that man may eventually attain to Divine estate. However far away it be in the eternities future, what aeons may elapse before any one now mortal may reach the sanctity and glory of

godhood, man nevertheless has inherited from his Divine Father the possibilities of such attainment—even as the crawling caterpillar or the corpse-like chrysalis holds the latent possibility, nay, barring destruction, the certainty, indeed, of the winged imago in all the glory of maturity.[17]

John Widtsoe

Apostle John Widtsoe was another LDS leader who attempted to provide an intellectual and theological defense of the Mormon doctrine of God. In his work *A Rational Theology*, he describes what he as a Mormon Apostle believes about God and exaltation. In a chapter titled "The Gods of This Earth," Widtsoe pulls no punches:

> *Plurality of Gods.* Since innumerable intelligent beings are moving onward in development, there must be some in almost every conceivable stage of development. If intelligent beings, far transcending the understanding of man, be called gods, there may be many gods. God, angel and similar terms denote merely intelligent beings of varying degree of development. The thought, however, that there is a plurality of gods and other divine beings of varying grades, is of fundamental truth, which may be applied in every-day life, for it gives the assurance that it is possible for all, by self-effort and by gradual steps, to attain the highest conceivable power.[18]

In light of this, who, then, is God the Father?

> *God, the Father.* God, the Father, the greatest personage concerned in our progression, is the supreme God. He is the Father of our spirits. He is the being of highest intelligence with whom we deal. To our senses and understanding he is as perfection. In his fullness he cannot be fathomed by the human mind. It is, indeed, useless for man to attempt to define in detail the great intelligent beings of the universe.[19]

Note well what Apostle Widtsoe *doesn't* say. He *doesn't* say God the Father is the greatest personage *period*, but the greatest personage "concerned in our progression." God the Father is not the highest intelligence *period*, but the highest intelligence "with whom we deal." And notice as well the use of the plural "intelligent beings of the universe." This same kind of hesitation is seen as he continues:

> God, the Father, the supreme God of whom we have knowl-
> edge, is the greatest intelligence in the infinite universe, because
> he is infinite in all matters pertaining to us and transcends
> wholly our understanding in his power and wisdom. We know
> no greater God than the omniscient, omnipotent Father.

God is the supreme God "of whom we have knowledge," and is
infinite "in all matters pertaining to us." Hence, "we know no greater
God," though, obviously, a greater god exists, since there had to be
gods preceding God the Father, who was once a man, and has progressed to Godhood. We may not know these other gods, but their
existence is as sure in LDS teaching as the Eternal Law of Progression
itself.

Bruce R. McConkie

I have often commented that I'm glad I am not Bruce R. Mc-
Conkie. This is because of all the LDS Apostles of recent memory,
he is the one about whom I have heard it said most often: "Well, that
was just his opinion." As far as Apostles go, he is the one that LDS
missionaries like to disagree with the most. As soon as you cite
something from McConkie's most famous work, *Mormon Doctrine*,
an encyclopedic compendium on the teachings of the LDS Church,
you hear, "Oh, that's just his speculation." Yet, when Ezra Taft Benson eulogized McConkie as his funeral, he saw things a bit differ-
ently:

> "Often when a doctrinal question came before the First Pres-
> idency and the Twelve," he continued, "Elder McConkie was
> asked to quote the scripture or to comment on the matter. He
> could quote scripture verbatim and at great length." He "pro-
> vided the entire Church with an example of gospel scholarship.
> He could teach the gospel with ease because he first understood
> the gospel."[20]

A quick glance at the currently published LDS manuals of reli-
gion also reveals that right after Joseph Smith comes Joseph Fielding
Smith and Bruce R. McConkie as the *most often cited* LDS authorities.
While McConkie may have been more than a little irascible,[21] when

it comes to the LDS doctrine of God, I have yet to find any LDS person who was able to demonstrate that what he said was out of line with the official position of the Church.

McConkie's writings, which are quite voluminous, contain a great deal of material on our particular subject of interest. However, we will focus upon only a few of the possible citations. Apostle McConkie often placed his words in an apologetic context, always keeping an eye upon the critics of the Church, both within and without. For example, notice his definition of monotheism from *Mormon Doctrine*:

> *Monotheism* is the doctrine or belief that there is but one God. If this is properly interpreted to mean that the Father, the Son, and Holy Ghost—each of whom is a separate and distinct godly personage—are one God, meaning one Godhead, then true saints are monotheists.[22]

This is hardly the definition of monotheism, for then the Egyptians could be called monotheists for worshiping a triad of Gods who are simply united in purpose. But even here, McConkie is straightforward in confessing three separate and distinct godly personages. Likewise, when defining "plurality of gods" in the same work, McConkie writes,

> Three separate personages—Father, Son, and Holy Ghost—comprise the Godhead. As each of these persons is a God, it is evident, from this standpoint alone, that a plurality of Gods exists. To us, speaking in the proper finite sense, these three are the only Gods we worship. But in addition there is an infinite number of holy personages, drawn from worlds without number, who have passed on to exaltation and are thus gods.[23]

Note especially the phrase, "these three are the only Gods we worship." This is a disputable phrase, for many LDS say they worship only the Father.[24]

In either case, by now we should be accustomed to hearing LDS speaking of "Gods" and we should understand exactly what is in view when we hear such words.[25]

McConkie likewise confesses that "an infinite number of holy personages" also exist who are rightly called gods. And did he likewise believe as Joseph Smith regarding the means of exaltation to godhood? It certainly seems so:

> Endowed with agency and subject to eternal laws, man began his progression and advancement in preexistence, his ultimate goal being to attain to a state of glory, honor, and exaltation like the Father of spirits. During his earth life he gains a mortal body, receives experience in earthly things, and prepares for a future eternity after the resurrection when he will continue to gain knowledge and intelligence (D & C 130:18–19). This gradually unfolding course of advancement and experience—a course that began in a past eternity and will continue in ages future—is frequently referred to as a course of eternal progression. . . . In the full sense, eternal progression is enjoyed only by those who receive the fullness of the Father; they have all power, all knowledge, and all wisdom; they gain a fullness of truth, becoming one with the Father. All other persons are assigned lesser places in the mansions that are prepared, and their progression is not eternal and unlimited but in a specified sphere. . . . Those who gain exaltation, having thus enjoyed the fullness of eternal progression, become like God[26] (*Mormon Doctrine*, 238–239).

So that he can conclude:

> Man and God are of the same race, and it is within the power of righteous man to become like his Father, that is to become a holy Man, a Man of Holiness.[27]

Is this not what we have seen consistently throughout the literature we have surveyed? Surely it is.

The Encyclopedia of Mormonism

Before we conclude our examination, I would like to call one last witness to the stand. In 1992 a major publication appeared in LDS bookstores called *The Encyclopedia of Mormonism*.[28] This major work represents the contributions of numerous LDS scholars and writers. Does it, likewise, speak of these doctrines? It most assuredly does. One of the plainest sections comes from the pen of Dr. Stephen Robinson of Brigham Young University. Speaking of God the Father, Robinson wrote:

The Father, Elohim, is called the Father because he is the literal father of the spirits of mortals (Heb. 12:9). This paternity is not allegorical. All individual human spirits were begotten (not created from nothing or made) by the Father in a premortal state, where they lived and were nurtured by Heavenly Parents. These spirit children of the Father come to earth to receive mortal bodies; there is a literal family relationship among humankind. Joseph Smith taught, "If men do not comprehend the character of God, they do not comprehend themselves" (TPJS, p. 343). Gods and humans represent a single divine lineage, the same species of being, although they and he are at different stages of progress. This doctrine is stated concisely in a well-known couplet by President Lorenzo Snow: "As man now is, God once was: as God now is, man may be" (see Godhood). . . . The important points of the doctrine for Latter-day Saints are that Gods and humans are the same species of being, but at different stages of development in a divine continuum, and that the heavenly Father and Mother are the heavenly pattern, model, and example of what mortals can become through obedience to the gospel (see Mother in Heaven).[29]

Robinson is hesitant to affirm much about the pre-exalted state of Elohim, the Father, but his emphasis upon God being of the "same species of being" as man should not be missed. Earlier, in writing a section on "LDS Doctrine Compared with Other Christian Doctrines," Robinson wrote,

Just as God organized preexisting matter to create the universe, so he organized preexisting intelligence to create the spirits that eventually became human beings. Consequently, Latter-day Saints do not view God as the total cause of what human beings are. Human intelligence is uncreated by God, and therefore independent of his control.[30]

What about the Godhead? We read,

Unique to LDS theology in modern times is a view of the Godhead as consisting of three separate beings, two possessing bodies of flesh and bone and one possessing a spirit body. An official declaration concerning the Godhead states: "The Father has a body of flesh and bones as tangible as man's; the Son also; but the Holy Ghost has not a body of flesh and bones, but is a personage of Spirit" (*D & C* 130:22). Latter-day Saints take the Bible, both Old and New Testaments, in a literal, anthropomorphic sense, attributing to God both a human form and emotions. They accept both a "oneness" and "threeness" of the Godhead as taught in the Bible. However, they reject the traditional doctrine of the Trinity, and believe instead that the Godhead is one in mind, purpose, and testimony, but three in number.[31]

Is God a man, according to the *Encyclopedia of Mormonism*?

Latter-day Saints perceive the Father as an exalted Man in the most literal, anthropomorphic terms. They do not view the language of Genesis as allegorical; human beings are created in the form and image of a God who has a physical form and image (Gen. 1:26). The Prophet Joseph Smith explained, "The Father has a body of flesh and bones as tangible as man's; the Son also; but the Holy Ghost has not a body of flesh and bones, but is a personage of Spirit" (*D & C* 130:22). Thus, "God is a Spirit" (John 4:24) in the sense that the Holy Ghost, the member of the Godhead who deals most often and most directly with humans, is a God and a spirit, but God the Father and God the Son are spirits with physical, resurrected bodies. Latter-day Saints deny the abstract nature of God the Father and affirm that he is a concrete being, that he possesses a physical body, and that he is in space and time.[32]

Such plain statements complete our investigation, using the scholarly modern testimony (the *Encyclopedia of Mormonism*) to the abiding validity of the concepts announced by Joseph Smith nearly 150 years earlier.

Is the Church Backing Away From This Doctrine?

Recent comments by Mormon Prophet Gordon Hinckley have added fuel to the fires of speculation that the LDS Church is, at the very least, de-emphasizing at least *part* of the doctrine that we have seen plainly taught from the very inception of the LDS Church. Many have commented on the fact that Mormonism has been seeking a wider acceptance as a "Christian" Church while maintaining a unique identity. The President of the Mormon Church, Gordon Hinckley, seems to indicate that this observation has a real basis.

Some point out that Hinckley worked for many years in "public relations," coordinating the LDS Church's media contacts, and therefore may be more "sensitive" to the issue of "appearance" than previous (and following) Presidents of the Church. I hesitate to even address these statements, since they do not appear in any kind of official publication of the Church. Indeed, they would not qualify for our previous study, because they are not found in LDS publications, but in non-LDS popular media! Mormons would rightly object to the citation of these sources to define their beliefs. Yet because these statements have been widely circulated, we will consider briefly what has been said.

Shortly after the April 1997 General Conference of the LDS Church, an article appeared in the *San Francisco Chronicle* (April 13 edition).[33] A reporter was interviewing Gordon Hinckley:

Q: There are some significant differences in your beliefs. For instance, don't Mormons believe that God was once a man?

A: I wouldn't say that. There was a little couplet coined, "As man is, God once was. As God is, man may become." Now that's more of a couplet than anything else. That gets into some pretty deep theology that we don't know very much about.

Q: So you're saying the church is still struggling to understand this?

A: Well, as God is, man may become. We believe in eternal progression. Very strongly. We believe that the glory of God is intelligence and whatever principle of intelligence we attain unto in this life, it will rise with us in the Resurrection. Knowledge, learning, is an eternal thing. And for that reason, we stress education. We're trying to do all we can to make of our people the ablest, best, brightest people that we can.

The person who has read the preceding documentation might be more than a little surprised by the statement, "That gets into some pretty deep theology that we don't know very much about." And we note that Hinckley only affirms the second half of Lorenzo Snow's couplet, that being that we can become like God. The assertion that God was once a man is left in a state of ambiguity.

A few months later a PBS program aired that contained another interview with Hinckley.[34] Richard Ostling is quoted:

RICHARD OSTLING: President Gordon Hinckley says the concept of God having been a man is not stressed any longer,
but he does believe that human beings can become gods in
the afterlife.

PRESIDENT GORDON HINCKLEY: Well, they can achieve to a
godly status, yes, of course they can, eternal progression. We
believe in the progression of the human soul. Ours is a for-
ward-looking religion. It's an upward-looking religion. We
believe in the eternity and the infinity of the human soul,
and its great possibilities.

Hinckley's words sound very much the same as in the previous
statement. We are not provided with the basis, in Hinckley's own
words, for Ostling's summary that "the concept of God having been
a man is not stressed any longer." But we can guess on the basis of
his words found in the August 4, 1997 issue of *Time*.[35] Here we are
given more of a direct quotation than in the preceding sources:

And not just the converts. In an interview with *Time*, President Hinckley seemed intent on downplaying his faith's dis-
tinctiveness. The church's message, he explained, "is a message
of Christ. Our church is Christ-centered. He's our leader. He's
our head. His name is the name of our church." At first, Hinckley seemed to qualify the idea that men could become gods, suggesting that "it's of course an ideal. It's a hope for a wishful
thing," but later affirmed that "yes, of course they can." (He
added that women could too, "as companions to their husbands. They can't conceive a king without a queen.") On
whether his church still holds that God the Father was once a
man, he sounded uncertain, "I don't know that we teach it. I
don't know that we emphasize it. . . . I understand the philosophical background behind it, but I don't know a lot about it,
and I don't think others know a lot about it."

Again, I stress that these are not in any way official sources. If
these words were found in the *Ensign*, the official LDS magazine,
they would carry far more weight than they do. If Hinckley were to
say in a General Conference address that he doesn't "know a lot
about" God being a man, we would have some real reason to wonder.
But even given the sources, it is hard to avoid asking a rather simple
question: How can the President of the LDS Church say that he

doesn't know a lot about a doctrine that we have traced through every level of LDS teaching and through every era of the Church's existence? While one could hope that these scattered statements in non-LDS sources bodes a change in the direction of the Mormon Church's theology, eventually leading to a *renunciation* of the concept of eternal progression, such a conclusion would be very premature. Even if Gordon Hinckley were to be found less than firm in his conviction of this doctrine (a fact that would raise all sorts of questions concerning the consistency of LDS teachings, the nature of truth in Mormonism, etc.), it would take a wholesale repudiation of the authority of the previous prophets and apostles who so plainly taught eternal progression to give us a true turnabout in LDS doctrine. Such a repudiation has yet to appear.

In a sermon delivered October 4, 1997, at the General Conference, President Hinkley made reference to these recent reports concerning his views of these doctrines and said, "I think I understand them thoroughly." He indicated, "it is unfortunate that the reporting may not make this clear." Those in attendance laughed when Hinkley told them not to worry. Hence we find no repudiation of the historic teaching by the modern prophet.

In Summary

Official Mormon teaching is clear. God and man are of the same species. The difference between them is a matter of exaltation and progression over aeons of time. God was once a man, a mortal, just as we are. He lived on another planet in a condition very similar to ours, and gained exaltation on the same principles that are made available to men today. The worthy Mormon man who is sealed for time and eternity to his wife in the LDS Temple and who continues faithful to the end in obedience to gospel ordinances and principles, will be exalted, in due time, to the status of a god. He will have "eternal increase," beget spirit children, and be worshiped as a god and creator of other worlds. In those worlds he will raise up his spirit children so that they, too, might become exalted. This is the eternal law of progression, the concept of exaltation to godhood, and as we have seen over and over again, in Mormonism this is the gospel. That this is the LDS teaching cannot possibly be doubted.

Now we will respond to this viewpoint by presenting from the

Scriptures the Christian doctrine of God. We do not enter here primarily upon issues such as the Trinity, the person of Christ, or the relationship between the divine Persons. There is a simple reason for this: it is a major mistake to think that what separates Mormonism and Christianity is a matter of perceptions of the Trinity. Instead, the fundamental issue is monotheism versus polytheism, one eternal God versus an exalted man. By now this should be plainly seen from the data that has been presented. We err greatly when we attempt to discuss the Trinity in regard to Mormonism without first focusing upon the primary issue: Is there only one true and eternal God? Are we gods in embryo or creations of the Almighty and Eternal Creator? To this issue we now turn.

8

THE GOD CHRISTIANS WORSHIP

The most fundamental truth of the Christian faith is this: There is one God. Everything else—who He is, what He has done in Christ, how we will spend eternity—flows from this fundamental statement of absolute monotheism. The certainty of the Gospel itself is rooted in the reality that there is one God who sovereignly reigns over all things, so that there is no "rival god" or some "higher power" that might step in and "change the rules" somewhere down the road.

It was this truth that I shared many years ago with the first two LDS missionaries with whom I became acquainted. When we came to the end of our discussions, there was one basic truth I wanted to make sure they understood. "Gentlemen," I said to them, "we have talked about many things. But most importantly we have discussed our very different views of God. Both cannot be correct. If I am right, you are wrong, desperately so, and vice versa. We are not worshiping the same God, that is for certain. But most importantly, I want you to understand that I worship a God who does not change, who has eternally been what He is today, and will be tomorrow and into eternity to come. My salvation is based upon the Word and promise of an unchanging and eternal God. That is what makes it certain and perfect. Your salvation is based upon the words of a God who was once something other than he is now. He has changed, progressed, grown. Just over the period of the past one hundred and fifty years he has changed what is required of final and full salvation, and you have no assurance that he will not change the requirements again tomorrow. When you tire of a changing or changeable god, I hope you will remember what I have shared with you during these discussions."

Thousands of witnessing opportunities later, I am still sharing the same fundamental message with LDS people. Everything ultimately comes down to a simple fact: Mormons and Christians worship different Gods. We may use the same terminology on a host of issues, but we differ all along the line simply because we start at completely different places. We begin with the one eternal God, while Mormons begin with eternal matter, intelligences, and the law of eternal progression. The two systems, then, will end up differing with each other on a basic, definitional basis, all along the line. Therefore, when I share the Gospel of Jesus Christ with LDS people, I do so with an eye to introducing them first and foremost to the God whose Gospel I wish to share.

The primary thrust of this book is not to provide a full-orbed discussion of the Christian doctrine of God. I have focused upon the LDS position for the simple reason that the teachings we have examined are not generally known to the Christian community. However, in this chapter I wish to provide a brief, though hopefully sufficient, defense of the Christian belief in absolute monotheism. We will look to the Bible and hear its testimony to the fact that there is one true and eternal God who is unchanging and immutable, unique in all ways, and the Creator of *all* things. Obviously, I offer this information in response to the repeated claims we have read from LDS leaders that God was once a man, that there are other gods beside Him, that He has progressed and changed over time, that He is not unique in any particularly meaningful sense, and that He is not, in reality, the Creator of *anything* ("organizer" not being the same as "creator").

We must be wise, however, in how we approach even a brief study of the Almighty. God is not a specimen to be studied under a microscope. We in our scientific age think we have the right (and the ability) to test *anything*, ask *any* question, cross *any* border in our "search for knowledge." Rarely is human activity marked any longer by the old-fashioned idea of *reverence*. Yet, at the very start, I must emphasize that we tread upon holy ground when we look to God's own revelation of himself. As a Christian, I approach God as my Maker, the one who sustains me at every moment. He is the Potter, I am the clay. He has formed me and made me. I have no ability or right to sit in judgment on Him, and, in fact, unless He deigned to stoop down to communicate with me and reveal himself in His creation and His Word, I would have no ability to know anything about Him. God determines the boundaries of what we can *truly* know about Him. The Scriptures say,

> The secret things belong to the LORD our God, but the things revealed belong to us and to our sons forever, that we may observe all the words of this law. (Deut. 29:29)

And we must constantly be reminded, in light of our penchant for arrogance and pride,

> "For My thoughts are not your thoughts, neither are your ways My ways," declares the LORD. "For as the heavens are higher than the earth, so are My ways higher than your ways and My thoughts than your thoughts" (Isa. 55:8–9).

As we will soon see, the Bible has very harsh words for any man who does not see himself as God sees him: as a creature made for the glory of God.

One God

> "Hear, O Israel! The LORD is our God, the LORD is one! You shall love the LORD your God with all your heart and with all your soul and with all your might. These words, which I am commanding you today, shall be on your heart" (Deut. 6:4–6).

Christianity begins with the following Jewish prayer, for here the God who would reveal himself in Jesus Christ in Bethlehem revealed to His ancient people the fact that He alone is God. The LORD, Yahweh,[1] is the God of Israel. Yahweh is not a "committee" of gods, so to speak. Yahweh is one.[2] As the one God of Israel, He is to be loved with all the heart, soul, and might. Jesus said this is the greatest commandment.[3] Monotheism allows for undivided devotion to the one true God, and this is the command found in the Shema, the central prayer of the Jewish people. God's people stood out sharply against the heathen nations that surrounded them. Rather than believing in many gods, the Jews confessed these words:

> Behold, to the LORD your God belong heaven and the high-
> est heavens, the earth and all that is in it. (Deut. 10:14)

Such a claim was downright blasphemous to the peoples around
Israel, for it inherently said that *their* gods were not real and had no
existence! But such was the revelation God made through Moses.[4]

Humans are an interesting lot. We learn things and then forget
what we learned—with frightening speed and regularity. If God's
dealing with His people Israel teaches us anything, it is that God has
to repeat the same truths to us over and over again. Even though He
taught His people from the start that He alone is God, the people of
Israel were constantly falling into idolatry. Centuries after Moses,
Isaiah was the mouthpiece God used to make some of His highest
statements about himself and His relationship to our world. Seeing
that the people of Israel were steeped in idolatry and were constantly
being lured away from single-hearted devotion to Him, Yahweh con-
venes a "court" and puts the gods of the peoples on trial. This "trial
of the false gods" reveals so much about God that it is truly a much-
neglected treasure. By challenging the false gods, He reveals to us
those things that are unique about himself. This trial is found between Isaiah chapters 40 and 48. We will quote often from this section, but before we do, I wish to address a common objection.

Frequently LDS with whom I have dialogued will say, "Isaiah is
talking about idols in these passages. The assertion that there is only
one God is only relevant to this planet and to the false gods men
make. It has nothing to do with the existence of other gods elsewhere." Aside from the fact that Isaiah and his audience would never
have considered the idea of gods "elsewhere" in the cosmos to begin
with, does the objection carry validity?

As we will see as we examine the many passages that teach monotheism, a number of truths intertwine to create the fabric of God's
claim to uniqueness. I have organized these passages into major topics, but many could easily fit into another category as well. And it is
this fact that leads us to realize that God's claims in response to the
false gods of the peoples are *expansive* and *exhaustive*. That is, one
of the claims God makes is that He is the only true God because He
is the *Creator of all things*. His claim of creatorship is *never limited to
a particular area or time period*. There is no allowance made for hem-
ming in God's creative activity. Consequently, the idea that there are

gods "outside" Yahweh's creative work is unacceptable. In the same way, God claims absolute knowledge of not only past events but future events as well. He also claims to know *why* things happened the way they did. This points again to something the false gods and idols cannot do. Only the true God can. From this we learn many things, but most important, that time itself falls within the creative realm of God's work. If God created time, what about these other "gods" that are "out there somewhere"? Are they limited by Yahweh's creative work? The idea that God is the Creator of all things, including time, simply does not fit with the King Follett Discourse.

As we examine each passage, we will find many other elements that do not fit within the parameters of the objection outlined above. For example, the single most often cited passage refuting the LDS doctrine of eternal progression is Isaiah 43:10:

> "You are My witnesses," declares the LORD, "and My servant whom I have chosen, in order that you may know and believe Me and understand that I am He. Before Me there was no God formed, and there will be none after Me."

Here Yahweh (the LORD), in His suit against the false gods, calls as a witness His own people, Israel. He chose Israel for a purpose: that they might know and believe Him. He showed great patience in continually revealing this truth to His people. What is the central aspect of His revelation of himself to Israel? "Before Me there was no God formed, and there will be none after Me."[5] It is as if God is saying, "Israel, I alone am God. There are no true gods beside me. There were none before Me, for I am eternal. And there will be none after Me, for I do not age and will not pass away. There is no room for other gods, for I alone am God, the Creator."

The significance of this passage to the LDS concept of eternal progression is obvious: it cuts the entire scheme in half. To the Mormon, there *were* other gods before the God of this world. Now, immediately someone might object, "But we have nothing to do with those gods. They do not exist in this particular eternity."[6] Let's quickly examine this. God does not say, "There were no *relevant* Gods formed before Me." He says, "There was *no God* formed before Me." But the text further undermines this objection. We must remember that in modern Mormon theology, Elohim is the Father, and Jehovah is the Son, Jesus. Note that Jehovah is speaking. With this in mind, observe that He is saying, "Before Me there was no El (singular of Elohim) formed." Is it true, *even granting the idea of limiting this verse to this earth or this eternity*, that there was no God before Jehovah? Certainly not! Elohim, the Father, *begat* the spirit "Jehovah" in the spiritual pre-existence! Hence, even granting the limitation of the passage placed upon it by this objection, it *still* refutes the law of eternal progression as applied to this world! It is simply impossible to consistently fit a belief in a plurality of gods into the Christian Scriptures.

The other common objection to this passage goes like this: "Isaiah is simply talking about idols, false gods." In a sense this is true, as all gods other than He are, by nature, false gods. But this in no way changes the import of the passage. God is not saying, "There are no false gods or idols other than Me." He is the true God; He is denying the existence of any *other* true Gods, any others who are worthy of worship. This is a theme found *throughout* the trial of the false gods:

> "Thus says the LORD, the King of Israel and his Redeemer, the LORD of hosts:[7] 'I am the first and I am the last, and there is no God besides Me. Who is like Me? Let him proclaim and declare it; Yes, let him recount it to Me in order, from the time that I established the ancient nation. And let them declare to them the things that are coming and the events that are going to take place. Do not tremble and do not be afraid; have I not long since announced it to you and declared it? And you are My witnesses. Is there any God besides Me, or is there any other Rock?[8] I know of none'" (Isa. 44:6–8).

Again, Yahweh speaks to His people and *reminds* them (note the phrase, "have I not long since announced it to you and declared it?") what they should already know about Him. He is the first and the last. Such a phrase is exhaustive. Is the God of Joseph Smith the first and the last? Only in a most limited way could anyone ever say, "Yes," that being "first God in this particular creation/eternity, and last for this particular creation/eternity, though there were many in previous creations/eternities, and there will be many others in future creations/eternities." But God's purpose is plain: "There is no God besides Me."[9] Idolatry is inherently foolish simply because there is no worthy object of worship other than the one true God, Yahweh Elohim, or as it normally appears in the English text, the LORD God.

God then asks, "Who is like Me?" There is no answer given, for the question is asked rhetorically only. Yet Mormonism can give an answer, for in LDS theology there are many like Yahweh, in the sense that Yahweh is not the first God (even of this creation/eternity!) and is, in fact, just one of the spirit children of Elohim (albeit the eldest).

God then challenges anyone who would claim to be like Him to do what only He can do: foretell the future with exacting and minute detail and accuracy. God knows the future, not because He has some kind of crystal ball into which He looks, but because, as these passages assert over and over again, He is the Creator of all things, including time—past, present, and future. His knowledge of the future is as certain as His knowledge of any other thing that has come into existence by the exercise of His will and power.

God comforts His people, His witnesses, the people of Israel. They need not be fearful of the gods of the peoples, for those gods do not exist. He then asks a question that we must ask of our LDS friends: "Is there any God besides Me?" How do we answer this question? The Christian answers, "Of course not." The Mormon has to answer, especially since this is Jehovah speaking, "Yes, there most certainly is." Not only do the General Authorities of the LDS Church affirm the existence of other "gods," but even within the "Godhead" of Mormonism you have three separate deities, as we have seen. Besides Jehovah, there is also Elohim, the Father, who begat Him. But who agrees with God's answer? The Christian does, for God says, "I know of none." Is God being honest? If so, are we to assume that He might be ignorant of the existence of these other gods? Surely not, for the Scriptures say,

> Great is our LORD and abundant in strength; His understanding is infinite. (Ps. 147:5)

The only logical conclusion, then, is that there *is no other God*, since God himself says He does not know of any. Joseph Smith may have said there were—but one of the tests of whether a man is a true prophet or not is this:

> If a prophet or a dreamer of dreams arises among you and gives you a sign or a wonder, and the sign or the wonder comes true, concerning which he spoke to you, saying, "Let us go after

other gods (whom you have not known) and let us serve them," you shall not listen to the words of that prophet or that dreamer of dreams; for the LORD your God is testing you to find out if you love the LORD your God with all your heart and with all your soul. You shall follow the LORD your God and fear Him; and you shall keep His commandments, listen to His voice, serve Him, and cling to Him. But that prophet or that dreamer of dreams shall be put to death, because he has counseled rebellion against the LORD your God who brought you from the land of Egypt and redeemed you from the house of slavery, to seduce you from the way in which the LORD your God commanded you to walk. So you shall purge the evil from among you. (Deut. 13:1–5)

God takes His truth very seriously. This is not a matter of theological finery—it is the difference between idolatry and worship, salvation and eternal punishment. Joseph Smith has led millions to follow "gods whom you have not known." Did not Smith himself say that we had imagined and supposed that God "was God from all eternity"? And is this not exactly what God is saying in these passages in Scripture? Yet Smith went on to say, "I will refute that idea, and take away the veil, so that you may see." These are the words of a false prophet, and God's view of false prophets is plainly stated in verse 5 above.

> "Declare and set forth *your case*; indeed, let them consult together. Who has announced this from of old? Who has long since declared it? Is it not I, the LORD? And there is no other God besides Me, a righteous God and a Savior; there is none except Me. Turn to Me and be saved, all the ends of the earth; for I am God, and there is no other" (Isa. 45:21–22).

Still, in the courtroom God demands that the defense present its case even though the verdict has been known for a very long time. In fact, so fundamental is the truth that there is only one God, Paul could speak in these terms:

> However at that time, when you did not know God, you were slaves to those which by nature are no gods.[10] (Gal. 4:8)

Any god other than Yahweh is, *by nature*, no god. There is no God besides Yahweh, "a righteous God and a Savior." We should note with great concern the fact that here the absolute monotheism of the Bible is presented *in the context of salvation itself.* Monotheistic belief is not optional. There is only one God who can save. When we direct people to God for salvation, are we uncertain as to whom they should believe in and trust? All the ends of the earth have only one to turn to if they are to be saved: Yahweh says He is God, and there is no other. There are no other Saviors (Isa. 43:11) but the one true God. We can see why God is so harsh on false prophets who lead the people after other gods. It is just as damaging as preaching a false gospel, in that it leads people away from the only Gospel that can save. A god other than the One here presented *is unable to save anyone,* for such a god, quite simply, does not exist.

Unique

One of the greatest truths about God that is utterly denied by LDS theology[11] is God's *uniqueness.* There simply is no meaningful way for a Mormon theologian to say that their Elohim is "unique." There were gods before him, and there will be gods after him. Only his particular experience may be called "unique."

The Christian, on the other hand, boldly proclaims the absolute *uniqueness* of God. God is unique *in His being.* That is, there is nothing or no one like God. He alone is God. We cannot compare Him to anything, for everything else is created and finite, while He is uncreated and infinite.

Again, this is not the result of Greek metaphysical reflection—it is the plain assertion of inspired Scripture. Read carefully the following passage and allow it to speak to this issue:

> Who has directed the Spirit of the LORD, or as His counselor has informed Him? With whom did He consult and who gave Him understanding? And who taught Him in the path of justice and taught Him knowledge and informed Him of the way of understanding? Behold, the nations are like a drop from a bucket, and are regarded as a speck of dust on the scales; behold, He lifts up the islands like fine dust. Even Lebanon is not enough to burn, nor its beasts enough for a burnt offering. All the nations are as nothing before Him, they are regarded by Him as less than nothing and meaningless. To whom then will you

liken God? Or what likeness will you compare with Him? (Isa. 40:13–18)

Amazingly, LDS theology strives to provide answers to the questions that God asks in this passage. Who taught Him? His parents, of course, upon some far away world. Who taught Him in the path of justice and taught Him knowledge? Some teacher long ago, far away. If, as Joseph Smith said, God was once a man, then He *learned and grew* just as we learn and grow, and was once easily likened to all the other mortals living upon the same planet He did.[12]

This is not the God here described, nor is it the God worshiped by Christians. The questions God asks are rhetorical. There are no answers. If you can come up with answers to those questions for the God you worship, you have the wrong God, for you can then find plenty to which you can compare your God. But the God of Abraham is incomparable. This tremendous passage continues:

> Do you not know? Have you not heard? Has it not been de-clared to you from the beginning? Have you not understood from the foundations of the earth? It is He who sits above the vault of the earth, and its inhabitants are like grasshoppers, who stretches out the heavens like a curtain and spreads them out like a tent to dwell in. He it is who reduces rulers to nothing, who makes the judges of the earth meaningless. Scarcely have they been planted, scarcely have they been sown, Scarcely has their stock taken root in the earth, but He merely blows on them, and they wither, and the storm carries them away like stubble. "To whom then will you liken Me that I would be his equal?" says the Holy One. Lift up your eyes on high and see who has created these stars, the One who leads forth their host by number, He calls them all by name; because of the greatness of His might and the strength of His power, not one of them is missing. Why do you say, O Jacob, and assert, O Israel, "My way is hidden from the LORD, And the justice due me escapes the notice of my God"? Do you not know? Have you not heard? The Everlasting God, the LORD, the Creator of the ends of the earth does not become weary or tired. His understanding is inscru-table. (Isa. 40:21–28)

This is the only God worthy of worship and adoration. And God expects us to know this truth—He upbraids those who have forgotten, by asking, "Do you not know? Have you not heard?" That this has *always* been known is plainly proclaimed. There is no excuse for idolatry, no defense for polytheism. In comparison with the true God, earth's inhabitants are "like grasshoppers." Are we truly to believe this is being said of an "exalted man" who was once a mortal like you and I? Here is the God who disposes with men as He pleases, lifting one up, sending another to destruction. He does not come from a star,[13] but upholds all the stars in their places. This is the true Creator, the Maker of heaven and earth, and the men who dwell on the earth.

The sovereignty of God is often placed in the context of demonstrating who God really is. Note these passages:

> I am the LORD, and there is no other; besides Me there is no God. I will gird you, though you have not known Me; that men may know from the rising to the setting of the sun that there is no one besides Me. I am the LORD, and there is no other, the One forming light and creating darkness, causing well-being and creating calamity; I am the LORD who does all these. (Isa. 45:5–7)

> Remember the former things long past, for I am God, and there is no other; I am God, and there is no one like Me, declaring the end from the beginning, and from ancient times things which have not been done, saying, "My purpose will be established, and I will accomplish all My good pleasure" (Isa. 46:9–10).

None but the true God can say, "My purpose will be established." A God who has become deified by obedience to external laws and principles is not one who can make such comments as these. The trial of the false gods results in a unanimous verdict: All of creation admits Yahweh is the only true God.

Certainly Isaiah provides us with tremendous insights into the nature and character of the one true God and great evidence of the uniqueness of Yahweh, but we are not limited to these passages. Jeremiah, likewise, recorded words of a similar nature:

> There is none like You, O LORD; You are great, and great is Your name in might. Who would not fear You, O King of the nations? Indeed it is Your due! For among all the wise men of

the nations and in all their kingdoms, there is none like You. (Jer. 10:6–7)

So, too, the psalmist extolled the uniqueness of God:

> The LORD is high above all nations; His glory is above the heavens. Who is like the LORD our God, who is enthroned on high, who humbles Himself to behold the things that are in heaven and in the earth? (Ps. 113:4–6)

Why would it be a humbling thing for an exalted man to "behold the things that are in heaven and in the earth," when such an exalted man *came* from these places? But the true God humbles himself to even look upon creation itself, so high above that creation is He in His essence and being. We can do little more than bow in reverence, awe, and fear before our Creator.

I have often tried to share with LDS the sense of worship and awe that fills my soul referring to many of these same passages. But we must remember that for many LDS who went through the pre–1990 Temple Endowment ceremonies, a God who is infinite, eternal, unchanging, and omnipresent is not a precious truth of the Scriptures, but a doctrine of the devil himself. A strong resistance to these truths is normally present. And such is completely understandable if you believe God was once such as you are—a mortal man, subject to the same limitations you are—the Christian concept of worshiping God *simply because He is God* has no basis or meaning. We need to remember this, for it will form the foundation of our conclusions regarding the relationship of Christians and Mormons.

I have many times in the past shared with LDS correspondents the following thoughts from Job 40:1–5 where Job, faced with the awesomeness of God and his own creatureliness, can only manage to place his hand over his mouth:

> Then the LORD said to Job, "Will the faultfinder contend with the Almighty? Let him who reproves God answer it." Then Job answered the LORD and said, "Behold, I am insignificant; what can I reply to You? I lay my hand on my mouth. Once I have spoken, and I will not answer; even twice, and I will add no more" (Job 40:1–5).

Job learned something we all need to learn: We have no basis for answering back to God. For this reason, I have often answered Mormon inquirers, "May God grant you an interview as he did with Job: Job 40:1–5." We all need an experience in which the Lord, by His grace, reveals to our soul a little of His own majesty and, in so doing, shows us what we really are: creatures formed by His power and sustained by His hand.

Unique in His Spirituality

God is unique in the fact that He does not have creaturely existence; that is, He does not exist in the same *mode* or *way* that we do. He is utterly unlike us in many ways, far beyond our creaturely categories, and, most important, He is not limited by time and space. Theologians have referred to this as His spirituality, not in the sense of His being one spirit among many, but that He exists as *spirit* and is therefore "omnipresent." We can think of omnipresence as a "lack of spatial limitations," just as His eternal existence means He is not limited by time.

The Lord Jesus knew well God's spiritual nature. When speaking with the woman at the well in Samaria, He diffused the controversy regarding the *place* of worship by pointing out a basic truth:

> God is spirit,[14] and those who worship Him must worship in spirit and truth. (John 4:24)

The Lord's point is striking: The worship of God is not a matter of *where* but of *how*. Whether Mount Gerazim (where the Samaritans thought one must worship) or in Jerusalem, it does not matter. Spatial location is irrelevant, as space does not limit God, for He is spirit.[15] The important thing is *how* we worship (in spirit and in truth).

Some have argued that it is not Jesus' primary intention here to address the nature of God. And that is quite true, it isn't. He is, in fact, addressing the matter of worship. But in doing so, He bases His response upon a belief that was a given, a truth that had been revealed in the Scriptures long before: God is not limited to time and space. It is a grave error to think God is like a man, as we saw before, and God's people were told many times that they erred greatly to think that location is relevant to God's being. For example, Jeremiah recorded the word of the LORD, saying,

> "Can a man hide himself in hiding places so I do not see him?" declares the LORD. "Do I not fill[16] the heavens and the earth?" declares the LORD. (Jer. 23:24)

Likewise, Solomon knew the truth that no man-made temple could contain God's presence:

> "But will God indeed dwell with mankind on the earth? Behold, heaven and the highest heaven cannot contain You;[17] how much less this house which I have built" (2 Chron. 6:18).

God's omnipresence flows logically and necessarily from the fact that He created all things. How could His creation be greater than He is? How could there be anyplace in His creation beyond His presence?

Another aspect of God's spirituality is the assertion that God, as to His absolute being, is not visible to human eyes. Indeed, one of the clearest evidences of the deity of Christ is that He is said to be the "image of the invisible God" (Col. 1:15), and that He is the one who makes the Father known. No one has seen God at any time (John 1:18), but we have come to know God through the revelation made in Jesus Christ. Only an infinite Person can reveal another infinite Person, and this tells us much about Jesus Christ. But as to God's *nature*, we are told that He is invisible and must choose to reveal himself in forms sensible to us. Hence, Paul's doxology in writing to Timothy:

> Now to the King eternal, immortal, invisible, the only God,[18] be honor and glory forever and ever. Amen. (1 Tim. 1:17)

Some argue that the term "invisible" only means "not seen," rather than "not *able to be* seen." Yet later in the same letter Paul explains his point:

> Who alone possesses immortality and dwells in unapproachable light, whom no man has seen or can see.[19] To Him be honor and eternal dominion! Amen. (1 Tim. 6:16)

The true God is not liable to representation by the physical universe, for He is invisible and infinite and therefore incapable of comparison with anything in the created order, which must be, by nature, finite. This brings us to the very nature of idolatry, for to represent God in any way that is untrue is, at its root, an act of idolatry. God forbade His people from making any kind of likeness that was meant to represent His being:

> You shall not make for yourself an idol, or any likeness of what is in heaven above or on the earth beneath or in the water under the earth. You shall not worship them or serve them; for I, the LORD your God, am a jealous God, visiting the iniquity of the fathers on the children, on the third and the fourth generations of those who hate Me, but showing lovingkindness to thousands, to those who love Me and keep My commandments. (Ex. 20:4–6)

There is a reason for this. Wayne Grudem commented on this passage:

> The creation language in this commandment ("heaven above, or . . . earth beneath, or . . . water under the earth") is a reminder that God's *being*, his essential mode of existence, is different from everything that he has created. To think of his being in terms of anything else in the created universe is to misrepresent him, to limit him, to think of him as less than he really is. To make a graven (or "carved" or "sculptured") image of God as a golden calf, for example, may have been an attempt to portray God as a God who is strong and full of life (like a calf), but to say that God was like a calf was a horribly false statement about God's knowledge, wisdom, love, mercy, omnipresence, eternity, independence, holiness, righteousness, justice, and so forth. Indeed, while we must say that God has made all creation so that each part of it reflects something of his own character, we must also now affirm that to picture God as *existing* in a form or *mode of being* that is like anything else in creation is to think of God in a horribly misleading and dishonoring way. . . . Thus, God does not have a physical body, nor is he made of any kind of matter like much of the rest of creation.[20]

As strong as it may sound, we cannot possibly be honest with the biblical evidence and teaching, and the statements of LDS leaders we have examined, and not honestly warn our LDS friends that to worship the God of Joseph Smith is, quite simply, to engage in idolatry. To even think of God in terms of a creature—a man—is to denigrate His being beyond words. Likewise, to worship any god other than the one true God who made all things is to place one's very soul in eternal peril:

> For you shall not worship any other god, for the LORD, whose name is Jealous, is a jealous God.[21] (Ex. 34:14)
> I am the LORD your God who brought you out of the land of Egypt, out of the house of slavery. You shall have no other gods before Me. (Deut. 5:6–7)

Unique in Not Being a Creature Like Man

The sin of idolatry includes thinking of God in human categories. This is not to say that God has not used human terminology to express himself and His existence—surely He has.[22] But we are warned over and over again not to think of God *as if He were a creature like us*. Note these words from Isaiah 29:16:

> You turn things around! Shall the potter be considered as equal with the clay, that what is made would say to its maker, "He did not make me"; or what is formed say to him who formed it, "He has no understanding"?

And the *New International Version* has a useful rendering of the same passage:

> You turn things upside down, as if the potter were thought to be like the clay! Shall what is formed say to him who formed it, "He did not make me"? Can the pot say of the potter, "He knows nothing"?

The first Hebrew word in the verse,[23] *hephek*, translated "turn things around" in the NASB and "turn things upside down" in the NIV, often means simply "perversity." It refers to a turning of something, and in this context, the "turning" is of the relationship between the thing made and the one who made it. One might literally render the first phrase, "Perversity, if the thing molded (clay) is to be considered like the one who molded it." It is perverse (*hephek*) for clay to think the potter is of the same "kind" as itself. Pots that "think" the potter is a pot are *hephek*. They are turning things upside down. So, too, when men think God is like man *on the level of being*, this is perverse. It is unnatural, a "turning of things upside down." And yet, is this not a perfect description of the central tenet of LDS theology itself? "God himself was once as we are now, and is an exalted man" is exactly how Joseph Smith put it. "The important points of the doctrine for Latter-day Saints are that Gods and humans are the same species of being" is how Stephen Robinson of BYU states it. Both are *hephek*, as God has said through Isaiah.

In the Psalms, God likewise warns against this kind of perverse notion:

> These things you have done and I kept silence; you thought that I was just like you; I will reprove you and state the case in order before your eyes. (Ps. 50:21)

"You thought I was just like you." What a charge! What a condemnation of the sinful attitudes of men toward God! And what a mistake for man to make. "I will reprove you and state the case in order before your eyes." God will not allow man to continue long in his rebellion. God will make His case, and demonstrate beyond all doubt His deity and providence. One commentator said,

> They did not understand that Yahweh is the Wholly Other One, who is free in his judgment as well as in his grace. He cannot be boxed in by humans. At his own time God will come to rebuke and then judge his people openly.[24]

All through Scripture it is considered the height of folly to forget a simple lesson: God is God, man is not. Sinful man chafes against his creatureliness and God's eternity. But only one response exists for the man who refuses to stay within the bounds set upon him by his Maker:

> On the contrary, who are you, O man, who answers back to God? The thing molded will not say to the molder, "Why did you make me like this," will it? (Rom. 9:20)

Answering back to a man—no matter how exalted—is one thing, but answering back to God is sheer folly, for He is unique and utterly unlike us.[25] We are never more in line with God's purpose in our creation than when we remember who we truly are, and who He truly is.

Eternal

Joseph Smith said he would refute the idea that God had always been God. In so doing, he separated himself and all who would follow him from the Christian faith. We have already seen a number of passages witness to the eternal nature of God *as God*. One of the clearest, however, comes from Moses:

> Before the mountains were born or You gave birth to the earth and the world, even from everlasting to everlasting,[26] You are God.[27] (Ps. 90:2)

From everlasting *to* everlasting. Without limitation. Not as a mere "intelligence" like all men, but *as God* He has existed eternally. There has never been a time *when God was not God*. Because any Mormon must confess that according to standard LDS doctrine there was a time—even in some other "eternity," there was still a time—when God was not God, but was yet to be exalted, and at that time worshiped and served another God. That alone is enough to make it tremendously clear: Such a god is not the God of Moses and Psalm 90:2, nor the God known to other writers of Scripture:

> For thus says the high and exalted One Who lives forever, whose name is Holy, "I dwell on a high and holy place, and also with the contrite and lowly of spirit in order to revive the spirit of the lowly and to revive the heart of the contrite. (Isa. 57:15)

> Of old You founded the earth, and the heavens are the work of Your hands. Even they will perish, but You endure; and all of them will wear out like a garment; like clothing You will change them and they will be changed. But You are the same, and Your years will not come to an end. (Ps. 102:25–27)

The psalmist here makes the same contrast as Moses in Psalm 90:2: creation, the work of God, is temporal, passing, limited. God, the true God, is not.

We struggle with God's eternity. We cannot grasp it. Our lives are conditioned by the passing of time. Our language itself is based upon tenses: past, present, future. We are creatures, and as such we have been created to exist *temporally*, that is, within the realm of time. God is not a creature, and does not exist *temporally*, but *eternally*. Rather than thinking of eternity as a long, long time, think of it as a *way* of existence that does not involve a progression of events and moments. That is how God lives. Boggle the mind? Too high for your thoughts? Remember what He said: "My ways are higher than your ways."

One of the results of existing eternally is that God is therefore unchanging. He is not growing, progressing, evolving, or in any way moving from a state of imperfection to a state of perfection. Again, this is not the result of influence from Greek philosophy: it is the teaching of Scripture itself. Indeed, the very fact that God is *unchangingly faithful* to His promises to Israel is based upon the understanding that Yahweh himself does not change with time:

> For I, the LORD, do not change; therefore you, O sons of Jacob, are not consumed. (Mal. 3:6)

If man is anything, he is changeable. Yet God says He does not change. Change involves movement over time, yet God is eternal, and therefore does not change as man does.[28] *Our very salvation is dependent upon God's unchanging nature, for His faithfulness is based upon His being the same yesterday, today, and tomorrow.*[29]

> God is not a man,[30] that He should lie, nor a son of man, that He should repent; has He said, and will He not do it? Or has He spoken, and will He not make it good? (Num. 23:19)

What is the solid foundation of God's trustworthiness? He is God, not man. Man lies. Man changes his mind. Man speaks many things, but cannot fulfill his promises. But God is not man. There is a fundamental distinction between God and man on the level of *being*. The same theme is struck many centuries later in Hosea:

> I will not execute My fierce anger; I will not destroy Ephraim again. For I am God and not man,[31] the Holy One in your midst, and I will not come in wrath. (Hos. 11:9)

Creator of All Things

We have seen that Mormonism lacks a Creator. That is, the God of Mormonism "organizes" preexisting matter but does not have the power or ability to create matter *ex nihilo* (out of nothing). Nor, indeed, can God *create* the spirit of man, but instead *begets* the spirits of men. On the issue of where the universe *en toto* came from, Mormonism cannot provide a coherent answer. When faced with the errors of infinite regression and related philosophical problems inherent with the Eternal Law of Progression, Mormonism is found wanting.[32]

Throughout this work I have described God as the Creator of "all things" or as the maker of "heaven and earth." These phrases come from Scripture itself. Some today, however, not finding scriptural terminology sufficient, need a more expansive definition. I emphasize that whenever I speak of God creating "heaven and earth," I am just as firmly asserting that God is the Creator of all matter, all space, and all time that ever has been or ever will be, anywhere, in this universe or any other that might be proposed. The claim is *exhaustive* in its scope, for that is the claim made by God himself in His Word.

The Scriptures claim that God's creative activity is *prima facie* evidence of His absolute and *sole* deity. Over and over again this point is made throughout the Word of God:

> By the word of the LORD the heavens were made, and by the breath of His mouth all their host. . . . For He spoke, and it was done; He commanded, and it stood fast. (Ps. 33:6, 9)

The psalmist did not believe that God *organized* preexisting matter, but that God *made* the heavens by His word. "He spoke, and it was done; He commanded, and it stood fast." All that exists—heaven and earth being exhaustive, in Hebrew thought, of creation itself—does so at God's command.

> Who has performed and accomplished *it*, calling forth the generations from the beginning? I, the LORD, am the first, and with the last. I am He. (Isa. 41:4)

Yahweh created *all* things, including "the generations." The eternal One, Yahweh, the first and the last, is the Lord of time itself. Later in the same chapter God mocks the idols who are *not* "supratemporal," existing beyond the realm of time. He challenges them to do two things that only the true God can do to perfection. One is easy to see: Tell us the future. This is a common challenge, one God can fulfill because He *created* time and is not limited to it. But we often miss the second challenge. God asks the idols to tell us what has taken place in the past and, even more important, *the purpose of what happened in the past.* It is one thing to recount past events, but to know *why* they happened—only the Sovereign Lord of eternity itself can do that. Hear His challenge to all would-be gods:

> Let them bring forth and declare to us what is going to take place; as for the former events, declare what they were, that we may consider them and know their outcome. Or announce to us what is coming; declare the things that are going to come afterward, that we may know that you are gods; indeed, do good or evil, that we may anxiously look about us and fear together. Behold, you are of no account, and your work amounts to nothing; he who chooses you is an abomination.[33] (Isa. 41:22–24)

The Christian worships the Lord of time itself and trusts in His unchanging nature. His promises are sure and everlasting because *He* is sure and everlasting. But what of the person who rejects the true God and embraces falsehood? God mocks the false idols, but He also has strong words for the person who *chooses* such idols. "He who chooses you is an abomination." We dare not miss the meaning of the LORD at this point. The Hebrew term that is used here is found elsewhere in the Old Testament. How does God view the idolater? The very same term is used of the idols themselves in Deuteronomy 7:26: They are an abomination to God. But to see how serious this sin is in God's eyes, realize that the very same Hebrew word, *to-evah,* "abomination," is used in Leviticus 18:22 and 20:13 *in reference to homosexuality itself.* God says homosexuality is *to-evah,* and He says the person who chooses a god other than the very Creator and Lord of time itself is, likewise, *to-evah.*

God has more strong words for false gods through the prophet Jeremiah:

> But the LORD is the true God; He is the living God and the everlasting King. At His wrath the earth quakes, and the nations cannot endure His indignation. Thus you shall say to them, "The gods that did not make the heavens and the earth shall perish from the earth and from under the heavens"[34] (Jer. 10:10–11).

Yahweh is the true God—all others are pretenders. He reigns supreme over His creation. And listen to the judgment He pronounces. To all "gods that did not make the heavens and the earth" he declares the death sentence: they will perish from the earth and from under the heavens. Did the Mormon God make the heavens and the earth? No, he only *organized* this world, and if you take the modern LDS approach, only this particular creation or eternity. But in either case, the LDS view of God *fails* the biblical test provided here by God himself.

> Thus says the LORD, your Redeemer, and the one who formed you from the womb, "I, the LORD, am the maker of all things, stretching out the heavens by Myself[35] and spreading out the earth all alone. (Isa. 44:24)

This passage presents numerous difficulties for the LDS viewpoint. Yahweh speaks. He claims to be the Maker, the one who formed man. Indeed, He claims to be the Maker of *all* things. But the final two phrases are simply beyond explanation for the Mormon Church. Yahweh (remember, this is the Son, a second and less exalted God than Elohim in modern LDS theology) says that He stretches out the heavens "by Myself" and the earth "all alone." Remember the scene we recounted from the *current* LDS Temple ceremonies in which Elohim directs Jehovah *and Michael* to go down and "organize" the earth? This passage is *directly* contradictory to the assertions found in the Endowment ceremony, which, as we saw, is considered to have been given *by revelation*. Yahweh did not stretch out the heavens under the orders of some greater god and in company with Michael. He *alone* is the Creator:

> For thus says the LORD, who created the heavens (He is the God who formed the earth and made it; He established it and did not create it a waste place, but formed it to be inhabited), "I am the LORD, and there is none else" (Isa. 45:18).

And so we come full circle: the Creator is Yahweh, "and there is none else." The glorious truth of monotheism is interwoven with the fact of God as Creator. Neither truth exists without the other.

The Maker of Man

Not only did God create all the material universe but Yahweh himself created the spirits of men:

> The burden of the word of the LORD concerning Israel. Thus declares the LORD who stretches out the heavens, lays the foundation of the earth, and forms the spirit of man within him.[36] (Zech. 12:1)

Yahweh not only created on a *grand scale*, but on a *personal* one as well. He formed the spirit of man within man. He is the personal Creator, the one who made man himself. Here the realm of God's creation is extended to the very spiritual nature of man. We would do well to remember the words of Joseph Smith in the King Follett Discourse, quoted earlier: "God never had the power to create the spirit of man at all." But is this what the Scriptures teach? Certainly not. Over and over again the Bible informs us (for we need to be reminded often) we are creatures, formed and made by Another.

> When I consider Your heavens, the work of Your fingers, the moon and the stars, which You have ordained; what is man that You take thought of him, and the son of man that You care for him? Yet You have made him a little lower than God, and You crown him with glory and majesty! (Ps. 8:3–5)

What is man? The psalmist asked that question and identified man as a creation, one *made by God* and yet crowned with glory and majesty. Man is the highest of God's creations and, as an image bearer of God, is worthy of honor and respect. But man is a *creature*, a *creation* of God, and will always, due to that fact, be separated from God on the scale of *being*. Everything that is created is finite and dependent; God is infinite and independent from all things. His *aseity*, or independence and self-existence, has already been seen. We now turn briefly to a look at man, focusing here solely upon the question of man's nature as a creation, and the *means* by which God created man.

We have already seen that God forms the spirit of man within him (Zech. 12:1). Likewise, we know that God created man for a particular purpose, one that is defined in terms of *God* (not in terms of the creature man):

> Everyone who is called by My name, and whom I have created for My glory, whom I have formed, even whom I have made. (Isa. 43:7)

Men are created for the glory of God. Our lives are defined on the basis of *God's* will, *God's* plan, *God's* decrees. This is why Paul could tell believers:

> Whether, then, you eat or drink or whatever you do, do all to the glory of God. (1 Cor. 10:31)

This fundamental truth (often lacking in modern Christian proclamation) is reflected in the first question of the Westminster Shorter Catechism, which asks,

> Q. What is the chief end of man?
> A. Man's chief end is to glorify God and to enjoy him forever.[37]

Man slips down the slope into idolatry when he views himself in any way other than as the creature of God, bound *by his creation itself* to live in such a way as to honor and glorify his God.

The chief testimony to the creation of man is found in Genesis, the book of origins. And, most relevant to our purposes, we turn immediately to Genesis 1:26, a passage often cited in LDS literature:

> Then God said, "Let Us make man in Our image, according to Our likeness; and let them rule over the fish of the sea and over the birds of the sky and over the cattle and over all the earth, and over every creeping thing that creeps on the earth." God created man in His own image, in the image of God He created him; male and female He created them.

The use of this passage by LDS apologists is illustrated by Stephen Robinson:

> Latter-day Saints believe that humankind is created in the image of God (Gen. 1:26–28). We take this quite literally to mean that God has a physical image and that humanity is created *in* it. By definition, an image is the representation of physical qualities. As Adam is created in the likeness and image of God, so after the Fall Adam begets Seth in *his* own likeness and image (Gen. 5:3). The language of orthodox Christians in making the "image" in which Adam was created a nonphysical image, a spiritual image, necessitates taking the word *image* figuratively. This is fine with me—the passage can be coherently interpreted that way—but it is another instance of the LDS taking Scripture *literally* where the "orthodox" make it merely fig-

urative and then charge *us* with being unbiblical![38]

Dr. Robinson asserts that "by definition" an image is the representation "of physical qualities."[39] But is this the case with the Hebrew terms used here? The answer is, no, it is not. The original terms, *tselem* and *damuth*, are capable of a wide variety of meanings. Grudem notes:

> The word *image* (*tselem*) means an object similar to something else and often representative of it. The word is used to speak of statues or replicas of tumors and of mice (1 Sam. 6:5, 11), of paintings of soldiers on the wall (Ezek. 23:14), and of pagan idols or statues representing deities (Num. 33:52; 2 Kings 11:18; Ezek. 7:20; 16:17; et al.). The word *likeness* (*demût*) also means an object similar to something else, but it tends to be used more frequently in contexts where the idea of similarity is emphasized more than the idea of being a representative or substitute (of a god, for example). King Ahaz's model or drawing of the altar he saw in Damascus is called a "likeness" (2 Kings 16:10), as are the figures of bulls beneath the bronze altar (2 Chron. 4:3–4), and the wall paintings of Babylonian chariot officers (Ezek. 23:14–15). In Ps. 58:4 the venom of the wicked is a "likeness" of the venom of a snake: here the idea is that they are very similar in their characteristics, but there is no thought of actual representation or substitution.[40]

Man is the image bearer of God, but we have already seen that the God who makes man is not a man, but is spirit. Furthermore, whatever the image of God is, it *separates* man from the rest of creation, for only man has this image. An ape has a physical image, but not the image of God. So the idea that the image has to do with corporeality, hence making God an exalted man, is without basis in the Genesis passage. What is more, while Adam *begat* Seth in his image (showing that the image of God would be hereditary and would continue in the human family), God *created* Adam in His. God did not *beget* Adam, but *created* Adam. Such might seem a simplistic observation, but when we remember the statements of LDS leaders defining the power of *creation* as primarily existing in the sense of *procreation*, the distinction is an important one.

We might note an internal problem in the LDS position at this point. If Mormons wish to believe that in Genesis 1:26 we are talking about *corporeality*—a physical image—then we must point out that when Joseph Smith changed this passage in his *Inspired Translation*,[41] he had God speak these words to "His Only Begotten," that is, to the Son. Smith plainly indicates that this is the Father speaking to the Son. However, at this point in time the Son did not have a physical body, for this was before the Incarnation! Hence, to get around this, the Mormon must say that the spirit body has a physical image as well, and it is this image that is meant. But as soon as it is admitted that the physical image could not be the focus of these words, the issue becomes moot.[42]

Biblical Testimony to Man's Createdness

Over the years I have found that many LDS react *emotionally* to the strong testimony of the Scriptures to the nature of man. This is especially true when God likens man to inanimate objects, or even (as we saw in Isaiah 40:22) to grasshoppers! Such *would be* a rather unkind thing to do *if* God were an exalted man, one of our own species! But God is not, as He makes plain over and over again:

> Woe to the one who quarrels with his Maker—an earthenware vessel among the vessels of earth! Will the clay say to the potter, "What are you doing?" Or the thing you are making say, "He has no hands"? (Isa. 45:9).

Just like Isaiah 29:16, we have here the *assumption* of a doctrine that is found throughout the inspired text: God is God, man isn't. I am reminded of the popular cartoon featuring Wile E. Coyote and the Roadrunner. The coyote is the classic example of someone who "just doesn't get it." The Roadrunner is too fast—and too smart. He's way out of Wile E.'s league. But, despite failing for many decades now, the coyote keeps trying. The Roadrunner often mocks Wile E., and we all laugh. Yet in Scripture, God himself uses sarcasm—regularly—to point out the foolishness of man's idolatry. So we hear God saying, in effect, "Oh man, man! I am God, *and you aren't.*" God likens rebellious men to an earthenware vessel, a mere inanimate object, yet arrogant enough to argue with his Maker! The *King James Version* renders the same term "potsherd," a mere broken piece of a pot! The whole idea of something that is *made* responding back to its *maker* is the absurdity that Isaiah is presenting. In the same way, it is absurd for man to think of himself, the pot, as being the same as the Potter. We are clay, molded by the Potter. The one who forgets this truth is in danger of playing the role of Wile E. Coyote—constantly needing to be reminded of his proper place.

> Know that the Lord Himself is God; it is He who has made us, and not we ourselves; we are His people and the sheep of His pasture. (Ps. 100:3)

Yahweh is Elohim (this is what the Hebrew says), and it is Yahweh who made us. It is in the context of *creation* that God is called our "Father" in the Old Testament, *not* the context of *generation*. This theme is repeated over and over in Scripture:

> Is this the way you repay the Lord, O foolish and unwise people? Is he not your Father, your Creator, who made you and formed you? (Deut. 32:6, NIV)
> But now, O Lord, You are our Father, we are the clay, and You our potter; and all of us are the work of Your hand. (Isaiah 64:8)
> Do we not all have one father? Has not one God created us? Why do we deal treacherously each against his brother so as to profane the covenant of our fathers? (Mal. 2:10)

Each of these passages tells us something important about how we can *properly* identify God as "our Father" in the Old Testament. The first passage defines the term "Father" as "Creator," the one who made and formed each individual. The second again uses "Father," but immediately refers to man as "clay" and God as the "Potter," emphasizing the *ontological distinction* that exists between Creator and created, God and man. And in Malachi the use of "father" is defined solely in the terminology of creation. All men can call God "Father" in this sense, for He is their *Maker* (just as the writer to the Hebrews uses the same phraseology in Hebrews 12:9, describing God as the Father of our spirits). But there is a special way in which believers call God "Father." They are His children by *adoption*, not by *procreation*, and by faith in Jesus Christ. This is a much more intimate, special use of the term "father," and goes far beyond the creative aspect seen in these passages.

So we see that Yahweh Elohim, the Lord God, is the Maker of man. Every breath we take, every thought we have, comes from His hand. He is our sustainer, and we are His creation. We have the privilege of looking out over the vast reaches of space and realizing that not a particle exists in all that vastness but that He made it. This is the God who is described by Paul as the one who "calls into being that which does not exist" (Rom. 4:17), and is the one who prepared the worlds "by the word of God, so that what is seen was not made out of things which are visible" (Heb. 11:3). This is the God Christians worship and adore, for "our God is in the heavens; He does whatever He pleases" (Ps. 115:3; 135:6). It is of Him that we confess, "And as for His stretched-out hand, who can turn it back?" (Isa. 14:27). We know that "all the gods of the peoples are idols, but the LORD (Yahweh) made the heavens" (Ps. 96:5). It is to this eternal Creator, our Maker and Lord, we sing:

> Worthy are You, our Lord and our God, to receive glory and honor and power; for You created all things, and because of Your will they existed, and were created. (Rev. 4:11)

9

ANSWERS TO COMMONLY CITED PASSAGES

Before we conclude our study and present some final thoughts, I would like to *briefly* respond to a few passages that are commonly presented in support of the LDS doctrine of God. We have seen that the *united* and *consistent* testimony of Scripture is that there is one eternal God, unchangeable, and that man is His creation. God is infinite, man is finite. Yet a few passages, taken out of the context of Scripture and isolated from the many passages that speak more clearly to the issue, are used to teach otherwise. We have already noted some of the problem passages in other chapters, especially in endnotes attached to their citation by LDS leaders. I would like to look at two of the most popular citations, and then focus upon a modern presentation of the LDS viewpoint and the passages pressed into service there.

I Said You Are Gods

John chapter ten is one of the most beautiful in all of Scripture, for it speaks of the Lord Jesus' relationship to His people in the terms of the Shepherd and His sheep. In the midst of talking about the glorious salvation that belongs to those who know and trust Christ, Jesus asserts that He and the Father are one in their bringing about the final and full salvation of all those who are given by the Father to the Son (vv. 28–30). When the Lord says, "I and the Father are one,"[1] He offends the Jews, who realize that such a claim implies Deity. No mere creature can be fully one with the Father in bringing about redemption itself! This prompts the dialogue that concerns us here:

> "I and the Father are one." The Jews picked up stones again to stone Him. Jesus answered them, "I showed you many good works from the Father; for which of them are you stoning Me?" The Jews answered Him, "For a good work we do not stone You, but for blasphemy; and because You, being a man, make Yourself out to be God." Jesus answered them, "Has it not been written in your Law, 'I SAID, YOU ARE GODS'? If he called them gods, to whom the word of God came (and the Scripture cannot be broken), do you say of Him, whom the Father sanctified and sent into the world, 'You are blaspheming,' because I said, 'I am the Son of God'?" (John 10:30–36).

The use of this passage in LDS literature is widespread. "I said, you are gods" is used to substantiate the idea of a plurality of gods, and men becoming gods. Yet even a brief review of the passage demonstrates that such is hardly a worthy interpretation, and some of the leading LDS apologists today avoid trying to press the passage that far, and for good reason.[2] The unbelieving Jews seen in this passage with murder in their hearts are hardly good candidates for exaltation to godhood. Furthermore, the Lord Jesus uses the *present tense* when He says, "You *are* gods." So, obviously, He is not identifying His attackers as divine beings, worthy of worship by their eventual celestial offspring! What, then, is going on here?

When we allow the text to speak for itself, the meaning comes across clearly. As usual the context is determinative. The Jewish leaders were acting as Jesus' judges. They were accusing Him of blasphemy, of breaking God's law. Their role as judges in this instance is determinative, for the Lord is going to cite a passage *about* judges from the Old Testament. The Jews make it plain that they understand Jesus' words to contain an implicit claim of equality with God (v. 33). It is at this point that the Lord quotes from Psalm 82:6, which contains the important words "I said, you are gods." But when we go back to the passage from which this is taken (and surely the Jewish leaders would have known the context themselves), we find an important truth:

> God takes His stand in His own congregation; He judges in the midst of the rulers. How long will you judge unjustly and

show partiality to the wicked? Vindicate the weak and father-less; do justice to the afflicted and destitute. Rescue the weak and needy; deliver them out of the hand of the wicked. They do not know nor do they understand; they walk about in dark-ness; all the foundations of the earth are shaken. I said, "You are gods, and all of you are sons of the Most High" (Ps. 82:1–6).

Here we have the key to the passage, for this is a psalm of judgment against the rulers of Israel. God takes His stand in His own congregation, that being His own people, Israel. He judges in the midst of the "rulers." The Hebrew term here is "Elohim," which could be translated "gods." The *NASB*, however, recognizes that the context indicates who is being discussed, for the next verse reads, "How long will you *judge unjustly and show partiality to the wicked*?" Who judges unjustly and shows partiality? Human judges, of course—human rulers among the people. Hence, the *NASB* rendering of "Elohim" as "rulers." It is important to recognize the use of the term *Elohim* in verse 1, for the very same term appears in verse 6 and is what lies behind Jesus' citation in John 10:34. Before moving on in the text, it should be noted that even at this point recognizing that this passage is talking about *unjust human rulers* removes this passage from the realm of possible passages to cite in support of a plurality of gods. Certainly Jesus was not, by citing this passage, calling His accusers true divine beings.

When we get to verse 6, we find that God has placed the judges of Israel in a position of being "gods" among the people. They were entrusted with the application of God's law. God calls them to vindicate the weak and fatherless and to do justice to the afflicted and destitute (v. 3). This is their task, their duty. But they are failing that duty. They are not acting as proper, godly judges. Verse 6, then, begins the pronouncement of judgment. Jesus only cites the beginning of the judgment—which was enough to make His point. But since many today do not immediately know the context the way the Jews did, we need to point it out. The rest of the phrase Jesus quotes is this: "Nevertheless you will die like men and fall like any one of the princes." Such is hardly the terminology one would use of divine and exalted beings! And this explains the use of the present tense verb "You *are* gods" in John 10:34. Jesus is saying His accusers *are*, right then, the judges condemned in Psalm 82. And what kind of judges were they? Unrighteous judges, who were judging unjustly. Jesus was calling His accusers false judges, and they well knew it.

That this is the meaning of Jesus' use of the passage is seen by going back to John chapter ten. Jesus refers to these rulers as those "to whom the word of God came." Surely this is an apt description of the rulers who were set to judge in God's place. Once He has made His application and identified His accusers as false judges, He then asks, "Do you say of Him, whom the Father sanctified and sent into the world, 'You are blaspheming,' because I said, 'I am the Son of God'?" Here He points to their judgment of blasphemy and contrasts their errant decision with the Father's sanctification and sending of the divine Son. The folly of their false judgment is manifest to all. This is the meaning of the passage, and pressing it to support the idea that men can, after aeons and aeons of evolution, *become* gods, only shows how far removed the LDS position is from biblical Christianity.

The Right Hand of God

> But being full of the Holy Spirit, he gazed intently into heaven and saw the glory of God, and Jesus standing at the right hand of God; and he said, "Behold, I see the heavens opened up and the Son of Man standing at the right hand of God" (Acts 7:55–56).

This passage is often used by LDS to prove that God and Jesus are two separate beings and that God has a "right hand." Of course, Christians believe that God the Father is a different *Person* than the Son, as the doctrine of the Trinity has always taught. But what of the idea that here you have two separate beings, two separate gods?

First, the passage comes from the martyrdom of Stephen the deacon. Upon uttering these words, the Jews rush upon Stephen and stone him.[3] There is something in what he says that causes them to become enraged, and certainly we can understand what it was. These men were responsible, by and large, for the crucifixion of Christ. When Stephen says he sees the Son of Man standing at the right hand of God, they realize that Stephen is proclaiming the exaltation of the Messiah—the very Messiah that they had rejected.

Second, we note that Stephen does not say that he saw two gods.

He saw *the glory of God* and Jesus standing on the right hand of God. Stephen did not see God the Father, he saw the Son.

Finally, what does "the right hand of God" mean? Any impartial review of the biblical usage of the phrase answers the question beyond doubt. The right hand of God is a position of honor and glory. It is not a *location* in space but a *position of power*. Dozens of references in the Old Testament bear this out.[4] Stephen saw the exalted Christ standing in glory, awaiting the arrival of His faithful servant. Nothing in the passage suggests a plurality of *gods*, but does suggest the Trinitarian plurality of *persons*.

A Modern Apologetic

In the recent book *How Wide the Divide?*[5] LDS scholar Stephen Robinson attempts to present a biblically based argument for the idea that men can become "gods," though in a rather relativistic way. While Robinson is not as bold as LDS leaders at this point, the passages he uses and the way he threads them together is representative of the best Mormonism has to offer. I would like to allow the argument to be heard in its full form, so that the impact of the use of scriptural passages can be felt. Then we will examine the argument closely and see that it does not hold up. Robinson begins,

> In the matter of deification, Latter-day Saints believe that God intends through the gospel of Jesus Christ to transform those who are saved by Christ to be like Christ. Moreover, we believe that God will succeed in what God intends. Since Latter-day Saints take seriously and literally the scriptural language about becoming the children of God (Rom. 8:16), it makes sense to us that the children grow up to be like their Father. According to Scripture, God is the Father of spirits (Heb. 12:9). We are his offspring (Acts 17:29), and offspring grow up to be what their parents are. Certainly through the atonement of Christ we have been begotten sons and daughters of God (1 Pet. 1:13), we partake of the divine nature (2 Pet. 1:4), and we have been designated heirs to all he has (Rom. 8:15–17; Rev. 21:7), which is all that the Father has.[6] (John 3:35)

The argument *sounds* very good. It claims to be taking biblical passages "seriously and literally." It makes sense that children grow up to be like their parents, too. And if one had not already examined passage after passage where God speaks as the Potter and of us as the clay, one might be swayed by such an argument. We will look at each passage cited below. The argument concludes,

> After all, when Christ appears, the sons and daughters of God will be like him (1 John 3:2), changed into the same image from glory to glory (2 Cor. 3:18). We receive his glory (John 17:22–23) and sit on his throne (Rev. 3:21). We become joint heirs with Christ to all that the Father has (Rom. 8:15–17; Rev. 21:7; 1 Cor. 3:22), and we partake of his divine nature (2 Pet. 1:4). What could it possibly mean to "partake of the divine nature" if the divine nature is not extended to us and does not become part of us? To Latter-day Saints the glorified and resurrected Christ illustrates in his person what the saved can become through his grace. For us the logic of the Scriptures is inescapable: (1) Jesus Christ is divine, and (2) through the atonement and the grace of Christ the saved become one with Christ, become like him (1 John 3:2) and receive his image and glory (John 17:21–23; 2 Cor. 3:18). Therefore, (3) through the atonement of Christ the saved become in some sense divine. If A equals B, and B equals C, how shall one resist concluding that A equals C?[7]

The repetitive use of the same passages adds to the biblical aura of the argument. The new Christian, or the person unfounded in Scripture, may well find such an argument appealing, and the growth of Mormonism certainly proves that *someone* is buying into it. But does the argument hold?

First, we point out that the argument *ignores* the totality of the testimony of Scripture that we have seen to the fundamental, *ontological* difference between God and men. It *assumes* that God and men are of the same species. The parent/child argument is based upon this assumption. If calling God our Father is instead a matter of *adoption*, rather than *nature* (as it is), the argument falls apart. Further, the logic of the Scriptures is indeed inescapable, but not as it is presented. Jesus Christ is divine—eternally so. He is without beginning or end. Hence, when the second point is presented, a major flaw is concealed: We shall be *like* Him, but not *in being*, for one thing will always separate the eternal Creator from us: He has eternally been what He is. We have not. Consequently, the range of meaning we can assign to the word "like" is limited by this simple consideration, one that I insist is based firmly upon the many biblical passages already presented. So when we get to the final step of the argument, it does not hold, for we are not like Christ in His eternity and divinity.

But let us look at the passages cited and see if any of them overthrows the testimony of Scripture to the divine truth that God has eternally been God, is our Creator in the sense of the Potter and the clay, and is *not* of our "species."

> That they may all be one; even as You, Father, are in Me and I in You, that they also may be in Us, so that the world may believe that You sent Me. The glory which You have given Me I have given to them, that they may be one, just as We are one; I in them and You in Me, that they may be perfected in unity, so that the world may know that You sent Me, and loved them, even as You have loved Me. (John 17:21–23)

Robinson uses this passage in the context of our receiving the glory of Christ and sitting upon the throne of God. This comes especially from verse 22, "The glory which You have given Me I have given to them." Does this passage then teach deification of human beings?

This passage comes from Christ's high priestly prayer to the Father. He is praying specifically for His own people whom the Father has given to Him. He prays that they may have a supernatural unity—the unity of the Church of Jesus Christ. The point that Robinson misses is that the glory mentioned is connected with this unity, for He says, "that they may all be one." This is not speaking to the individual believer's exaltation to godhood. In fact, it has no application to the *being* of believers at all. It does, however, speak strongly to glory that rests upon Christ's Church when, united in the truth, faith, and love, she stands boldly for Christ's name in the world. The Church is then surely "glorious," as the apostle Paul put it:

> Husbands, love your wives, just as Christ also loved the church and gave Himself up for her, so that He might sanctify her, having cleansed her by the washing of water with the word, that He might present to Himself the church in all her glory, having no spot or wrinkle or any such thing; but that she would be holy and blameless. (Eph. 5:25–27)

More popular among LDS apologists is the use of Romans 8:

> For you have not received a spirit of slavery leading to fear again, but you have received a spirit of adoption as sons by which we cry out, "Abba! Father!" The Spirit Himself testifies with our spirit that we are children of God, and if children, heirs also, heirs of God and fellow heirs with Christ, if indeed we suffer with Him so that we may also be glorified with Him. For I consider that the sufferings of this present time are not worthy to be compared with the glory that is to be revealed to us. For the anxious longing of the creation waits eagerly for the revealing of the sons of God. (Rom. 8:15–19)

The argument is, "If we are joint heirs with Christ, then we receive everything Christ has. Since Christ is God, we receive godhood." But the passage speaks of our position as *adopted* children of God, not as children *by nature*, which would be required if the Father/child argument is to hold up. But on the level of receiving whatever Christ has, we again see a problem in that it assumes that Christ *received* Deity. He did not. The Son has eternally been God and did not enter into the state of being "God" at some point in time.[8] *Deity is not a possession to be transferred to fellow heirs.* Receiving an inheritance does not *change our being*. When I receive an inheritance, it does not change *me*; it only changes my status. No matter how highly a human is exalted, *he remains a human*. And so we go back to the fundamental difference between Christianity and Mormonism: Christians accept God's statement that He has eternally been God, while Mormons reject this or redefine it out of existence. An exalted man *is still a creature*, while God is the Creator.

> For in Him we live and move and exist, as even some of your own poets have said, 'For we also are His children.' Being then the children of God, we ought not to think that the Divine Nature is like gold or silver or stone, an image formed by the art and thought of man. (Acts 17:28–29)

This is certainly the strongest passage that can be mustered, again, if we ignore everything that the Word says in the Old Testament regarding the fundamental revelation of God's existence. Isolated from the rest of the Bible, the phrase "we are His children" could be used to support the idea that God has literal physical offspring. But again, the context keeps us from making this mistake. Paul's point is not to teach that God is an exalted man, but that God *is living* and is not "an image formed by the art and thought of man," made of silver and gold. Since men are living and thinking beings, and God is our Creator (remember the plain teaching that "Father" means "Creator" when we are referring to man's being, as in Deuteronomy 32:6; Isaiah 64:8; Malachi 2:10), it follows that God cannot be a mere idol, but must be a living Being. We dare not go beyond this immediate context and end up contradicting everything else the Bible says about the nature of God.

> Whether Paul or Apollos or Cephas or the world or life or death or things present or things to come; all things belong to you. (1 Cor. 3:22)

This passage is used due to the presence of the phrase "all things belong to you." Yet Paul goes on to say, "and you belong to Christ; and Christ belongs to God" (v. 23). Even if this were to refer to some kind of omnipotent power (which it obviously does not), it would still not change the fact that all things have not *always* belonged to believers, and hence, they are not eternal gods. The chasm that exists between the created and the Creator is not bridged by such a statement. Later Paul said to the same congregation:

> But we all, with unveiled face, beholding as in a mirror the glory of the Lord, are being transformed into the same image from glory to glory, just as from the Lord, the Spirit. (2 Cor. 3:18)

This is another passage that obviously uses the word "image" in a metaphorical sense, rather than in a physical way, contrary to Robinson's own argument on Genesis 1:26. If we already *have* the image of God, and this is physical, why do we need to be transformed into it? But, of course, we are talking about the image of Christ—Christlikeness—that is being worked into our lives through the sanctifying operation of the Spirit of God. It is indeed glorious—not in the outward sense of the glory of God seen by angels, but glorious in the sense that God is glorified in our salvation and sanctification and in our living lives that reflect Christ and His love. There is nothing here that even begins to suggest that this "image" involves being something *other than* what we are by creative fiat: human beings.

> Beloved, now we are children of God, and it has not appeared as yet what we will be. We know that when He appears, we will be like Him, because we will see Him just as He is. (1 John 3:2)

We shall indeed be like Christ, and what a promise it is. But we must remember that Christ is the God-man, unique in every way. In Him the divine and the human meet, and so it can be said that we can be like Him, for He became man and rose from the dead as man. As the perfect human, we can become like Him as He works His will in our lives. But again, this in no way means that we cease being what we are (creatures) and become what only God is (eternal).

> Furthermore, we had earthly fathers to discipline us, and we respected them; shall we not much rather be subject to the Father of spirits, and live? (Hebrews 12:9)

We noted in the preceding chapter that this passage borrows from the Old Testament the phraseology of Father as Creator that is so well attested there. It can in no way be suggested that God in a physical body begets spirits through literal sexual activity. He makes them (Zechariah 12:1).

> Seeing that His divine power has granted to us everything pertaining to life and godliness, through the true knowledge of Him who called us by His own glory and excellence. For by these He has granted to us His precious and magnificent promises, so that by them you may become partakers of the divine nature, having escaped the corruption that is in the world by lust. (2 Peter 1:3–4)

We have indeed been granted everything we need pertaining to life and godliness, for which we should be eternally thankful. We have been *granted*, by His grace, precious and magnificent promises—promises of redemption, sanctification, and eventually, glorification, all to the praise of His glorious grace. It is by those promises—not by nature, not by Eternal Law of Progression, not by priesthood authority—that we may "become partakers of the divine nature." Here we are told that this must mean that the divine nature is extended to us, and so becomes a part of us. As far as it has application to the finite creature that man is, that is true. But it does not even begin to follow from the text that we therefore can be called "gods." Peter himself only sees this participation in the light of the modifying clause that follows, "having escaped the corruption that is in the world by lust." Our participation in the divine nature is a participation in *holiness* and *incorruption*. It refers only to those aspects of our nature than *can* be like the divine nature. If Peter meant this passage in the way it is often used by LDS, he certainly passed over a golden opportunity to talk about our being "gods in embryo" and the like. But, of course, he didn't understand it in that way. We participate in the divine life when we walk in holiness, as much of both 1 and 2 Peter points out.

> He who overcomes, I will grant to him to sit down with Me on My throne, as I also overcame and sat down with My Father on His throne. (Rev. 3:21)
> Then He said to me, "It is done. I am the Alpha and the Omega, the beginning and the end. I will give to the one who thirsts from the spring of the water of life without cost. "He who overcomes will inherit these things, and I will be his God and he will be My son" (Rev. 21:6–7).

Both of these beautiful passages come from the book of Revelation, and both speak of the same wonderful promise: True believers will overcome the persecution and opposition of the world and will be richly rewarded in heaven. Neither passage promises that they will cease to be human beings; neither passage in any way teaches anything other than that *in Christ* we shall be glorified, and we will. True Christians will be glorified *human beings*, always creatures, always worshipers of the one true and eternal God.

10

THE DIVIDE IS VERY WIDE

I love the Mormon people. In our culture today, that might sound strange. Secular folks could not possibly understand what I mean, especially since I have written an entire work demonstrating, from LDS sources and from the Bible, that Mormonism is *not* Christianity. And since Mormons *claim* to be Christians, how can I say I love Mormons when I say that one of their most often repeated claims is not true?

But the Christian reading this work will understand exactly what I mean. The Bible is very plain in telling us how we are to act as followers of Christ. We are to "speak the truth in love" (Eph. 4:15), even while we "refute those who contradict" (Titus 1:9) and "expose the unfruitful works of darkness" (Eph. 5:11). Christian love does not ignore the truth, it revels in it. Indeed, there is no Christian love where truth is ignored or compromised. They go hand in hand, for "love rejoices with the truth" (1 Cor. 13:6).

It is my love for the LDS people that compels me to missions work in Utah and Arizona. And it forms a major component in my writing this book. If I love someone, I will tell them the truth, even if I know they may not appreciate my efforts. As Paul was forced to say to the Galatians when writing them a difficult letter, "Have I become your enemy by telling you the truth?" (Gal. 4:16).

I believe it is not a sign of true, honest, uncompromising love to have the kind of disagreements I have with LDS people—disagreements that involve eternal issues, and yes, the eternal destiny of those involved—and yet dismiss those disagreements because it is uncomfortable to talk about them. We would never allow such a mindset to exist in any other area of our lives, but when it comes to this, we seem to lose our common sense and allow our emotions to run away with our thinking. If my Mormon friend is worshiping another god and has been deceived, how can I remain silent and still claim I am showing Christian love?

And so in part I write out of love for the LDS people. But even more so, I have written out of love for *Christian* people. This book is meant to equip the saints, to provide them with the necessary facts—both from a biblical perspective as well as from a dogmatic LDS perspective—upon which to act in deciding such issues as fellowship, interaction, and evangelism. Christians need to know the truth about LDS teaching, and I have sought diligently to present it. I hope that the Lord will be pleased to re-ignite in the hearts of many a pastor and layperson a love for the great truths of God's uniqueness, immutability, and creatorship through the process of their evaluating and struggling with these issues.

Again I Ask, Is the Mormon My Brother?

I believe we are now equipped to answer the question that has prompted our journey together. The question is not asked on the level of common humanity—is the Mormon a fellow human being, a fellow image bearer of God? The answer to that would obviously be yes, of course. All humans are related to one another in that sense.

But our question is asked on the level of Christian spirituality. Is the Mormon my brother? Can I fellowship with him as I fellowship with other brothers and sisters in Christ? This question is obviously related to the question, "Is Mormonism Christian?" We can now provide a biblical answer to that question.

On the personal level of one-on-one relationships, we must start by admitting that we cannot judge the heart of any single individual. God has not given us that ability. We must judge on matters of truth, not on the basis of having some supernatural ability to see into someone's spirit. On that level I cannot even say with certainty that some of my best friends in *Christian* fellowship are going to persevere to the end. I've seen too many fall by the wayside to make that mistake.[1] So I may well fellowship with individuals who, in the end, will not be with me in glory. I do not believe that I can say with certainty that every person sitting with me even in my own church is, without question, an heir of grace.

On a little wider scale as well, I gladly admit that God's grace goes far beyond denominational barriers. I have brothers and sisters in Christ in many traditions and denominations. Some of my best friends are Presbyterians, Baptists, or involved in nondenominational or community churches. I fellowship with Lutherans and even an occasional Episcopalian! We may disagree on some very important but nonessential issues—and I may not be able to be a part of their particular denomination or church as a result. But I can join hands with them and pray with them and for them because we share a common heritage and, more important, a common *God*.

But when we come down to answering the big question, we have to focus upon what defines Christianity and what defines Mormonism. I will gladly admit that there may be LDS people who are LDS in name only. That is, they were raised in Christian churches and converted to Mormonism without a full knowledge of what the LDS Church really teaches about God, Christ, and salvation. I have met these individuals and have personally helped a number of them come to understand the issues involved. But what about the person who is LDS *by conviction* and accepts the teachings of the LDS Church on core issues? What must I say, on the basis of the evidence we have examined, concerning their state?

Mormonism is not Christianity. It is fundamentally different. While it differs in hundreds of minor details, what is most important to us is that it differs in the most *definitional and fundamental* aspects from the Christian faith. Christianity worships one God. Christianity knows that there is one God who has eternally been God and is the Creator of *all* things—exhaustively. Everything else in the Christian faith, from the Trinity to the Atonement to the Gospel to the Resurrection, flows from and is defined by this fundamental truth. And it is here that we cannot help but hear the words of Joseph Smith when, addressing the idea that God has been God from all eternity, he said, "I will refute that idea and take away the veil so that you may see." Smith cannot refute God's truth and, of course, he failed to do so. But the result is beyond question: Mormonism, the system he founded, is not Christianity. It is a false religion with a false god. And if Mormonism is a false religion, then the believing Mormon is deceived and lost. There can be no other honest answer.

If we are truly concerned with pleasing God and rightly handling His truth, we will have to go one step further. As we saw in Isaiah 41:24, choosing to worship a false god is a fearful choice. The true God takes His sole rights to worship very seriously. When speaking to the idols, God says, "He who chooses you is an abomination" (to-evah). The teaching that God was once a man and that men can become gods involves simple *idolatry*, for it makes of God something that He is not and lowers Him to the level of His creation. *There is no salvation in such a god, and those worshiping this god are under the wrath of the true and living God.*

Surely this is the conclusion that many have reached before, and rightly so. Some might argue that we took the long way around to what should be an obvious conclusion. But hopefully the conclusion we have reached is solidly based upon a fair reading of the sources, both pro and con.

What Now?

What should be the response of the believing Christian to these facts? Let me divide my answer into two parts—first with regard to worship, and second with regard to evangelism.

I know that I personally have been reminded, through working on this text, of the importance of Christian worship and the high *privilege* I have to regularly engage in the corporate worship of God by His people. It is a wonderful gift of grace to be able to join together with like-minded people and worship God in spirit *and in truth*. I am reminded that we are praying to the same God, who is powerful to save and to answer prayer. I cannot so pray with a Mormon person. We are worshiping different gods. His god differs fundamentally from mine. How, then, can we join together in prayer, since prayer is an act of worship itself? Why would I ask an exalted man to meet my needs? I cannot begin to understand how true, Christian prayer—which is always focused upon the *majesty* and *awesomeness* of God—could be shared with a person fostering the idea in his or her mind and heart that he or she may someday become a god or goddess. The disparity is too great, and as Scripture says, "Can two walk together, except they be agreed?" (Amos 3:3, KJV).

If Christian churches wish to make a strong impact upon the LDS faith, we will have to ask God to refocus our attention upon *what really matters*. Our worship will be life-changing if, in fact, it is focused upon God and His Word. Do we revel in His being the Creator of all things? Do we rejoice that He is unchanging and ever faithful? Are these realities that truly warm our hearts and drive us, out of love for Him, to service in His name? When Mormon people see Christians who are excited about their faith *and excited about the truth*, we will have more opportunities of sharing our wonderful God and His glorious Gospel with them.

But finally, I believe we should be prompted to engage in full-scale, no-apologies-given evangelism of those within the Mormon fold. I am not merely talking about "dialogue," but *evangelism*. As difficult as the task may be, I firmly believe the LDS people to be deceived and misled. They are very much in the position of the Galatians before Paul came with the gospel, for they are "slaves to those which by nature are no gods" (Gal. 4:8). As sincere and kind as many Mormons are, you will find sincere and kind Buddhists and Muslims, too. Sincerity and kindness is not the measure. Knowledge of the one true God is first and foremost, and this is a knowledge not only missing but denied in Mormonism.

Yes, your Mormon friend or relative or co-worker speaks of Christ and the Gospel and faith and the Bible and so much more. And yes, that makes the task all the more difficult and at times frustrating. We must climb the language barrier and patiently remove the veritable minefield of objections and false notions that have been placed in the way of the Gospel's progress in their lives. The task calls for a *tremendous* amount of patience. But we have the promise that patience is one of the works the Spirit performs in our hearts, and we have His promise that He will honor the proclamation of His truth.

Mormons and Christians—the divide between us is immeasurably wide because we worship different gods. We start at opposite poles. The Mormon is not my brother, but I wish he could be, and I pledge myself anew to serve my God in presenting the awesome God of Scripture to the members of the Church of Jesus Christ of Latter-day Saints.

11

HOW WIDE THE DIVIDE?

In 1997 a landmark book appeared in Christian bookstores titled *How Wide the Divide?* authored by Dr. Craig Blomberg of Denver Theological Seminary and Dr. Stephen Robinson of Brigham Young University. The book presents a dialogue, in a fashion, between Blomberg and Robinson on four vital subjects: Scripture, God and Deification, Christ and the Trinity, and Salvation. The work is landmark because it is the first such "dialogue" to appear in print.[1] Since it was published by a major Christian publisher (InterVarsity Press), it created quite a stir. It exposed the Christian public to a form of LDS apologetics it had never seen before.

How Wide the Divide? is very important to our own examination as it touches very clearly upon the central issue that concerns us: What does Mormonism teach concerning God, and are the fundamental differences that exist between Christians and Mormons on this issue sufficient to end all discussion of fellowship and restrict us solely to the realm of evangelization, proclamation, and refutation? The answer given by *How Wide the Divide?* is an ambiguous one at best,[2] and a deceptive one at worst.

There is much I would like to say concerning all aspects of the work, but I must confine myself to those issues that are directly relevant to our current study.[3] The chapter titled "God and Deification" begins with an essay written by Dr. Stephen Robinson. This essay begins with these words:

> In the LDS view God is omniscient, omnipresent, infinite, eternal, and unchangeable.[4]

The person who has read carefully the more than one hundred pages of citations of LDS writers concerning the nature of God, his progression to godhood, his physical body, etc., may have to stop a moment to consider how it is that an LDS scholar can begin an essay on the doctrine of God with such a claim. This is only the beginning of a process that I must honestly call the "Christianizing" of the doctrines of Joseph Smith that Dr. Robinson pursues throughout *How Wide the Divide?* Though Robinson plainly recognizes the language barrier that exists between Mormons and Christians (and claims to be one of the "few" who has learned to speak the evangelical language, p. 163), he takes advantage of that barrier with frightening consistency. Robinson is quite aware of the fact that his position is liable to criticism as "unorthodox." The book is filled with preemptive strikes against anyone who would point this out. Over and over again he insists that he is presenting an orthodox view. One example comes from the section on salvation:

> For example, when I say that I believe in Jesus Christ or in justification by faith in Christ, I often hear in return, "Oh, no you don't, and I can prove it," accompanied by a flurry of proof-texts culled from sources supposedly more reliable than I am on the subject of what *I* believe. But it is just as absurd to try to prove to me by prooftexting LDS literature that I do not believe what I think I do as it is for me to try to argue to Calvinists that they don't really believe in irresistible grace or eternal security. Stop and think about it. If I could compile enough snippets of citations from Calvinist writings to support my thesis or make it credible, would I convince you that you do not really believe what you think you do? Of course not![5]

Of course this is only relevant to what Dr. Robinson personally believes. It is not relevant to what *Mormonism teaches*. This comes up in the next paragraph:

> However, even when I occasionally do convince evangelicals that I as a Mormon really do believe A, B, and C, their next response is equally predictable and equally frustrating. "Yes," they will say, "I now believe that you believe these things. It is wonderful to see someone break away from those nasty Mormon beliefs and find Jesus." And once again I cannot convince them, no matter what I say, that I am not an aberration, but that

I am actually fairly representative of contemporary LDS orthodoxy. I am certainly not aware of any rift between myself and
Joseph Smith, Brigham Young, or Gordon B. Hinckley, our present LDS leader.[6]

As we have already seen, we determine LDS orthodoxy not by
reference to Brigham Young University faculty, but by looking to the
General Authorities of the LDS Church to define and explain Mormon doctrine. As we saw in the preceding chapter, LDS apologists,
including BYU faculty, can provide us with less than representative
viewpoints when it suits their purposes and agendas. And certainly
the greatest problem with *How Wide the Divide?* is just this: it presents as LDS orthodoxy a view of God, Christ, and even salvation that
is *not* what one will hear when attending the General Conference in
Salt Lake City, or when reading the current manuals on religion published by the Church. Rather than making it plain throughout that
we are here getting the *personal* views of Robinson and Blomberg, it
consistently uses the sweeping language of "Evangelicals and Mormons believe . . . ," leading to some very skewed and inaccurate perceptions.

In light of our study of the LDS doctrine of God and exaltation,
the comments of Dr. Robinson regarding this subject are most interesting. It should be remembered that I have already presented,
briefly, the "minimalist" viewpoint of Robinson regarding what is and
what is not "official" Mormon theology, and what sources we can and
cannot use in making that determination. Since he does not accept
as having binding authority a large portion of the teaching of the
General Authorities, he can say the following:

> Those who are exalted by his grace will always be "gods"
> (always with a small g, even in the *Doctrine and Covenants*) by
> grace, by an extension of *his* power, and will always be subor-
> dinate to the Godhead. In the Greek philosophical sense—and
> in the "orthodox" theological sense—such contingent beings
> would not even rightly be called "gods," since they never be-
> come "the ground of all being" and are forever subordinate to
> their Father. Any teaching beyond this involves speculation
> without support from either the Bible or the other LDS scrip-
> tures, and these are waters I refuse to swim in. I grant that some
> LDS do indulge in speculation on this point (it is a favorite

jumping off place for LDS fundamentalists)—but they go beyond the teaching of the LDS Church and the advice of LDS leaders when they do.[7]

There are many points that must be addressed in this presentation. First, in an overall response, I must point out that such a summary does not even begin to do justice to the *consistent* teaching of the LDS hierarchy on the subject of eternal progression to godhood. Even the use of the phrase "exalted by his grace" flies in the face of the constant drumbeat of obedience, worthiness, and striving for perfection that was found in every level of data that we examined earlier.[8] Indeed, as Antoine Ivins, a General Authority, expressed it at one of the General Conferences of the Church,

> And if we limit it to those two senses, then by the grace of Jesus Christ alone, we are saved; but I have never felt like limiting it to that significance alone. I feel that salvation moves over into the realm of exaltation, and that before a man is completely saved he must be exalted in the presence of God, and to be exalted his deeds must justify that exaltation.[9]

And in the same vein, Apostle McConkie, speaking at Conference, said, "By the grace of God, and through his mercy, we have had restored to us in this day the fullness of the everlasting gospel: all of the laws, ordinances, and principles by obedience to which we can be both saved and exalted in our Father's kingdom."[10] Robinson's expression simply does not fit with the King Follett Discourse, which is cited literally *hundreds* of times by LDS authorities.

In particular, I note how Dr. Robinson's minimalism leads to an error in this section. Robinson insists that when speaking of exalted human beings, Mormonism speaks of them as gods "always with a small g, even in the *Doctrine and Covenants*." Yet elsewhere he accepts as doctrinally binding the official statements of the First Presidency and/or the Quorum of the Twelve Apostles.[11] Surely Dr. Robinson knows, then, of this statement from the First Presidency titled "The Origin of Man," dated 1909:

> Man is the child of God, formed in the divine image and endowed with divine attributes, and even as the infant son of an earthly father and mother is capable in due time of becoming a man, so the undeveloped offspring of celestial parentage is

capable, by experience through ages and aeons, of evolving into a God.[12]

The First Presidency of the LDS Church is not afraid to use the term "God"—with a capital *G*, no less—of exalted human beings in an "official pronouncement." Why is Dr. Robinson uncomfortable with this? Certainly we would encourage discomfort in thinking in any such categories (Isa. 29:16), but we should be honest in dealing with the official LDS sources and admit that the capitalized form "God" has been used of exalted humans, and if Lorenzo Snow's famous couplet, "As man is, God once was; as God is, man may become," means anything at all, Mormons use the capitalized form of God for an exalted man (God the Father) all the time.

But probably most significant is the fact that Robinson not only refuses to "swim" in waters beyond the bare assertion of a nebulous form of divinization of humans but he identifies as unscriptural "speculation" the vast majority of the plain teachings we have read from General Authorities and official church publications regarding the status of those who achieve godhood. If it is definitional of "LDS fundamentalists" to "speculate" upon such things, then the General Authorities of the Church for the past one hundred fifty years have been heavily infested with "LDS fundamentalists"! This is simply part of a book-wide effort on Dr. Robinson's part to paint his own position as "mainstream," and the position that has been taken by such notables as Bruce R. McConkie and George Q. Cannon as "extreme" or "fundamentalist." Robinson does not come out and identify individuals like this—but the reader can examine the statements provided in the earlier chapters in this work and make the connections for himself.

Before leaving this section and noting some other problems with the discussion of God and deification in *How Wide the Divide?* I feel it is important to note an element of Robinson's position that was touched on above. One of the key statements in the entire book, in my opinion, is found on page 91:

> Latter-day Saints believe that after the end these "gods" will, by God's grace, be engaged in the sorts of activities that God engages in now.

This is not the only place where this idea appears in Robinson's writings. In his earlier work *Are Mormons Christians?* he wrote:

> If through the gospel of Jesus Christ and the grace of God we receive the fullness of god (Ephesians 3:19) so that we also can be called gods, humans will never become "ultimate" beings in the abstract, philosophical sense. That is, even as they sit on thrones exercising the powers of gods, those who have become gods by grace remain eternally subordinate to the source of that grace; they are extensions of their Father's power and agents of his will. They will continue to worship and serve the Father, the Son, and the Holy Ghost forever, and will worship and serve no one and nothing else. . . . And that, in a nutshell, is the LDS view. Whether in this life or the next, through Christ human beings can be given the powers of God and the authority of God. Those who receive this great inheritance can properly be called gods. They are not gods in the Greek philosophic sense of "ultimate beings," nor do they compete with God, the source of their inheritance, as objects of worship. They remain eternally his begotten sons and daughters—therefore, never equal to him nor independent of him.[13]

If exaltation to godhood is, in fact, an act of "grace," then a rather obvious question presents itself: Since God himself was exalted to the status of godhood in the same way that men will be, does it not follow that He, too, is a "god" by the "grace" of some other "god" somewhere else? It seems this is an area that Dr. Robinson doesn't want to "swim" in, yet it is one that any serious student cannot help but ponder. Robinson is intent upon making sure that God himself is safeguarded, in some way, by insisting that whatever else exalted men might be in the future, they will be that by grace and they will remain dependent upon God as their Father. Does it not logically and necessarily follow, then, that God himself, who was once a man, is likewise still dependent upon the "grace" of the "god" who exalted Him to His current position? If we will be "gods" only by an extension of *God's* power, does it not follow that He is a "god" only by the extension of His own "God's" power? Is God not likewise limited in His actions by His dependence upon this other being? And could it not be said that we might be better off worshiping this other deity, by whose grace the "god" of this world acts? It seems to me that no matter how hard one tries, it is simply impossible to avoid the inherent self-contradictions that are part and parcel of Joseph Smith's system. Even when one tries to insert safeguards into the system, exaltation to godhood will always lead one to utter confusion.

One of the means used by LDS in general and by Robinson in particular to escape the presentation of the Bible regarding God's nature is to postulate the existence of "multiple eternities." Eternity becomes a word that does not mean what it *normally* means in theological discussion. Instead, eternity becomes that which marks the period of deification for a particular God. In other words, "eternity" begins when God becomes a god. Hence, the "god" of this eternity can be said to be supreme and eternal, but only in the context of this particular "eternity." Obviously, there was a "previous eternity" (whatever such a phrase means) when the "god" of this eternity wasn't even a god. Note Robinson's words:

> In the same vein, I suggest that no biblical passage intends to inform us about the condition or career of God before the beginning or after the end of eternity. The Bible neither affirms nor denies what God may or may not have done or have been in any theoretical prior eternity.[14]

Of course the whole idea of multiple eternities is beyond biblical thought in the first place. As we saw, God is the Creator of *all* things, including time itself, so the idea that God is limited in time or space, and hence only exists in one "eternity" but not in some other "eternity," is not only unbiblical but *anti*biblical in its content. But it is meaningless to say the Bible says nothing about God "before" the "beginning" of eternity. Such a phrase is double-speak. There is no "before" eternity because eternity has no beginning. If it has a beginning it is not eternity.[15]

In his effort to make the divide that separates Christians and Mormons a little less wide, Robinson says,

> God is *God*, and Mormons attribute to God every honor, power, glory, and perfection that evangelicals do.[16]

On the basis of what we have read from LDS sources and seen from Scripture up to this point, I can safely say, with all due respect to Robinson, that such a statement is utterly untrue. I could wish that Robinson ascribes every honor, power, glory, and perfection to God that I do, but the simple fact is, he doesn't. At the very foundation, I attribute to God *self-existence* and *eternity*. No matter how hard he tries, Robinson cannot do so. He has to redefine both terms to even make the attempt. My God has always been God in this or any other eternity you might wish to propose. If it exists, be it matter or time itself, my God made it. He has always been God and will always be God. He did not become a God at some time in the past, in this or any other eternity. He is not what He is today because some other "god" exalted Him to that position by grace, works, or a combination thereof. Hence, Mormons in general, and even Robinson in particular, do *not* attribute to God every honor, power, glory, and perfection that I and other evangelicals do.

What is most amazing about the presentation found in *How Wide the Divide?* is that oftentimes Robinson presents concepts and ideas with all seriousness that would not find acceptance *within the faculty of BYU itself.* For example, Robinson says,

> Many evangelicals are convinced, wrongly, that Latter-day Saints believe in a finite, limited, or changeable God, even though that notion is repugnant to us.[17]

Compare this with the citation of Brigham Young, cited in an official LDS publication, on this very topic:

> It appears ridiculous to the world, under their darkened and erroneous traditions, that God has once been a finite being (*Deseret News* [Nov. 16, 1859]: 290).[18]

Perhaps Robinson might point out that God is *no longer* a finite being, and Brigham Young was only saying he had *once* been a finite being. Yet we still find Robinson running right up against the plain statements of one of his fellow professors at BYU, Dr. David Paulsen. Professor Paulsen's doctoral thesis at the University of Michigan in 1975 was titled, "Comparative Coherency of Mormon (Finitistic) and Classical Theism."[19] Paulsen writes,

> Although God is never explicitly characterized in the datum discourse as finite, His finitism is plainly entailed by the doctrine of eternalism. It is not the case that everything other than God is ontologically dependent on Him. He did not create everything *ex nihilo*. God has always acted within a physical environment of uncreated mass-energy, a social environment of other selves, and within a framework of eternal laws and prin-

ciples. These aspects of the world which are coeternal with His condition and limit Him.

Paulsen goes on to say that "God has revealed that He is a person with a corporeal body who exists in time and space," and he quotes Orson Pratt in support, who likewise insists that "The true God exists both in time, space, and has as much relation to them as man or any other being." But then he says,

> Perhaps most startling (and to many most offensive, but when fully understood, I believe most inspiring) is the Mormon view that God, the Father . . . once dwelled on an earth and earned the honorific title "God" through a process of growth and development. This doctrine was most fully articulated by Joseph Smith at the 1844 conference of the church. The doctrine is . . . radically heretical from the perspective of Christian orthodoxy. . . ."[20]

This is followed by a lengthy citation of the King Follett Discourse, a passage we have examined in detail. Paulsen says, "It should be clear that Mormon theism is committed to redefining many of the attributes classically ascribed to God."[21] Indeed! He goes on to quote B. H. Roberts: "The attribute of 'Omnipotence' must needs be thought upon . . . as somewhat limited." Paulsen then says, "But, the being who is God has not always been God—i.e., he has not always qualified for the honorific title 'God'—a distinction earned through a process of growth and development toward Godliness."[22] In conclusion, he says,

> God, then, according to Mormon theology is not unconditioned or unlimited. . . . Nor has he always been "God." At some distant point in an infinite past, He earned the right to be "God" through a process which men, as his children, are now repeating.[23]

If, as Robinson suggests, evangelicals are in error to believe that Mormons believe in a finite, limited, or changeable God, and if he is correct in saying that Mormons (not only Dr. Robinson—he uses the plural pronoun "us") find such an idea "repugnant," how does he explain these statements by his colleague Dr. Paulsen? Of the two, certainly Paulsen is far more in line with Joseph Smith's King Follett Discourse than is Robinson.

One other example and we will conclude. With reference to "polytheism," a term I have often used of LDS teaching (and, I think, with great reason), Robinson writes,

> Clearly Prof. Blomberg feels that such a Godhead is unlikely and that defining the Godhead so runs a risk of polytheism—but that is not the LDS belief. It would horrify the Saints to hear talk of "polytheism."[24]

I remember discussing this electronically with some LDS a few years ago. One of the LDS participants accidentally sent a private message, originally destined for a list of Mormons only, to the public echo where I could see it. Commenting on the argument about my use of the term "polytheists," he wrote, "What's all the fuss over the term polytheists? We are polytheists. What's the problem?" Now, I don't expect my anonymous correspondent to carry much weight. But what about Dr. Eugene England, also of BYU?

> Despite the context of this scripture—a discussion by Paul of belief in idols—Brigham Young, B. H. Roberts, Joseph Fielding Smith, and many others have used it as a brief explanation of how it is possible to be both a Christian polytheist (technically a henotheist) and a monotheist: how we can talk sometimes in an adventuresome mode about multiple orders of godhood, and how we can consider the advanced spheres that exist in the infinities, and yet at the same time, without contradiction, we can talk in a worshipful mode about our one God and his perfect knowledge and supreme redemptive power in the sphere of our world.[25]

The term "polytheist" may not be the term of choice for Mormons. However, it is technically and logically accurate in light of their doctrine as it has been documented in this book.

The Divide is VERY Wide

At the end of *How Wide the Divide?* we find a conclusion written by both authors. In it we find a listing of agreements and differences. At the top of the list of "agreements" we find the following words:

> On the one hand, we jointly and sincerely affirm the follow-

ing foundational propositions of the Christian gospel as we both understand it.

1. The Father, the Son, and the Holy Spirit are one eternal God.[26]

Christians and Mormons do *not* agree that the Father, Son, and Holy Spirit are one eternal God. The only way to make such a statement is to so redefine every word used as to make the entire effort meaningless. The mere unity of purpose of Mormonism is not even remotely close to the majestic unity of being that is the Christian Trinity. So why would an evangelical scholar and a Mormon scholar agree to such a statement? And if a Christian layperson comes across this book, and this book only, would they not be *badly* misled concerning the real issues and the full teaching of the LDS Church?

It is suggested by a number of people today that we should encourage someone such as Dr. Robinson. Encourage the movement away from LDS orthodoxy and toward an emphasis upon common beliefs and orthodox perspectives. So what if Robinson is incorrect to represent Mormonism as portraying exaltation as a matter primarily of grace rather than obedience and worthiness? Isn't the emphasis upon grace important enough in and of itself? These same folks point to recent events in a group like the Worldwide Church of God, which has undergone a process of "becoming orthodox," abandoning and even repudiating its cultic and heretical past. Could this not happen in Mormonism, too?

In response to this viewpoint, I briefly suggest two thoughts. First, I rejoice in the brave actions of the leaders of the Worldwide Church of God. But there is a vast difference between openly repudiating past errors and embracing the truth of the Gospel of Christ, on the one hand, and, on the other, attempting to *rewrite* past teachings and doctrines while trying to maintain the authority and sanctity of the past leaders who taught heresy. I do not see anyone *repudiating* Joseph Smith's King Follett Discourse (including Robinson) and calling for others to do so. When I see the General Authorities of the LDS Church honestly coming out and saying, "Joseph Smith was wrong about many of the doctrines he taught," then I will grant that what has happened in the Worldwide Church of God *might* take place in Salt Lake City, too.

Second, I find no biblical warrant for seeking "dialogue" or "common ground" with the Mormon faith. It is a postmodernistic viewpoint of truth that sees more value in "agreements" than in "disagreements." When Paul repudiated the Judaizers in his letter to the churches of Galatia, he did not seek to point out the areas of agreement he had with the false teachers. He said they were anathema because they compromised the Gospel of Christ, which is the power of God unto salvation. When he warned the Colossian Christians against the errors of Gnosticism, he did not list areas of agreement with the false teachers and then counterbalance this with a carefully worded and crafted list of disagreements "for future dialogue." He identified that religious system as a falsehood that would only lead one to destruction.

I believe we should encourage every Mormon to adopt more orthodox views of God and salvation—by openly proclaiming the truth of God, exposing the errors of Joseph Smith and his followers, and calling all LDS everywhere to the worship of the one true and eternal God, their Creator and Maker. We do not show Christian love or concern to muddle the issues with relativistic "dialogue." Paul said the Galatians had once worshiped those who by nature were not gods (Gal. 4:8). Mormons, no matter how kind, friendly, or well-meaning they may be, are worshiping a god that does not exist; Joseph Smith's exalted man is "by nature" not a god. We show true concern when we have the temerity to speak this truth in love.

12

A MORMON DOCTRINE, OR MERE SPECULATION?

At the beginning of the LDS movement, Joseph Smith recorded this revelation:

> Wherefore, confound your enemies; call upon them to meet you both in public and in private; and inasmuch as ye are faithful their shame shall be made manifest. Wherefore, let them bring forth their strong reasons against the Lord. Verily, thus saith the Lord unto you—there is no weapon that is formed against you shall prosper; And if any man lift his voice against you he shall be confounded in mine own due time (*D & C* 71:7–10).

Early Mormon missionaries were willing to enter into public dispute on the issues of religion. But as the years went by, this changed. For generations now the standard LDS response to outside challenge has been to turn a deaf ear and say nothing in reply. But beginning with Dr. Hugh Nibley of Brigham Young University, things have begun to change. An entire generation of LDS apologists has appeared, taking up the cause of Mormonism and providing a defense of the unique claims of the Church of Jesus Christ of Latter-day Saints.

Many Christians make the grave error of thinking that there is no way that a system like Mormonism, replete with its concept of God as an exalted man, could ever muster a robust defense of its own position. And from one perspective, that is true, in that there is no meaningful way of defending the simple idolatry that is the LDS theology of God. However, I have often warned audiences and correspondents against the danger that often accompanies a recognition of how *far removed* LDS teaching is from biblical revelation and the Christian faith. The danger lies in thinking that it is merely a matter of pointing out the logical inconsistencies, providing a few Bible verses, and that should take care of the problem. Certainly no Mormon could ever argue against such a plain truth as monotheism and the eternality of God! And the mindset that accompanies such an idea is that either the Mormon is simply *ignorant* of the facts or *not intelligent* enough to see through the smokescreen. Armed with such false assumptions, many a believer has run directly into the buzzsaw of a sharp, well-read Mormon and brought disrepute upon the Gospel as a result.

At the outset the arguments provided by LDS apologists often sound plausible. And since Mormon apologetics has, by and large, been focused inward, that is, upon the LDS people themselves, many Mormons find the arguments convincing and confirmatory of their beliefs. For certain, a large portion of the books produced in opposition to Mormonism have failed to take into account any of the better apologetic arguments now popular among the LDS.

Remaking Mormonism

One of the tasks of some of the modern proponents of the LDS cause seems to be to remake Mormonism in a mold that fits better in the modern setting. Whether purposefully or not, modern defenders of Joseph Smith are often found softening, or even directly denying, doctrines and teachings that have been taught within the LDS Church since its inception. And, of course, if this doctrine is referred to in "anti-Mormon" literature, it is claimed that the authors of such works are acting in bad faith, purposefully misrepresenting the LDS faith.

One such doctrine that is now identified as "mere speculation," rather than a teaching of the LDS Church, is the doctrine that God the Father (Elohim) in a physical body *begat*, literally, the body of Jesus Christ here on earth. The physical parentage of Jesus Christ has often been a focus of attack on the part of Christians who seek to respond to the claims of Mormonism. Yet if one is to believe the current crop of LDS apologists, it is a doctrine that is nothing more than speculation, and certainly not representative of the official teaching of the LDS faith.

In their 1992 book *Offenders for a Word: How Anti-Mormons Play Word Games to Attack the Latter-day Saints*,[1] BYU professors Daniel C. Peterson and Stephen D. Ricks attempt to respond to the historical teaching of the LDS Church regarding the physical parentage of Christ. Note their own words:

> We will ignore the fact that these scattered nineteenth-century speculations were never canonized by the Mormon Church, and that no comparable statements occur in Latter-day Saint scripture. We will pass over the unfairness of holding Mormons to statements that they and their own leaders have never deemed authoritative and binding (and we will deprive ourselves of the great entertainment that would ensue were we to call our Protestant critics to account for every speculation advanced by their pastors and reformers of the past five centuries). . . . The speculations that most incense the critics are simply literalistic interpretations of the divine paternity alluded to in the title "Son of God." While certain early Mormon leaders may occasionally have reinterpreted the concept of "virgin birth," they never for a moment suggested that Jesus was begotten by a mortal man, nor that his father was any other personage than God. . . . And for a denial, it cannot be repeated too often, that the Latter-day Saints have never accepted as official doctrine.[2]

In a footnote Peterson and Ricks cite numerous Christian critiques of Mormonism that note this doctrine. They focus upon Walter Martin, saying he "finds these rare and isolated speculations 'shocking and vile,' and makes the obligatory allusions to Greek mythology."[3]

From the above citation, then, we can conclude that the idea that God the Father physically begat Jesus Christ is a mere "scattered nineteenth-century speculation" that was "never canonized by the Mormon Church." These "speculations" have never been considered "authoritative and binding." They were merely "literalistic interpretations of the divine paternity" based upon the title "Son of God." They amount only to a reinterpretation of the Virgin Birth and have *never* been accepted as official doctrine.

A colleague of Peterson and Ricks, Stephen Robinson, likewise downplays this doctrine. In *How Wide the Divide?* Robinson makes these comments:

> Unfortunately, popular speculations on the LDS side have sometimes also been tasteless and indelicate. . . . While it is true that certain LDS leaders (mostly in the nineteenth century) have offered their opinions on the conception of Jesus, those opinions were never included among the official doctrines of the church and have, during my lifetime at least, not appeared in official church publications—lest they be taken as the view of the church. Yet those who would misrepresent the LDS Church (and also a vocal minority of its own eccentrics) continue to insist on the unofficial speculations of nineteenth-century members rather than on the *official* views of the church then or now.[4]

We can add to the conclusions of Peterson and Ricks the following from Robinson: this doctrine is again a speculation, based primarily on the nineteenth-century "opinions" of certain unnamed LDS leaders and "members." These opinions have never been included among the official doctrines of the LDS faith and have not appeared in *any official church publications during the lifetime of Stephen Robinson.* Those who say otherwise (which would include this author) are "misrepresenting" Mormonism.

For most Mormons, and for most Christians who have not read widely in LDS sources, such should be sufficient. Three LDS scholars, all Ph.D.s, have pronounced the idea that God the Father literally and physically begat the Son in the flesh a mere nineteenth-century speculation. What more could be said?

The problem is, history stands inalterably opposed to *every single claim* made by all three authors. As we will now document, this doctrine has been taught *consistently by every single General Authority of the LDS Church who has addressed this topic up to this present day!* What is more, we will find *numerous* official LDS publications *written within the past thirty years* that likewise teach this very doctrine. And just as important, we will not find a single LDS General Authority *denying* this doctrine. I will leave the reader to determine the issue of motivations, misrepresentation, and simple honesty in debate that arise when faced with the kind of documentation that follows.

Nineteenth-Century Teachings

Since it is said that this doctrine is primarily found in the nineteenth century, we should take the time to find out if those LDS leaders that modern apologists *admit* "speculated" on this topic were, in fact, saying, "This is my speculation and opinion only," or whether, in fact, they *taught* this doctrine as a divine truth, consistent with the rest of LDS theology. However, as we will see, *the vast majority of the statements presenting this doctrine come from the twentieth century!*

The most vocal proponent of the idea that God the Father, possessing a physical body, begat the physical body of Jesus Christ was Brigham Young, second Prophet and President of the LDS Church. We have already noted earlier that President Young stated that if he was given the chance to correct a sermon (i.e., proofread the transcript) when it was recorded, it was then as good "scripture" as the people deserved. What did President Young say about this doctrine?

> He [God] created man, as we create our children; for there is no other process of creation in heaven, on the earth, in the earth, or under the earth, or in all the eternities, that is, that were, or that ever will be.[5]
>
> The birth of the Savior was as natural as are the births of our children; it was the result of natural action. He partook of flesh and blood—was begotten of his Father, as we were of our fathers.[6]
>
> When the Virgin Mary conceived the child Jesus, the Father had begotten him in his own likeness. He was not begotten by the Holy Ghost. . . . Now, remember from this time forth, and for ever, that Jesus Christ was not begotten by the Holy Ghost. I will repeat a little anecdote. I was in conversation with a certain learned professor upon this subject, when I replied, to this idea—"if the Son was begotten by the Holy Ghost, it would be very dangerous to baptize and confirm females, and give the Holy Ghost to them, lest he should beget children, and be palmed upon the Elders by the people, bringing the Elders into great difficulties."[7]
>
> When the time came that His first-born, the Savior, should come into the world and take a tabernacle, the Father came Himself and favored that spirit with a tabernacle instead of letting any other man do it. The Savior was begotten by the Father

of His spirit, by the same Being who is the Father of our spirits, and that is all the organic difference between Jesus Christ and you and me.[8]

As this is one of Young's plainest statements, we should note some particulars. Young says God favored his firstborn, the Savior, with a tabernacle. The term "firstborn" in LDS theology refers to the idea that Jesus Christ is the first begotten spirit child of God (Elohim) in the spiritual preexistence. Once Elohim became a God, his firstborn spirit offspring was Jesus, also known (in modern LDS theology) as Jehovah.[9] The term "firstborn" needs to be differentiated from "only-begotten" in Mormon teaching.[10] If one listens carefully to the leaders of the Church, and even to the missionaries who visit in your home, you will note the use of a short, three-word modifier when Mormons refer to "only-begotten." They consistently say, "Jesus is the only-begotten *in the flesh*." It took me some time to realize what this meant, but it goes back to this very concept. As we have seen, Mormons believe that Elohim has begotten literally *billions* of spirit offspring in heaven. Consequently, how can he be said to have an "only-begotten" Son? The key is recognizing that Jesus Christ is the only human being who was physically begotten by God the Father. This will become more and more clear as the citations stack up.

> The Father came down from heaven, as the Apostles said he did, and begat the Saviour of the world, for he is the only-begotten of the Father, which could not be if the Father did not actually beget him in person.[11]
>
> This matter was a little changed in the case of the Savior of the world, the Son of the living God. The man Joseph, the husband of Mary, did not, that we know of, have more than one wife, but Mary the wife of Joseph had another husband. On this account infidels have called the Saviour a bastard. This is merely a human opinion upon one of the inscrutable doings of the Almighty. That very babe that was cradled in the manger was begotten, not by Joseph, the husband of Mary, but by another Being. Do you inquire by whom? He was begotten by God our heavenly father.[12]

It is certainly striking that the Mormon Prophet would say that Mary had "another husband" and that husband was God our heavenly Father. In the same way, note the parallelism between Jesus *not* being begotten by Joseph, but *instead* being begotten by Elohim. And the reader should keep in mind throughout these passages the statement of LDS Scripture: "The Father has a body of flesh and bones as tangible as man's" (*D & C* 130:22). How, then, does a God who has a body of flesh and bones "beget" a child?

Mormon Apostle Heber Kimball likewise addressed this topic:

> In relation to the way in which I look upon the works of God and his creatures, I will say that I was naturally begotten; so was my father, and also my Saviour Jesus Christ. According to the Scriptures, he is the first begotten of his father in the flesh, and there was nothing unnatural about it.[13]

Kimball claims that Jesus was begotten just as he himself was begotten. "There was nothing unnatural about it." Certainly this is what Orson Pratt had in mind when he wrote the following startling and, indeed, highly offensive section:

> But it was the personage of the Father who begat the body of Jesus; and for this reason Jesus is called the Only Begotten of the Father; that is, the only one in this world whose fleshly body was begotten by the Father. There were millions of sons and daughters whom He begat before the foundation of the world, but they were spirits, and not bodies of flesh and bones; whereas, both the spirit and body of Jesus were begotten by the Father, the spirit having been begotten in heaven many ages before the tabernacle was begotten upon the earth. The fleshly body of Jesus required a Mother as well as a Father. Therefore, the Father and Mother of Jesus, according to the flesh, must have been associated together in the capacity of Husband and Wife; hence the Virgin Mary must have been, for the time being, the lawful wife of God the Father: we use the term lawful Wife, because it would be blasphemous in the highest degree to say that He overshadowed her or begat the Saviour unlawfully. It would have been unlawful for any man to have interfered with Mary, who was already espoused to Joseph; for such a heinous crime would have subjected both the guilty parties to death, according to the law of Moses. But God having created all men and women, had the most perfect right to do with His own creation, according to His holy will and pleasure; He had a lawful

right to overshadow the Virgin Mary in the capacity of a husband, and beget a Son, although she was espoused to another;
for the law which He gave to govern men and women was not
intended to govern Himself, or to prescribe rules for his own
conduct. It was also lawful in Him, after having thus dealt with
Mary, to give Mary to Joseph her espoused husband. Whether
God the Father gave Mary to Joseph for time only, or for time
and eternity, we are not informed. Inasmuch as God was the first
husband to her, it may be that He only gave her to be the wife
of Joseph while in this mortal state, and that He intended after
the resurrection to again take her as one of his own wives to
raise up immortal spirits in eternity.[14]

Such blunt language certainly causes us to consider a rather obvious problem: In LDS theology, Mary was Elohim's spirit child. Yet,
a Mormon apostle speaks of Mary as being Elohim's wife so that the
procreative act would be licit. It is this very idea that has caused
some LDS of my acquaintance to utterly reject as preposterous and
blasphemous the idea that God the Father would impregnate one of
His own spirit daughters. The term "incest" has been used by those
who rejected this view even as Mormons. Yet this is what Pratt
taught. Even if one, in the face of the evidence yet to be presented,
rejects the doctrine as being truly representative of Mormon theology (a difficult thing to do), it still follows that those who taught
such things are, beyond question, "heretics" in the true sense of the
word. How a person then deals with the fact that Mormon apostles
have taught heresy from the pulpit and in print is another issue.

If these were all the statements we could present on this topic,
we could understand the strong language of Dr. Peterson, Dr. Ricks,
and Dr. Robinson. We could hardly hold the modern LDS Church
accountable for a small number of statements, *especially* if we found
repeated affirmations of the Virgin Birth of Christ in later authoritative writings. But is this what we actually find? No. Instead we find
the vast majority of the *clearest* statements on this topic in the *twentieth century* and in *official LDS Church publications!* To those sources
we now turn.

The Twentieth Century

Two LDS authorities figure prominently in teaching the literal
physical parentage of Jesus Christ by the Father in the twentieth cen-

tury. They are James Talmage and Bruce R. McConkie. We will look at their statements first, and then provide other confirmatory proclamations by other LDS leaders. Finally, we will look at books published by the LDS Church that also contain and promulgate this doctrine, and we will finish by looking at the *Encyclopedia of Mormonism*.

James Talmage addressed the paternity of Christ at the April General Conference in 1915. Note especially his use of the term "sire" of God the Father:

> We belong to the Church of Jesus Christ, and much has been said concerning His proprietorship, His mastership, in the Church, the Church that bears His name. I take it to be a plain and simple principle that we cannot worship intelligently, and therefore acceptably unto the Lord, unless we know something of the attributes and of the will of Him whom we profess to worship. The relationship of the Christ to the Eternal Father has been set forth in such plainness that I do not think any wayfaring man amongst us can fail to understand. We recognize in Jesus Christ the Son of the Eternal Father, both in spirit and in body. There is no other meaning to attach to that expression, as used by the Eternal Father Himself—"Mine Only Begotten Son." Christ combined within His own person and nature the attributes of His mortal mother, and just as truly the attributes of His immortal Sire. By that fixed and inexorable law of nature, that every living organism shall follow after his kind, Jesus the Christ had the power to die, for He was the offspring of a mortal woman; and He had the power to withstand death indefinitely, for He was the son of an immortal Father. This simplicity of doctrine has shocked many, but the truth is frequently shocking just because of its simplicity and consequent grandeur. We must know something of the attributes of the Eternal Father, that we may the more fully comprehend His relationship to His Only Begotten Son.[15]

Note well the words of this General Authority of the LDS Church, for many LDS today continue to believe as he did. Jesus Christ had the power to die, he claims, because he was the son of a mortal mother, Mary. But he had the power to withstand death, and take up his life again, because he was the son of an "immortal Sire." Talmage admits this doctrine "shocks" many. First, Talmage, an authority of the Church, calls it "doctrine," not "speculation." He would seemingly be in a better position to know than modern LDS scholars who are not even authorities in the Church. Second, in reference to it being "shocking," why would it be if, in fact, it is merely a "reinterpretation" of the Virgin Birth, and is not to be taken literally? So here we have a twentieth-century General Authority preaching in the General Conference—hardly a "rare" nineteenth-century "opinion."

Talmage's book *Jesus the Christ* likewise refers often to this belief. We noted in an earlier chapter that *Jesus the Christ* has been published *by the LDS Church itself* in various of its editions. It is a widely read, generally accepted work that is considered completely "orthodox." Yet it also plainly teaches the doctrine under discussion. For example, the same thought presented above regarding Christ possessing the attributes of both man and God is seen in this quotation:

> As the Only Begotten of the Father and therefore the only Being born to earth possessing in their fulness the attributes of both Godhood and manhood. . . . What other man has lived with power to withstand death, over whom death could not prevail except through his own submission? Yet Jesus Christ could not be slain until His "hour had come," and that, the hour in which He voluntarily surrendered His life, and permitted His own decease through an act of will. Born of a mortal mother He inherited the capacity to die; begotten by an immortal Sire He possessed as a heritage the power to withstand death indefinitely. . . . Only such a One could conquer death; in none but Jesus the Christ was realized this requisite condition of a Redeemer of the world.[16]

Probably the most often cited passage on this topic also comes from the pen of Talmage:

> That Child to be born of Mary was begotten of Elohim, the Eternal Father, not in violation of natural law, but in accordance with a higher manifestation thereof; and, the offspring from that association of supreme sanctity, celestial Sireship, and pure though mortal maternity, was of right to be called the "Son of the Highest." In His nature would be combined the powers of Godhood with the capacity and possibilities of mortality; and this through the ordinary operation of the fundamental law of heredity, declared of God, demonstrated by science, and ad-

mitted by philosophy, that living beings shall propagate—after their kind. The Child Jesus was to inherit the physical, mental, and Spiritual traits, tendencies, and powers that characterized His parents—one immortal and glorified—God, the other human—woman.[17]

LDS apologists will forgive us if we simply believe what we are told by those with the authority to define LDS teaching. Since it is LDS leaders who use terms like "celestial Sireship" and "fundamental laws of heredity," we can hardly accept the charge of "misrepresentation" when we allow these words to have their normal meaning.

Talmage returned to this same emphasis, and the reality of God the Father being the Son's "immortal Sire," in his book *Jesus the Christ*:

> For this cause was Jesus the Father's Beloved Son—that He was ready to lay down His life for the sake of the sheep. . . . A natural effect of His immortal origin, as the earth-born Son of an immortal Sire, was that He was immune to death except as He surrendered thereto. The life of Jesus the Christ could not be taken save as He willed and allowed. The power to lay down His life was inherent in Himself, as was the power to take up His slain body in an immortalized state.[18]

I have personally had many LDS priesthood holders—individuals who are widely read in LDS materials and books—affirm this teaching, and the reason for it, that is here presented by Talmage. To identify this doctrine as "mere speculation" and "opinion" is to completely ignore mountains of clear teaching by duly appointed leaders.

But of all LDS authorities, Apostle Bruce R. McConkie provides the clearest, most pointed affirmations of this doctrine. In his book *Mormon Doctrine*, in defining the phrase "Only Begotten Son," he wrote,

> These name-titles all signify that our Lord is the only Son of the Father in the flesh. Each of the words is to be understood literally. Only means only; Begotten means begotten; and Son means son. Christ was begotten by an Immortal Father in the same way that mortal men are begotten by mortal fathers.[19]

What does "the same way that mortal men are begotten by mortal fathers" mean? McConkie has no hesitation:

> God the Father is a perfected, glorified, holy Man, an im-
> mortal Personage. And Christ was born into the world as the
> literal Son of this Holy Being; he was born in the same personal,
> real, and literal sense that any mortal son is born to a mortal
> father. There is nothing figurative about his paternity; he was
> begotten, conceived and born in the normal and natural course
> of events, for he is the Son of God, and that designation means
> what it says.[20]

"There is nothing figurative about his paternity" we are told.
McConkie is no nineteenth-century leader—he passed away in
1985! But these are only the beginning of the passages from which
this Mormon leader taught—with the force of doctrine itself—this
concept. I quote from *The Promised Messiah*:

> The great God, the Eternal Elohim, the Father of us all . . .
> in his love, mercy, and grace condescended to step down from
> his Almighty throne, to step down to a lesser and benighted
> state, as it were, and become the Father of a Son "after the man-
> ner of the flesh." . . . This then is the condescension of God—
> that a God should beget a man; that an Immortal Parent should
> father a mortal Son; that the Creator of all things from the be-
> ginning should step down from his high state of exaltation and
> be, for a moment, like one of the creatures of his creating. . . .
> We have spoken plainly of our Lord's conception in the womb
> of Mary; in reality the plain assertions are found in the revealed
> word, and we have but certified that the words mean what they
> say and cannot be spiritualized away. And as it is with reference
> to our Lord's mother, so it is as pertaining to his Father. The
> scriptures say that Jesus Christ is the Only Begotten Son. The
> problem is that the intellectually led ministry and laity of the
> day assume, as Satan leads them to do, that a name-title of this
> sort is simply figurative and does not have the same literal
> meaning as when the words are spoken in ordinary conversa-
> tion. Perhaps again the best service we can render, on the issue
> here involved, is somehow to get the message across that words
> mean what they say, and that if Christ is the Only Begotten of
> the Father, it means just that.
>
> Some words scarcely need definition. They are on every
> tongue and are spoken by every voice. The very existence of

intelligent beings presupposes and requires their constant use. Two such words are father and son. Their meaning is known to all, and to define them is but to repeat them. Thus: A son is a son is a son, and a father is a father is a father. I am the son of my father and the father of my sons. They are my sons because they were begotten by me, were conceived by their mother, and came forth from her womb to breathe the breath of mortal life, to dwell for a time and a season among other mortal men.

And so it is with the Eternal Father and the mortal birth of the Eternal Son. The Father is a Father is a Father; he is not a spirit essence or nothingness to which the name Father is figuratively applied. And the Son is a Son is a Son; he is not some transient emanation from a divine essence, but a literal, living offspring of an actual Father. God is the Father; Christ is the Son. The one begat the other. Mary provided the womb from which the Spirit Jehovah came forth, tabernacles in clay, as all men are, to dwell among his fellow spirits whose births were brought to pass in like manner. There is no need to spiritualize away the plain meaning of the scriptures. There is nothing figurative or hidden or beyond comprehension in our Lord's coming into mortality. He is the Son of God in the same sense and way that we are the sons of mortal fathers. It is just that simple. Christ was born of Mary. He is the Son of God—the Only begotten of the Father.[21]

It seems impossible to me that anyone could miss McConkie's point. How else could he possibly state it? If he is *not* teaching this doctrine, he is certainly doing everything in his power to confuse and mislead the reader! The reader should note: nowhere do *any* of these General Authorities say, "Now, this is merely my speculation on the topic—it's just an opinion which you can take or leave." As much as some professors at BYU might wish otherwise, these men meant what they said. Listen to how McConkie put it:

> And so, in the final analysis, it is the faithful saints, those who have testimonies of the truth and divinity of this great latter-day work, who declare our Lord's generation to the world. Their testimony is that Mary's son is God's son; that he was conceived and begotten in the normal way. . . . This is their testimony as to his generation.[22]

This doctrine is not only found in one or two of McConkie's

works. Rather, it is a doctrine that is found *throughout* the considerable literature he produced.

> Again the answer is perfect. There is a power beyond man's. When God is involved, he uses his minister, the Holy Ghost, to overshadow the future mother and to carry her away in the Spirit. She shall conceive by the power of the Holy Ghost, and God himself shall be the sire. It is his Son of whom Gabriel is speaking. A son is begotten by a father: whether on earth or in heaven it is the same.[23]

I will not multiply examples, but instead draw from McConkie's *Doctrinal New Testament Commentary* for my last citations. One does not normally fill doctrinal commentaries with mere speculations or opinions. For this reason these words should carry much weight:

> The express image of his person. What more need be said? God the Eternal Father is the Father; the Son of God is the Son. A father is a father, and a son is a son. The Father begets; the Son is begotten; they are Parent and Child; Sire and Son look alike, so much so that they are the express image of each other's persons. The substance composing the body of one is identical in appearance to that composing the body of the other. What could be plainer? . . . Begotten means begotten; it means Christ's mortal body was procreated by an Eternal Sire; it means God is the Father of Christ, "after the manner of the flesh."[24]

The phrase "Eternal Sire" does not lend itself very well to metaphorical interpretation, especially in the way McConkie consistently uses it. One thing is for certain: this General Authority believed this doctrine, taught it, and never once identified it as "speculation."

More Authorities Testify

One of the strongest sources we can turn to regarding this doctrine is the official pronouncement titled "The Father and the Son: A Doctrinal Exposition by the First Presidency and the Twelve." Under the subtitle "Father As Literal Parent," we find these words:

> Scriptures embodying the ordinary signification—literally

that of Parent—are too numerous and specific to require citation. The purport of these scriptures is to the effect that God the Eternal Father, whom we designate by the exalted name-title "Elohim," is the literal Parent of our Lord and Savior Jesus Christ, and of the spirits of the human race.[25]

Please take notice of the fact that this doctrinal exposition by the leadership of the LDS Church says that the Eternal Father, Elohim, is the "literal parent of our Lord and Savior Jesus Christ," as well as the parent of the spirits of the human race. How did God beget our spirits? With our "heavenly Mother," as we have seen earlier. So how, then, did Elohim become the literal parent of Jesus Christ? The answer is obvious. Later the same exposition states,

> Jesus Christ is the Son of Elohim both as spiritual and bodily offspring; that is to say, Elohim is literally the Father of the spirit of Jesus Christ and also of the body in which Jesus Christ performed His mission in the flesh, and which body died on the cross and was afterward taken up by the process of resurrection, and is now the immortalized tabernacle of the eternal spirit of our Lord and Savior. No extended explanation of the title "Son of God" as applied to Jesus Christ appears necessary.

In light of all that has come before, we can understand why this document says that "no extended explanation" of the title Son of God "appears necessary." It wasn't, until modern LDS concluded that such a doctrine is simply indefensible and began backpedaling very quickly from it.

Another LDS apostle, contemporary with Talmage, was Melvin Ballard. He is another witness as to how widely this teaching was disseminated:

> One of the great questions that I have referred to that the world is concerned about, and is in confusion over, is as to whether or not his was a virgin birth, a birth wherein divine power interceded. Joseph Smith made it perfectly clear that Jesus Christ told the absolute truth, as did those who testify concerning him, the Apostles of the Lord Jesus Christ, wherein he is declared to be the very Son of God. And if God the Eternal Father is not the real Father of Jesus Christ, then are we in confusion; then is he not in reality the Son of God. But we declare

that he is the Only Begotten of the Father in the flesh.

Mary told the story most beautifully when she said that an angel of the Lord came to her and told her that she had found favor in the sight of God, and had come to be worthy of the fulfilment of the promises heretofore made, to become the virgin mother of the Redeemer of the world. She afterwards, referring to the event, said: "God hath done wonderful things unto me." "And the Holy Ghost came upon her," is the story, "and she came into the presence of the highest." No man or woman can live in mortality and survive the presence of the Highest except by the sustaining power of the Holy Ghost. So it came upon her to prepare her for admittance into the divine presence, and the power of the Highest, who is the Father, was present, and overshadowed her, and the holy Child that was born of her was called the Son of God.

Men who deny this, or who think that it degrades our Father, have no true conception of the sacredness of the most marvelous power with which God has endowed mortal men—the power of creation. Even though that power may be abused and may become a mere harp of pleasure to the wicked, nevertheless it is the most sacred and holy and divine function with which God has endowed man. Made holy, it is retained by the Father of us all, and in his exercise of that great and marvelous creative power and function, he did not debase himself, degrade himself, nor debauch his daughter. Thus Christ became the literal Son of a divine Father, and no one else was worthy to be his father.[26]

How much plainer can it be expressed? Ballard speaks of the necessity of the Spirit being involved so that Mary could stand the presence of the "Highest." Ballard knows that some would say this degrades the Father. How does he respond to this charge? By saying that sexual activity, the power of creation itself, this "holy and divine function," is a good thing, and is "retained by the Father of us all." Ballard says God "exercised" that function, but in the process, did not "degrade himself, nor debauch his daughter." If this doctrine is all metaphorical, why the constant reference to sexual activity? The answer is obvious: It is plainly the intention of this LDS leader to assert that God the Father physically begat the body of Jesus Christ. There is no other possibility.

Apostle Marion G. Romney is yet another who taught this doctrine plainly, and that in the General Conference of the LDS Church:

> Now who is Jesus Christ, and how could he bring about the resurrection when no other man nor all men put together could do so? The Scriptures respond to these questions. They make it clear that the spirit person Jesus Christ—as are the spirits of all men—is the Son of God, our Eternal Father. In this respect he is like all other men. He differs from all other men, however, by reason of the fact that men's bodies are begotten of mortal men and are, therefore, subject to death, being descendants and inheritors from Adam, while Christ's physical body was begotten of God, our Heavenly Father—an immortal being not subject to death. Christ, therefore, inherited from his Father the faculty to live on indefinitely.[27] (CR1975Apr:123–24)

In an earlier Conference (1967), Henry D. Taylor had spoken to the same, seemingly very *common*, belief:

> Having been begotten of an immortal sire, Jesus possessed as a heritage the power to withstand death indefinitely. He literally and really gave up his life. It was not taken from him.[28]

Another Conference address example is provided by Hugh B. Brown in 1962:

> The answer is found in the fact that of all the sons of God, only Christ could qualify, because he was the only sinless man who ever walked the earth. Furthermore, he was the First Begotten, the eldest of the sons of God in the spirit, and the Only Begotten in the flesh, and therefore the only one who possessed the full powers of Godhood and manhood.[29]

Mormon Prophet Joseph Fielding Smith provided one of the more common passages cited concerning the paternity of Christ:

> CHRIST NOT BEGOTTEN OF HOLY GHOST. I believe firmly that Jesus Christ is the Only Begotten Son of God in the flesh. He taught this doctrine to his disciples. He did not teach them that He was the Son of the Holy Ghost, but the Son of the Father. . . . Christ was begotten of God. He was not born without the aid of Man, and that Man was God![30]

As President of the Quorum of the Twelve, Ezra Taft Benson made the following statement:

The Church of Jesus Christ of Latter-day Saints proclaims that Jesus Christ is the Son of God in the most literal sense. The body in which He performed His mission in the flesh was sired by that same Holy Being we worship as God, our Eternal Father. Jesus was not the son of Joseph nor was He begotten by the Holy Ghost. He is the son of the Eternal Father![31]

Robert A. Rees served as bishop of the Los Angeles First Ward. He gave a sacrament meeting talk on April 29, 1990, and provided an article to *Dialogue: A Journal of Mormon Thought* that is found in the Winter 1991 issue. It is titled "Bearing Our Crosses Gracefully: Sex and the Single Mormon." His words demonstrate how widespread is this belief. In it we find the following:

> Mormons differ from other Christians in our literal belief that we are begotten of God spiritually and that Christ was begotten of him physically. Paul says in Acts that we are God's offspring (17:28–29). We believe that our spiritual conception was sexual just as we believe that Christ's mortal conception was. Elucidating the latter, James E. Talmage says, "That child to be born of Mary was begotten of Elohim the Eternal Father, not in violation of natural law, but in accordance with a higher manifestation thereof" (1986, 81).

We have seen that the idea that this doctrine is mere speculation on the part of a few LDS leaders of the past century is about as accurate as saying the Chicago Bulls have won a couple of basketball games over the past few years or that Michael Jordan is a so-so player. But remember Dr. Robinson's assertion that this doctrine has not "appeared in official church publications" during his lifetime. Is this the case? Let's find out.

Thus Saith the Official Publications

If we assume that a publication copyrighted by the Corporation of the President of the Church of Jesus Christ of Latter-day Saints can be logically called "official," we find a number of statements concerning the literal paternity of Christ in "official" documents written over the last thirty years. For example, from the *Family Home Evenings* booklet of 1972 we read:

We must come down to the simple fact that God Almighty was the Father of His Son Jesus Christ. Mary, the virgin girl, who had never known mortal man, was his mother. God by her begot his Son Jesus Christ, and he was born into the world with power and intelligence like that of His Father. . . . Now, my little friends, I will repeat again in words as simple as I can, and you talk to your parents about it, that God, the Eternal Father, is literally the father of Jesus Christ. (Joseph F. Smith, Box Elder Stake Conference, Dec. 20, 1914, as quoted in *Brigham City Box Elder News* [Jan. 28, 1915]: 1–2).[32]

Following this statement the booklet shows an almost stick-figure, male, identified as "Daddy," and another figure, female, identified as "Mommy." There is a plus between them, with lines leading down to a child figure, marked "You." Right below this is a diagram with "Our Heavenly Father" in "Daddy's" place, "Mary" in "Mommy's" place, and "Jesus" in the child's place. If such a diagram, *meant to be used to explain LDS doctrine to children*, is not enough to convince a person of the meaning of this teaching, nothing will. This appears in an "official" publication, but certainly not the only place such doctrine can be found. The work *Messages for Exaltation: Eternal Insights from the Book of Mormon*,[33] says,

Christ has power over death. Since the Fall of Adam, every person born on earth has had within him the seeds of death. Christ was no exception. He inherited the ability to die from mortal mother, Mary. But he also inherited the ability to live forever from his immortal Father. This power over death was entirely dependent upon Christ's being the literal Son of God. From his immortal, glorified Father he inherited power over death. Thus with a mortal mother and an immortal Father, the sinless Christ could decide for himself whether to live or die. The choice was his. Milton R. Hunter expressed this power in these words: He, Jesus Christ, being literally the Only Begotten Son of God, was endowed with a double portion of divine attributes. He received a comparable proportion of divinity in the spirit world that we received through being spirit children of God, and He was also the offspring of the Eternal Father in mortality—thus He possessed a double portion of God's power.

This is exactly in line with the current *Doctrines of the Gospel*

Student Manual, Religion 231 and 232 (published by the Church of Jesus Christ of Latter-day Saints), 1986, p. 22, which states,

> C. Only Jesus Christ possessed the qualifications and attributes necessary to perform an infinite atonement. 1. As the Only Begotten Son of God, the Savior inherited the capacity to suffer for the sins of all the children of God.

The above referenced *Messages for Exaltation* also said,[34]

> He was *willing* to make payment because of his great love for mankind, and he was *able* to make payment because he lived a sinless life and because he was actually, literally, biologically the Son of God in the flesh. Thus he had the power to atone for the spiritual and physical deaths introduced by the Fall of Adam and Eve.

Is there not an obvious consistency through all these citations, going all the way back through Talmage to Brigham Young? There certainly is. And this consistency follows through to the modern *Encyclopedia of Mormonism*, as well. For example,

> For Latter-day Saints, the paternity of Jesus is not obscure. He was the literal, biological son of an immortal, tangible Father and Mary, a mortal woman (see Virgin Birth). Jesus is the only person born who deserves the title "the Only Begotten Son of God" (John 3:16; Benson, p. 3; see Jesus Christ: Only Begotten in the Flesh). He was not the son of the Holy Ghost; it was only through the Holy Ghost that the power of the Highest overshadowed Mary.[35]

Likewise, we also read,

> Ancient and modern scriptures use the title Only Begotten to emphasize the divine nature of Jesus Christ. Latter-day Saints recognize Jesus as literally the Only Begotten Son of God the Father in the flesh. . . . This title signifies that Jesus' physical body was the offspring of a mortal mother and of the eternal Father. . . . It is LDS doctrine that Jesus Christ is the child of Mary and God the Father, "not in violation of natural law but in accordance with a higher manifestation thereof" (JC, 81).[36]

Note the line, "It is LDS doctrine that Jesus Christ is the child of Mary and God the Father." Is this LDS writer trying to "misrepresent" Mormonism? Is he an "eccentric"? And are Christians to be accused of attacking a straw man when they object to this teaching? No, not at all. This is LDS doctrine, pure and simple, as one last citation shows:

> The fact of Jesus' being the literal Son of God in the flesh is crucial to the Atonement, which could not have been accomplished by an ordinary man. . . . To complete the Atonement by physical death and resurrection, it was necessary that Jesus be able to lay down his physical body and also be able to take it up again. He could do this only because he had life in himself, which he inherited from God his Father. . . . Christ inherited the ability to die from his mortal mother and the power to resurrect himself from his immortal Father. Dying was for him a voluntary, deliberate act for mankind, made possible only because he was the Only Begotten of the Father.[37]

Conclusion

It is not always easy to determine the teachings of the LDS faith. However, if one uses the resources that are available, the task is quite possible. And when it comes to the physical, literal parentage of Jesus Christ, the consistent teaching of the General Authorities of the LDS faith is without question. If LDS apologists like Daniel Peterson, Stephen Ricks, and Stephen Robinson wish to identify this teaching as merely a matter of speculation, they are certainly free to do so (though at the cost of consistency). I would not wish to be pressed into defending a doctrine such as this one! To call it "blasphemous" is to understate the issue. We should not forget, however, the words of Bruce R. McConkie, written to BYU professor Eugene England:

> It is not in your province to set in order the Church or to determine what its doctrines shall be. . . . This means, among other things, that it is my province to teach to the Church what the doctrine is. You do not have a divine commission to correct me or any of the Brethren. The Lord does not operate that way. If I lead the Church astray, that is my responsibility, but the fact still remains that I am the one appointed with all the rest involved so to do. The appointment is not given to the faculty at

Brigham Young University or to any of the members of the Church.[38]

But it strikes me that it would be rather easy for these men to disprove the doctrine: cite a consistent *denial* of the alleged "misrepresentation" on the part of critics of the LDS faith *from the very same sources* I have used. The simple fact is, *they can't*, because no such denial exists.

Appendix

THEOSIS—BECOMING A GOD?

> Latter-day Saints reject the doctrines of the Trinity as taught by most Christian churches today. Those creeds were canonized in the fourth and fifth centuries A.D. and do not reflect the thinking or beliefs of the New Testament church.

So began an article titled *Comparing LDS Beliefs with First-Century Christianity* in the March 1988 issue of *The Ensign*, the official magazine of the LDS Church.[1] The article raises a number of issues, but most significantly it presents the idea that the early Christian doctrine of *theosis*, that men become "gods" upon sanctification, is a parallel to the LDS concept that we have examined earlier in this work. The authors, Daniel C. Peterson and Stephen D. Ricks, both professors at Brigham Young University, followed up their article with a book titled *Offenders for a Word: How Anti-Mormons Play Word Games to Attack the Latter-day Saints.*[2] This work, too, attempted to present the idea that *theosis* in the writings of such early Christians as Irenaeus or Athanasius demonstrates that believing that men can become gods is not something that should be considered unorthodox, and certainly believing such a thing should not remove one from consideration as a Christian.

Between the time of the *Ensign* article and the publication of *Offenders for a Word* another book was published that likewise presented the doctrine of deification in the early church as evidence that the Mormons should not be excluded from the name "Christian" for their allegedly similar belief. This book by BYU professor Stephen Robinson was titled *Are Mormons Christians?*[3] It was far more widely distributed than the Peterson and Ricks work, and many in the Christian apologetics field noted the increased use of the doctrine of *theosis* by LDS apologists. Robinson turned to the concept yet again in his work co-written with Denver Seminary professor Craig Blomberg, *How Wide the Divide?*[4] This effort on the part of leading LDS scholars and apologists has been quite fruitful, not because the patristic sources actually support the thesis, but because most Christians, including those who would be concerned to share the Gospel with Mormons in the first place, are generally unfamiliar with the writings of the early church fathers. Your average Christian is not going to readily understand the issues at hand, nor are they going to be able to direct a believing Mormon to the resources they would need to properly evaluate the claims that are being made.

Let's Simplify

This topic can be somewhat difficult to follow, so I would like to summarize the issue right at the start, and then provide the necessary reasoning in the paragraphs that follow. It is quite true that some of the early Fathers (not all) spoke of men "becoming gods." Stephen Robinson was not making anything up when he quoted the early Church Father Irenaeus (c. A.D. 130–200), bishop of Lyon in Gaul, as saying, "Do we cast blame on him [God] because we were not made gods from the beginning, but were at first created merely as men, and then later as gods?"[5] The issue is not that these words and others like them were written. The issue is what these words *meant*.

The simple reason that LDS scholars are in error in pointing to these passages is that a fundamental, definitional aspect of their own beliefs is *completely missing* from the faith of the early Fathers. That is, there is no parallel to the LDS belief in eternal progression because the early Fathers believed something fundamentally different about the nature of God, making any parallel impossible. What did the Fathers believe that the Mormons do not? Or, what do the Mormons believe that the early Christians did not? The answer is simple: The early Christians believed that God had always been God, and they did *not* believe that God had once been a man who lived on another planet and progressed to godhood.

The LDS concept of deification cannot possibly be understood outside of the famous couplet "As man is, God once was; as God is, man may become." This concept cannot be split in two. That is, you cannot have the second half without the first. You cannot have men becoming gods without first recognizing the fact that God was once a man who also went through the process of exaltation to godhood. The two ideas go hand in hand, and neither exists on its own. The idea that men can become "gods" is based upon the idea that God and men are of the same "species." This is the heart and soul of the LDS concept.

But it is this very concept that is *completely and utterly denied* by every single one of the early Christians who are cited by LDS apologists in an attempt to draw some kind of parallel to Mormon belief. Irenaeus did not believe that God was once a man who had progressed to godhood—neither did any other early Christian writer. Instead, they insisted that there was only one true God, the Creator of *all things*, the very origin and ground of all existence, who himself is without beginning, without origin, without source. *Christians have always believed this about God.* Therefore, obviously, when some early Christians speak of "becoming gods," they mean it in a *very* different way than Mormonism does when it speaks of men becoming gods. Quite simply, they *never* speak in such a way as to compromise the absolute monotheism that lies at the heart of the Christian faith. LDS apologists are quite wrong in attempting to find in *theosis* a parallel to their own theology, for those who taught *theosis* were monotheists to the core. The entire concept of eternal progression in LDS theology is based, as I see it, upon Joseph Smith's belief as represented in the King Follett Discourse:

> We have imagined and supposed that God was God from all eternity. I will refute that idea, and take away the veil, so that you may see.[6]

By rejecting the eternity of God, which surely involves the strict monotheism of the Christian people, Joseph Smith separated himself fundamentally even from those who taught that men could be deified. Their concept obviously did not create "gods," while Joseph's did.

Scholarly Commentary

Patristic scholar G. L. Prestige said concerning *theosis*,

> All such expressions of the deification of man are, it must

be remembered, purely relative. They express the fact that man has a nature essentially spiritual, and to that extent resembling the being of God; further, that he is able to attain a real union with God, by virtue of an affinity proceeding both from nature and from grace. Man, the Fathers might have said, is a supernatural animal. In some sense his destiny is to be absorbed into God. But they would all have repudiated with indignation any suggestion that the union of men to God added anything to the godhead. They explained the lower in terms of the higher, but did not obliterate the distinction between them. Not only is God self-dependent, He has also all those positive qualities which man does not possess, the attribution of which is made by adding the negative prefix to the common attributes of humanity. In addition, insofar as humanity possesses broken lights of God, they are as far as possible from reaching the measure and perfection with which they are associated in the godhead. Real power and freedom, fullness of light, ideal and archetypal spirit, are found in Him alone. The gulf is never bridged between Creator and creature. Though in Christ human nature has been raised to the throne of God, by virtue of His divine character, yet mankind in general can only aspire to the sort of divinity which lies open to its capacity through the union with the divine humanity. Eternal life is the life of God. Men may come to share its manifestations and activities, but only by grace, never of right. Man remains a created being: God alone is *agenetos* [i.e., uncreated].[7]

Note well what Prestige says. He asserts that the early Fathers did not "obliterate the distinction" between God and man (Mormonism most definitely does, teaching that God was once a man who has progressed to godhood). Prestige says that "real power and freedom" are found in God *alone*, not in the creature man. And in as clear a denial of the concept presented by Mormonism as one could find, Prestige says, "The gulf is never bridged between Creator and creature." He closes by saying, "Man remains a created being: God alone is *agenetos*." Clearly, Prestige is saying that the early Fathers did not teach that men could become gods *in the sense that Mormonism would like us to believe.*

Some leading ideas about the nature of God may be illustrated in a few quotations from early writers. Tatian writes (*ad*

Gr. 4.1, 2), "Our God does not have his constitution in time. He alone is without beginning; He Himself constitutes the source (ἀρχή) of the universe. God is spirit. He does not extend through matter, but is the author of material spirits and of the figures (σχήματα) in matter. He is invisible and intangible."[8]

Prestige is giving what he sees as *representational* views of the early Fathers. Note the many things that are *directly* contradictory to LDS teaching. First, God is eternal—he does "not have his constitution in time." The LDS God has progressed to his current position—obviously, then, he undergoes a progression of time. Tatian states that God is without beginning; yet Mormonism speaks of God's once having been a man, so, obviously, he had to enter into the condition of a god at some point in time. Tatian says God is spirit; Mormonism says he is flesh. Tatian says that God is the "author" of "material spirits and of the figures in matter"; Joseph Smith taught that "God never had the power to create the spirit of man at all."[9] Tatian says that God is invisible and intangible; *Doctrine and Covenants* 130:22, says just the opposite. Prestige continues,

Athenagoras (*suppl.* 10.1) expresses allegiance to "one God, the uncreated, eternal, invisible, impassible, incomprehensible, uncontainable, comprehended only by mind and reason, clothed in light and beauty and spirit and power indescribable, by whom the totality has come to be." . . . But, in brief, this statement implies that God is transcendent and everlasting; free alike from limitations of time or space and from subjection to sense or affections; and possessed of supreme supernatural power and glory. Theophilus speaks similarly (*ad Aut.* 1.3) of the abstract qualities of the deity. "The form of God is ineffable . . . in glory He is uncontainable, in greatness incomprehensible, in height inconceivable, in might incomparable, in wisdom without peer, in goodness inimitable, in well-doing indescribable. . . . He is without beginning because He is uncreated, and He is unchangeable because He is immortal." And again, (*ib.* 2.3), "it belongs to God, the highest and almighty and the truly God, not only to be everywhere, but also to overlook all things and to hear all things, and yet, nevertheless, not to be contained in space."[10]

We again note the completely different view of God presented here than that of Mormonism. The God of the early Fathers is un-created, eternal, invisible, impassible, incomprehensible, and un-containable. The God of Mormonism entered into godhood at a par-ticular point, he has not eternally been God, he is not invisible (in the sense the church fathers meant the term), and he is certainly not impassible, incomprehensible, or uncontainable; many LDS *mock* these very aspects of the Christian doctrine of God. But Prestige did not stop there:

> His absolute independence is a corollary to His absolute goodness and wisdom, as well as to His absolute capacity to create. Thus the emphasis . . . on God being uncreated ($\dot{\alpha}\gamma\acute{\epsilon}$-$\nu\eta\tau o\varsigma$) implies that He is the sole originator of all things that are, the source and ground of existence; and the conception is taken as a positive criterion of Deity. The insistence that God is uncontained spatially ($\dot{\alpha}\chi\acute{\omega}\rho\eta\tau o\varsigma$) conveys a very necessary warning against Stoic pantheism. Though the created universe contributes an implicit revelation of God through His works, it is by no means a complete or perfect revelation of His being; He is infinitely greater than His creation. Thus Justin claims (*dial.* 127.2) that God is uncontained either in one place or in the whole universe since He existed before the universe came into being.[11]

That all of this is directly contradictory to the LDS doctrine of a finite, limited God who has a physical body of flesh and bone (*D & C* 130:22) and who was once a man is too obvious to require further comment. The early Fathers did *not* present the LDS concept of God in any way, shape, or form. One of the greatest patristic schol-ars, J. N. D. Kelly, has written,

> The classical creeds of Christendom opened with a decla-ration of belief in one God, maker of heaven and earth. The monotheistic idea, grounded in the religion of Israel, loomed large in the minds of the earliest fathers; though not reflective theologians, they were fully conscious that it marked the divid-ing line between the Church and paganism. According to Her-mas, the first commandment is to "believe that God is one, Who created and established all things, bringing them into existence out of nonexistence". It was He Who "by His invisible and mighty power and great wisdom created the universe, and by

His glorious purpose clothed His creation with comeliness, and by His strong word fixed the heavens and founded the earth above the waters." For Clement God is "the Father and creator of the entire cosmos" and for "Barnabas" and the *Didache* "our maker." His omnipotence and universal sovereignty were acknowledged, for He was "the Lord almighty, the Lord Who governs the whole universe," and "the master of all things." The reader should notice that at this period the title "almighty" connoted God's all-pervading control and sovereignty over reality, just as "Father" referred primarily to His role as creator and author of all things.[12]

The Misuse of Irenaeus

LDS apologists and scholars are quick to cite Irenaeus, bishop of Lyon, with reference to men becoming gods, as we noted above. It is important to investigate what Irenaeus said Christians believed about the nature of God:

> The disciple of the Lord therefore desiring to put an end to all such doctrines, and to establish the rule of truth in the Church, that there is one Almighty God, who made all things by His Word, both visible and invisible.[13]

And he also insisted that Christians were . . .

> . . . carefully preserving the ancient tradition, believing in one God, the Creator of heaven and earth, and all things therein, by means of Christ Jesus, the Son of God; who, because of His surpassing love towards His creation, condescended to be born of the virgin, He Himself uniting man through Himself to God, and having suffered under Pontius Pilate, and rising again, and having been received up in splendor, shall come in glory, the Savior of those who are saved, and the Judge of those who are judged, and sending into eternal fire those who transform the truth, and despise His Father and His advent.[14]

Both Stephen Robinson in his book, and Drs. Daniel C. Peterson and Stephen D. Ricks in their book, cite Irenaeus in *Against Heresies* 4:38, in the sections wherein they attempt to use the doctrine of *theosis* as supportive of LDS teachings (Robinson on pages 60–61, and Peterson and Ricks on page 77). The specific section they cite is as follows:

> For we cast blame upon Him, because we have not been made gods from the beginning, but at first merely men, then at length gods; although God has adopted this course out of his pure benevolence, that no one may impute to Him invidiousness or grudgingness. He declares, "I have said, Ye are gods, and ye are all sons of the Highest."[15]

At this point Robinson's citation breaks off with an ellipsis, and Peterson and Ricks cite only the first sentence. What Robinson leaves out is as follows:

> But since we could not sustain the power of divinity, He adds, "But ye shall die like men," setting forth both truths—the kindness of His free gift, and our weakness, and also that we were possessed of power over ourselves. For after His great kindness He graciously conferred good [upon us], and made men like to Himself, [that is] in their own power; while at the same time by His prescience He knew the infirmity of human beings, and the consequences that would flow from it; but through [His] love and [His] power, He shall overcome the substance of created nature.[16]

Then Robinson resumes his citation:

> For it was necessary, at first, that nature should be exhibited; then, after that, that what was mortal should be conquered and swallowed up by immortality. . . .[17]

Robinson ends his quote, but I continue,

> . . . and the corruptible by incorruptibility, and that man should be made after the image and likeness of God, having received the knowledge of good and evil.[18]

Now a few things on this citation. The material not found in the middle of Robinson's quote (or anywhere in Peterson and Ricks' version) is certainly not "LDS" in character, and would diminish the force desired by the quotation. Also, the final section, likewise not included, defines the *imago Dei* (image of God) in terms of the moral and rational character of man (i.e., the knowledge of good and evil), and LDS belief defines the image of God in a physical manner.

But what is most distressing to me is the fact that reading this passage in context utterly destroys the LDS position. I would invite everyone to read Irenaeus' words in *Against Heresies* 4:38, and see for themselves:

> If, however, any one say, "What then? Could not God have exhibited man as perfect from the beginning?" let him know that, inasmuch as God is indeed always the same and unbegotten as respects Himself, all things are possible to Him. But created things must be inferior to Him who created them, from the very fact of their later origin; for it was not possible for things recently created to have been uncreated. But inasmuch as they are not uncreated, for this very reason do they come short of the perfect.[19]

In Mormonism, God and man are of the same species.[20] Neither have eternally been what they are now; God is simply an exalted man. There is no concept of God as "uncreated" (*agenetos*) in LDS theology, yet this is where Irenaeus begins, with God as the Creator of all things, the source of all life. Irenaeus continues,

> There was nothing, therefore, impossible to and deficient in God, [implied in the fact] that man was not an uncreated being; but this merely applied to him who was lately created, [namely] man.[21]

Compare Irenaeus' teaching that man is created while God is not with the statement of LDS Scripture:

> Man was also in the beginning with God. Intelligence, or the light of truth, was not created or made, neither indeed can be (*D & C* 93:29).

Shortly after this, Irenaeus defines for us what "deification" means to him. Note his words:

> For the Uncreated is perfect, that is, God. Now it was necessary that man should in the first instance be created; and having been created, should receive growth; and having received growth, should be strengthened; and having been strengthened,

should abound; and having abounded, should recover [from the disease of sin]; and having recovered, should be glorified; and being glorified, should see his Lord. For God is He who is yet to be seen, and the beholding of God is productive of immortality, but immortality renders one nigh unto God.[22]

Notice that seeing "his Lord" is "productive of immortality," and that immortality "renders one nigh unto God." But in none of this does man ever cease to be "created." Nowhere does man become "uncreated" as God is. There is no breaking down of the dividing wall between the Creator and the creature.

I move to the beginning of the paragraph that these leading scholars of Mormonism have cited in their works. Please read carefully what is said by Irenaeus:

> Irrational, therefore, in every respect, are they who await not the time of increase, but ascribe to God the infirmity of their nature. Such persons know neither God nor themselves, being insatiable and ungrateful, unwilling to be at the outset what they have also been created—men subject to passions; but go beyond the law of the human race, and before that they become men, they wish to be even now like God their Creator, and they who are more destitute of reason than dumb animals [insist] that there is no distinction between the uncreated God and man, a creature of today.[23]

Please note that this material is a scant *one sentence* before the citations used by Robinson and Peterson and Ricks! And yet does it not describe the LDS belief almost perfectly? Indeed it does!

The Misuse of Jaroslav Pelikan

At the beginning of this chapter we noted the *Ensign* article that was written by Drs. Peterson and Ricks. They made a number of references to the works of Jaroslav Pelikan, at one point simply stating, "See appropriate index entries in Jaroslav Pelikan . . . and the index entry "Salvation—Defined As Deification.""[24] Yet a fair analysis of Pelikan's writings reveals that those who presented the concept of *theosis* were not, in any way, presenting a concept that compromised absolute monotheism. A review of the two works of Pelikan cited in the article (volumes 1 and 2) of his *Christian Tradition* series[25] make this quite clear. First, we note that the early Christians believed in *creatio ex nihilo* (1:36), and that "God alone made it [the creation], because he alone is God in his being ὄντως. By his sheer act of will he creates (δημιουργεῖ); and after he has merely willed, it follows that things come into being." Nowhere is such an ability predicated of the deified man. They denied the concept of the coeternity of God and matter (*ibid.*). Irenaeus is quoted as saying that God the Creator "is discovered to be the one and only God who created all things, who alone is omnipotent, and who is the only Father founding and forming all things, visible and invisible" (1:36–37). The concept of "strict monotheism" is predicated of the Fathers over and over again throughout Pelikan's works, and the "disgust" that Christians had for polytheism is noted as well (1:66).

Pelikan's chapter titled "Vindication of Trinitarian Monotheism" also affords important information. We read,

> According to the Christian doctrine of creation, neither matter nor time could be coeternal with God, who alone possessed true eternity. He also possessed true oneness. . . . Similarly, God was the beginning (ἀρχή) of all beings, not in the sense that he was the first in a series, but in the sense that he transcended all being and that all beings were dependent on him. It was orthodox doctrine that God was "beyond and above all things that are known and all things that exist." The distinction as well as the link between the Creator and his creation had to be maintained: immanence without pantheistic identification, transcendence without deistic isolation.[26]

But most significantly, we find the following section from Pelikan regarding the *nature* of the concept of *theosis*:

> The emphasis on the reality of the divine in revelation applied also to the divine in deification. Maximus had expressed this unequivocally in the formula: "All that God is, except for an identity in ousia, one becomes when one is deified by grace." . . . Yet the reality being discussed in the two questions was not the same; for in the clarification of what it meant to be deified, the qualification added by Maximus, "except for an identity of ousia," proved to be crucial. . . . A way had to be found, Palamas maintained, to preserve the reality of salvation as deification

without implying the absurd and blasphemous idea that those who were deified became "God by nature." . . . The absurdity and the blasphemy were avoided by the teaching that "the deifying gift of the Spirit is not the superessential ousia of God, but the deifying activity ($\grave{\varepsilon}\nu\acute{\varepsilon}\rho\gamma\varepsilon\iota\alpha$) of the superessential ousia of God." To avoid saying that deification made a human being God by nature, it was necessary to insist that grace was supernatural, that is, beyond nature. For if deifying grace were "according to nature," it would indeed produce an identity of nature and of ousia between the deifying God and the deified man. . . . But the illumination and the deifying activity of God which made its recipients participants in the divine nature could not be the very nature of God . . . the nature of God could not be shared, and hence deification could not be "natural" . . . so also here the participation of man in the divine nature through salvation as deification needed to be interpreted in such a way as to safeguard the unchangeability of God, without in any way jeopardizing the reality of the gift of deification.[27]

A selection of quotations from the early Fathers that substantiates the conclusions of Prestige and Kelly quoted above follows at the end of this chapter. I believe that it is incumbent upon anyone who would cite the concept of *theosis* as being reflective of a concept even remotely similar to the LDS view of a plurality of exalted beings to be able to demonstrate the *foundational* aspect of an anthropomorphic deity; that is, if one is going to parallel *theosis* with eternal progression, one must be able to demonstrate that the same Fathers who spoke of deification *also* spoke of God *becoming* God through a process of exaltation. As we have seen, this is not to be found in the Fathers. The Christian church has always believed God to be eternal—without origin, without source, totally independent of all else. The concept of God having *become* a god through a process is totally absent from the church fathers. Hence, the foundation upon which any parallel with the LDS concept of eternal progression would have to be laid is missing. Therefore, the bare citation of an early Father or two who presented an idea of deification does not in any way support the early existence of the LDS concept, for it is clear that the early Fathers had a *radically* different view of God.

The Witness of the Early Fathers

Ignatius (A.D. 110)

> On this account also they were persecuted, being inspired by His grace to fully convince the unbelieving that there is one God, who has manifested Himself by Jesus Christ His Son, who is His eternal Word, not proceeding forth from silence, and who in all things pleased Him that sent Him.[28]

Justin Martyr (c. A.D. 160)

> But as my discourse is not intended to touch on this point, but to prove to you that the Holy Ghost reproaches men because they were made like God, free from suffering and death, provided that they kept His commandments, and were deemed deserving of the name of His sons, and yet they, becoming like Adam and Eve, work out death for themselves; let the interpretation of the Psalm be held just as you wish, yet thereby it is demonstrated that all men are deemed worthy of becoming "gods," and of having power to become sons of the Highest; and shall be each by himself judged and condemned like Adam and Eve. Now I have proved at length that Christ is called God.[29]

> For those things which exist after God, or shall at any time exist, these have the nature of decay, and are such as may be blotted out and cease to exist; for God alone is unbegotten and incorruptible, and therefore He is God, but all other things after Him are created and corruptible.[30]

> "There will be no other God, O Trypho, nor was there from eternity any other existing" (I thus addressed him), "but He who made and disposed all this universe. Nor do we think that there is one God for us, another for you, but that He alone is God who led your fathers out from Egypt with a strong hand and a high arm. Nor have we trusted in any other (for there is no other), but in Him in whom you also have trusted, the God of Abraham, and of Isaac, and of Jacob."[31]

Aristides of Athens (A.D. 140)

> I say, then, that God is not born, not made, an ever-abiding nature without beginning and without end, immortal, perfect, and incomprehensible. Now when I say that he is "perfect," this means that there is not in him any defect, and he is not in need

of anything but all things are in need of him.[32]

Let us proceed then, O King, to the elements themselves that
we may show in regard to them that they are not gods, but perishable and mutable, produced out of that which did not exist
at the command of the true God, who is indestructible and immutable and invisible; yet He sees all things and as He wills,
modifies, and changes things.[33]

Tatian (A.D. 165)

Our God did not begin to be in time: He alone is without
beginning, and He Himself is the beginning of all things. God
is a Spirit, not pervading matter, but the Maker of material spirits, and of the forms that are in matter; He is invisible, impal-
pable, being Himself the Father of both sensible and invisible
things. Him we know from His creation, and apprehend His invisible power by His works.[34]

For matter is not, like God, without beginning, nor, as having no beginning, is of equal power with God; it is begotten,
and not produced by any other being, but brought into existence by the Framer of all things alone.[35]

Athenagoras (A.D. 177)

But to us, who distinguish God from matter, and teach that
matter is one thing and God another, and that they are separated
by a wide interval (for that the Deity is uncreated and eternal,
to be beheld by the understanding and reason alone, while matter is created and perishable), is it not absurd to apply the name
of atheism? . . . But, since our doctrine acknowledges one God,
the Maker of this universe, who is Himself uncreated (for that
which is does not come to be, but that which is not) but has
made all things by the Logos which is from Him, we are treated
unreasonably in both respects, in that we are both defamed and
persecuted.[36]

That we are not atheists, therefore, seeing that we acknowledge one God, uncreated, eternal, invisible, impassable, incomprehensible, illimitable, who is apprehended by the understanding only and the reason, who is encompassed by light, and
beauty, and spirit, and power ineffable, by whom the universe
has been created through His Logos, and set in order, and is
kept in being—I have sufficiently demonstrated.[37]

Irenaeus (c. A.D. 180)

The rule of truth which we hold, is that there is one God Almighty, who made all things by His Word, and fashioned and formed, out of that which had no existence, all things which exist. Thus saith the Scripture, to that effect "By the Word of the Lord were the heavens established, and all the might of them, by the spirit of His mouth." And again, "All things were made by Him, and without Him was nothing made."[38]

. . . let them learn that God alone, who is Lord of all, is without beginning and without end, being truly and forever the same, and always remaining the same unchangeable Being. But all things which proceed from Him, whatsoever have been made, and are made, do indeed receive their own beginning of generation, and on this account are inferior to Him who formed them, inasmuch as they are not unbegotten. Nevertheless they endure, and extend their existence into a long series of ages in accordance with the will of God their Creator; so that He grants them that they should be thus formed at the beginning, and that they should so exist afterwards.[39]

Tertullian (A.D. 197)

The object of our worship is the One God, He who by His commanding word, His arranging wisdom, His mighty power, brought forth from nothing this entire mass of our world, with all its array of elements, bodies, spirits, for the glory of His majesty; whence also the Greeks have bestowed on it the name of Κόσμος. The eye cannot see Him, though He is (spiritually) visible. He is incomprehensible, though in grace He is manifested. He is beyond our utmost thought, though our human faculties conceive of Him. He is therefore equally real and great. But that which, in the ordinary sense, can be seen and handled and conceived, is inferior to the eyes by which it is taken in, and the hands by which it is tainted, and the faculties by which it is discovered; but that which is infinite is known only to itself. This it is which gives some notion of God, while yet beyond all our conceptions—our very incapacity of fully grasping Him affords us the idea of what He really is. He is presented to our minds in His transcendent greatness, as at once known and unknown. And this is the crowning guilt of men, that they will not recognize One, of whom they cannot possibly be ignorant.[40]

Now, with regard to this rule of faith—that we may from this point acknowledge what it is which we defend—it is, you must know, that which prescribes the belief that there is one only God, and that He is none other than the Creator of the world, who produced all things out of nothing through His own Word. . . .[41]

God, however, must be One, because that is God which is supreme; but nothing else can be supreme than that which is unique; and that cannot possibly be unique which has anything equal to it; and that Matter will be equal with God when it is held to be eternal.[42]

But the Christian verity has distinctly declared this principle, "God is not, if He is not one;" because we more properly believe that has no existence which is not as it ought to be. In order, however, that you may know that God is one, ask what God is, and you will find Him to be not otherwise than one. So far as a human being can form a definition of God, I adduce one which the conscience of all men will also acknowledge,—that God is the great Supreme existing in eternity, unbegotten, unmade without beginning, without end.[43]

Novatian (A.D. 235)

Thus God the Father, the Founder and Creator of all things, who only knows no beginning, invisible, infinite, immortal, eternal, is one God; to whose greatness, or majesty, or power, I would not say nothing can be preferred, but nothing can be compared.[44]

Cyril (A.D. 350)

Whence came the polytheistic error of the Greeks? God has no body: whence then the adulteries alleged among those who are by them called gods?[45]

First then let there be laid as a foundation in your soul the doctrine concerning God that God is One, alone unbegotten, without beginning, change, or variation; neither begotten of another, nor having another to succeed Him in His life; who neither began to live in time, nor endeth ever. . . . This Father of our Lord Jesus Christ is not circumscribed in any place, nor is He less than the heaven. . . . He is in all things and around all. Think not that the sun is brighter than He, or equal to Him: for

He who at first formed the sun must needs be incomparably greater and brighter. He foreknoweth the things that shall be, and is mightier than all, knowing all things and doing as He will; not being subject to any necessary sequence of events, nor to nativity, nor chance, nor fate; in all things perfect, and equally possessing every absolute form of virtue, neither diminishing nor increasing, but in mode and conditions ever the same; who hath prepared punishment for sinners, and a crown for the righteous.[46]

Hilary (A.D. 356)

It is the Father to Whom all existence owes its origin. In Christ and through Christ He is the source of all. In contrast to all else He is self-existent. He does not draw His being from without, but possesses it from Himself and in Himself. He is infinite, for nothing contains Him and He contains all things; He is eternally unconditioned by space, for He is illimitable; eternally anterior to time, for time is His creation. Let imagination range to what you may suppose is God's utmost limit, and you will find Him present there; strain as you will there is always a further horizon towards which to strain. Infinity is His property, just as the power of making such effort is yours.[47]

Epiphanius (c. A.D. 370)

Reject also the opinion of those who say the body is in the image of God. For how were it possible for the visible to be close to the invisible? How the corporeal to the incorporeal? How the tangible to the illimitable?[48]

Gregory of Nazianus (A.D. 383)

God always was and always is, and always will be; or rather, God always is for "was" and "will be" are fragments of our time, and of changeable nature. But He is Eternal Being; and this is the Name He gives Himself when giving the Oracles to Moses in the Mount. For in Himself He sums up and contains all Being, having neither beginning in the past nor end in the future . . . like some great Sea of Being, limitless and unbounded, transcending all conception of time and nature, only adumbrated by the mind, and that very dimly and scantily.[49]

Augustine (c. A.D. 400)

> The first decision to be made is whether we should prefer to believe those who call us to the worship of many gods, or those who call us to the one God. Who can doubt that it is preferable to follow those who call us to one, especially when those worshipers of many agree that this one God is the ruler of all others? And certainly, rank begins at one. Those, therefore, are to be followed first who say that there is only one supreme God, the true God, who alone is to be worshiped. If truth does not shine forth from them, then a change is to be made.[50]

The Witness of Athanasius, Bishop of Alexandria

In closing, we look to the witness of Athanasius, the bishop of Alexandria. His testimony is very important and relevant to the LDS claims regarding *theosis* for two reasons: first, he was the great defender of the deity of Christ and the Council of Nicæa, and second, he is often referred to in their writings as a prime source of information on *theosis*. Space permits only a few citations from his works regarding the issue at hand. However, it is plain to see that his view of God, like the Christian writers before him, is utterly contrary to the LDS conception and, therefore, his view of *theosis* cannot be used to substantiate the LDS idea.[51]

> But if God is one, and at the same time Lord of heaven and earth, how could there be another God beside Him? or what room will there be for the God whom they suppose, if the one true God fills all things in the compass of heaven and earth? or how could there be another creator of that, whereof, according to the Savior's utterance, the God and Father of Christ is Himself Lord.[52]
>
> For the people of the Jews of old had abundant teaching, in that they had the knowledge of God not only from the works of Creation, but also from the divine Scriptures. And in general to draw men away from the error and irrational imagination of idols, He saith: "Thou shalt have none other gods but Me." Not as if there were other gods does He forbid them to have them, but lest any, turning from the true God, should begin to make himself gods of what were not, such as those who in the poets and writers are called gods, though they are none.[53]

But this being so, and nothing being outside Him, but both heaven and earth and all that in them is being dependent on Him, yet men in their folly have set aside the knowledge and service of Him, and honored things that are not instead of things that are: and instead of the real and true God deified things that were not, "serving the creature rather than the Creator," thus involving themselves in foolishness and impiety.[54]

For we must not think there is more than one ruler and maker of Creation: but it belongs to correct and true religion to believe that its Artificer is one, while Creation herself clearly points to this. For the fact that there is one Universe only and not more is a conclusive proof that its Maker is one. For if there were a plurality of gods, there would necessarily be also more universes than one. For neither were it reasonable for more than one God to make a single universe, nor for the one universe to be made by more than one, because of the absurdities which would result from this.

1. First, if the one universe were made by a plurality of gods, that would mean weakness on the part of those who made it, because many contributed to a single result; which would be a strong proof of the imperfect creative skill of each. For if one were sufficient, the many would not supplement each other's deficiency. But to say that there is any deficiency in God is not only impious, but even beyond all sacrilege. For even among men one would not call a workman perfect if he were unable to finish his work, a single piece, by himself and without the aid of several others.

2. But if, although each one was able to accomplish the whole, yet all worked at it in order to claim a share in the result, we have the laughable conclusion that each worked for reputation, lest he should be suspected of inability. But, once more, it is most grotesque to ascribe vainglory to gods.

3. Again, if each one were sufficient for the creation of the whole, what need of more than one being self-sufficient for the universe? Moreover it would be evidently impious and grotesque to make the thing created one, while the creators were many and different, it being a maxim of science that what is one and complete is higher than things that are diverse.

4. And this you must know, that if the universe had been made by a plurality of gods, its movements would be diverse and inconsistent. For having regard to each one of its makers,

its movements would be correspondingly different. But such difference, again, as was said before, would involve disarray and general disorder; for not even a ship will sail aright if she be steered by many, unless one pilot hold the tiller, nor will a lyre struck by many produce a tuneful sound, unless there be one artist who strikes it.

5. Creation, then, being one, and the Universe one, and its order one, we must perceive that its King and Artificer also is one. For this is why the Artificer Himself made the whole universe one, lest by the coexistence of more than one a plurality of makers should be supposed; but that as the work is one, its Maker also may be believed to be One. Nor does it follow from the unity of the Maker that the Universe must be one, for God might have made others as well. But because the Universe that has been made is one, it is necessary to believe that its Maker also is one.[55]

And this being so, no heretic shall object, "Wherefore rises the flesh, being by nature mortal? and if it rises, why not hunger too and thirst, and suffer, and remain mortal? for it came from the earth, and how can its natural condition pass from it?" Since the flesh is able now to make answer to this so contentious heretic, "I am from earth, being by nature mortal, but afterwards I have become the Word's flesh, and He 'carried' my affections, though He is without them; and so I became free from them, being no more abandoned to their service because of the Lord who has made me free from them. For if you object to my being rid of that corruption which is by nature, see that you object not to God's Word having taken my form of servitude; for as the Lord, putting on the body, became man, so we men are deified by the Word as being taken to Him through His flesh, and henceforward inherit life everlasting."[56]

. . . but rather let him marvel that by so ordinary a means things divine have been manifested to us, and that by death immortality has reached to all, and that by the Word becoming man, the universal Providence has been known, and its Giver and Artificer the very Word of God. For He was made man that we might be made God; and He manifested Himself by a body that we might receive the idea of the unseen Father; and He endured the insolence of men that we might inherit immortality. For while He Himself was in no way injured, being impassible and incorruptible and very Word and God, men who were suffering, and for whose sakes He endured all this, He maintained and preserved in His own impassibility.[57]

Thus they idly babble; but in this their perverseness I see nothing but unreasoning audacity and recklessness from the devil, since it is saying after his pattern, "We will ascend to heaven, we will be like the Most High." For what is given to man by grace, this they would make equal to the Godhead of the Giver. Thus hearing that men are called sons, they thought themselves equal to the True Son by nature such. And now again bearing from the Savior, "that they may be one as We are," they deceive themselves, and are arrogant enough to think that they may be such as the Son is in the Father and the Father in the Son; not considering the fall of their "father the devil," which happened upon such an imagination.[58]

Men were created of matter, and that passible; but God is immaterial and incorporeal. . . . For God creates, and to create is also ascribed to men; and God has being, and men are said to be, having received from God this gift also. Yet does God create as men do? or is His being as man's being? Perish the thought; we understand the terms in one sense of God, and in another of men. For God creates, in that He calls what is not into being, needing nothing thereunto; but men work some existing material, first praying, and so gaining the wit to make, from that God who has framed all things by His proper Word. And again men, being incapable of self-existence, are enclosed in place, and consist in the Word of God; but God is self-existent, enclosing all things, and enclosed by none; within all according to His own goodness and power, yet without all in His proper natures. As then men create not as God creates, as their being is not such as God's being, so men's generation is in one way, and the Son is from the Father in another.[59]

But a mutable thing cannot be like God who is truly unchangeable, any more than what is created can be like its creator. This is why, with regard to us, the holy man said, "Lord, who shall be likened unto thee," and "who among the gods is like unto thee, Lord;" meaning by gods those who, while created, had yet become partakers of the Word, as He Himself said, "If he called them gods to whom the word of God came." But things which partake cannot be identical with or similar to that whereof they partake.[60]

NOTES

Chapter 1

1. James White, *Letters to a Mormon Elder* (Minneapolis: Bethany House Publishers, 1993).
2. The *Deseret News 1997–1998 Church Almanac* indiates that Arizona has approximately 271,000 Mormon residents, or 1 in every 15 residents.
3. This is not to say they are seeking to be accepted as Protestants or Catholics. Note the words of BYU professor Stephen Robinson:

   > The statement is sometimes made that Latter-day Saints now want to be known as Christians, whereas in the past we did not. This statement is both true and false. If we define "Christian" generically as someone who accepts the New Testament proclamation of Jesus as Son of God and Savior, then the first part of the statement is true: Mormons *do* wish to be known as Christians. But the second half of the statement would then be false, since there has never been a time when we wished otherwise. However, if we define "Christian" as meaning traditional, historical, and creedal orthodoxy, then the first part of the statement would be false: Mormons do *not* now wish to be known as post-Nicene, "orthodox" Christians. But the second part of the statement would then be true, for Mormons have never wanted to identify with post-New-Testament Christianity.

   Craig L. Blomberg and Stephen E. Robinson, *How Wide the Divide?* (Downers Grove, Ill.: InterVarsity Press, 1997), 19–20. Whether the issue is "post-Nicene orthodoxy" or not will be examined later.
4. Examples abound. See Daniel C. Peterson and Stephen D. Ricks, *Offenders for a Word: How Anti-Mormons Play Word Games to Attack the Latter-day Saints* (Salt Lake City: Aspen Books, 1992), and a recent video production, *In Defense of Truth: A Candid Response to Anti-Mormon Criticism* (Keystone Foundation, 1997).
5. Bill McKeever and Eric Johnson, *Questions to Ask Your Mormon Friend* (Minneapolis: Bethany House Publishers, 1994).

6. That is, a defense, an *apologia*, as Peter put it (1 Pet. 3:15), the very root term of "apologetics."

7. Christianity is just as monotheistic as Judaism or Islam. The doctrine of the Trinity is *completely predicated upon absolute monotheism*. Any person who believes the Trinity in any way compromises absolute (ontological) monotheism simply does not understand the Trinity itself. See my book *The Forgotten Trinity* (Minneapolis: Bethany House Publishers, 1998) for details.

Chapter 2

1. Official leaders of the LDS Church, normally referring to the members of the First Presidency, the Quorum of the Twelve, and the Quorum of the Seventy.

2. Numerous works exist dealing with the *Book of Mormon* by way of criticism and refutation. One that has caused quite a stir amongst defenders of Mormonism comes from the liberal branch of Mormonism itself: *New Approaches to the Book of Mormon*, Brent Lee Metcalfe, ed. (Salt Lake City: Signature Books, 1993). Most Christian books responding to Mormonism include sections of critique of the *Book of Mormon*, including Ron Rhodes and Marian Bodine, *Reasoning from the Scriptures with the Mormons* (Eugene, Ore.: Harvest House Books, 1995), 87–133; Jerald and Sandra Tanner, *Mormonism: Shadow or Reality?* (Salt Lake City: Utah Lighthouse Ministry, 1982), 50–125; and my own brief comments in *Letters to a Mormon Elder* (Minneapolis: Bethany House Publishers, 1993), 131–157. Likewise, critiques of the prophecies of Joseph Smith found in the *Doctrine and Covenants* can be found in the same sources, and a large body of information debunking the most unique section of *The Pearl of Great Price*, known as the *Book of Abraham*, can be found in the Tanners' work *Mormonism: Shadow or Reality*, 294–370 and in my *Letters to a Mormon Elder*, 157–168.

3. As cited by Rulon T. Burton in *We Believe: Doctrines and Principles of The Church of Jesus Christ of Latter-day Saints* (Salt Lake City: Tabernacle Books, 1994), 718, LDS Collector's Library '97 CD-ROM. As I will be using this CD-ROM as my standard source throughout this work (making it easier for LDS to check my sources, as it is a widely owned and used resource), I will abbreviate it as LDSCL through the remainder of the book.

4. Ibid., LDSCL. This quote is cited by Burton as CR1977Apr:115. The reader will take note that CR stands for "Conference Report," hence indicating that this was taken from the report of the General Conference of the LDS Church, which is held semiannually in the Tabernacle in Salt Lake City. As we will note, this gives special authority to the citation, as it comes from General Conference. This specific citation would come from the April Conference of 1977.

5. Ibid., 719, CR1910Oct:41, LDSCL.

6. Ibid., 718, LDSCL.

7. George Q. Cannon, *Gospel Truth: Discourses and Writings of President George Q. Cannon, First Counselor to Presidents John Taylor, Wilford Woodruff and Lorenzo Snow (1880–1901)*, (Salt Lake City: Zion's Book Store, 1957), 272, 309.

8. *Teachings of the Living Prophets: Student Manual Religion 333*, prepared by the Church Educational System, published by The Church of Jesus Christ of Latter-day Saints, 1982.

9. Ibid., 20.

10. Ibid. Note as well the citation of the *Journal of Discourses* in this current, official publication of the LDS Church. This will become significant later.

11. Found in Joseph Fielding Smith, ed., *Teachings of the Prophet Joseph Smith*, (Salt Lake City: Deseret Book Press, 1938), 278, LDSCL.

12. *Teachings of the Living Prophets*, 21.

13. Ibid.

14. Joseph Fielding Smith, *Doctrines of Salvation: Sermons and Writings of Joseph Fielding Smith*, Bruce R. McConkie, ed. (Salt Lake City: Bookcraft, 1954–1956), 3:203, LDSCL.

15. L. G. Otten and C. M. Caldwell, *Sacred Truths of the Doctrine and Covenants*, 2 vols. (Springville, Utah: LEMB, 1982), 1:197, LDSCL.

16. *Gospel Principles* (The Church of Jesus Christ of Latter-day Saints, 1981), 51–52.

17. Ibid., 52.

18. James E. Talmage, *Articles of Faith* (Salt Lake City: The Church of Jesus Christ of Latter-day Saints, 1978), 7, LDSCL.

19. Ezra Taft Benson, *Conference Report*, October 1963, 17, cited in *Conference Reports of The Church of Jesus Christ of Latter-day Saints* (Salt Lake City: The Church of Jesus Christ of Latter-day Saints, 1880, 1897–1970), LDSCL.

20. Ibid.

21. *Journal of Discourses*, George D. Watt, ed., 26 vols. (Liverpool: F. D. Richards, et al., 1854–1886), 13:95, LDSCL. This sermon was preached in the Tabernacle, January 2, 1870.

22. McKeever and Johnson, *Questions to Ask Your Mormon Friend*, 41.

23. Daniel H. Ludlow, ed. *The Encyclopedia of Mormonism*, 4 vols. (New York: Macmillan Publishing, 1992), vol. 4, "Temple Ordinances," LDSCL.

24. Bruce R. McConkie, *Mormon Doctrine*, 2nd ed., rev. (Salt Lake City: Bookcraft, 1966), p. 779, LDSCL.

25. Ezra Taft Benson, *Teachings of Ezra Taft Benson*, (Salt Lake City: Bookcraft, 1988), 250, 252, LDSCL.

26. Ibid., 140.

27. Blomberg and Robinson, *How Wide the Divide?*, 68.

28. Joseph Smith is singled out because he was the "prophet of the restoration." He is constantly cited (most often in "non-canonical" sources) in official LDS publications. Joseph Fielding Smith put it bluntly in his work *Doctrine of Salvation*, 1:188, LDSCL,

    CHURCH STANDS OR FALLS WITH JOSEPH SMITH. Mormonism, as it is called, must stand or fall on the story of Joseph Smith. He was either a prophet of God, divinely called, properly appointed and commissioned, or he was one of the biggest frauds this world has ever seen. There is no middle ground.

Chapter 3

1. See Louis Berkhof, *The History of Christian Doctrines* (Grand Rapids: Baker Book House, 1975), G. L. Prestige, *Fathers and Heretics* (London: SPCK, 1940), and Richard Norris, *The Christological Controversy* (Philadelphia: Fortress Press, 1980).

2. Blomberg and Robinson, *How Wide the Divide?* 20, 92, 129, 138.

3. Ibid., 142.

4. I discuss this issue thoroughly in *The Forgotten Trinity* (Minneapolis: Bethany House Publishers, 1998).

5. Ontology is the study of the nature of being; hence, ontological monotheism is the assertion that there is one *Being* of God, one divine essence. This is to be distinguished from any belief that asserts the existence of multiple divine *beings*. Mormonism specifically denies ontological monotheism, as we shall see.

6. I. D. E. Thomas, *A Puritan Golden Treasury* (Edinburgh: Banner of Truth Trust, 1989), 34, quotes the great Puritan John Flavel:

> I know there is nothing in the Word or in the works of God that is repugnant to sound reason, but there are some things in both which are opposite to carnal reason, as well as above right reason; and therefore our reason never shows itself more unreasonable than in summoning those things to its bar which transcend its sphere and capacity.

Likewise, Blaise Pascal expressed the same truth in his *Pensees*, here taken from *Mind on Fire: A Faith for the Skeptical and Indifferent*, James M. Houston, ed., (Minneapolis: Bethany House Publishers, 1997), 136:

> The last step that reason must take is to recognize that there are an infinite number of things beyond it. It is merely feeble if it does not go so far as the grasp this reality.

7. Greek: γεννηθέντα.

8. Greek: ὁμοούσιον, Latin: *consubstantialem*.

9. For a study of the text of the creed itself, see J. N. D. Kelly, *Early Christian Creeds*, (New York: Longman, Inc. 1972). For background on the Council of Nicaea and its deliberations, see James White, "What Really Happened at Nicaea?" *Christian Research Journal* (July/August 1997), 28–34.

Chapter 4

1. For example, Robert J. Matthews, writing in *Scriptures for the Modern World*, said,

> I think it is evident from many statements by the Prophet Joseph Smith that the term "translated correctly" must include difficulties of transmission—not only language problems, but copying, omitting, adding to, and every other phenomenon that might enter into the process of transmitting the original word from the mind of the author through all the phases of its perilous journey to the printed page of the Bible that we hold in our hands today. The Prophet Joseph Smith said: "I believe the Bible as it read when it came from the pen of the original writers. Ignorant translaters, careless transcribers, or designing and corrupt priests have committed many errors." Elsewhere he observed that many things had either been taken from the Bible or lost before it was compiled.

Cited in Paul R. Cheesman and C. Wilfred Griggs, eds., *Scriptures for the Modern World*, Religious Studies Center Monograph Series, Volume 11 (Provo, Utah: Religious Studies Center, Brigham Young University, 1984), 78, LDSCL.

2. This is the view of Mormon Apostle John Widstoe, *Evidences and Reconciliations*, 3 vols., 1943–1951, reprint (3 vols. in 1), Compiled by G. Homer Durham, (Salt Lake City: Bookcraft, 1960), 117, LDSCL:

> The Eighth Article of Faith declares that "We believe the Bible to be the word of God as far as it is translated correctly." This implies that there are mistranslations in the Bible. Moreover, the Prophet Joseph Smith,

from the beginning of his ministry, gave some time to revising passages in the Bible which had been translated incorrectly or so rendered as to make the meaning obscure.

3. The LDS Church officially uses the *King James Version* of the Bible, although Joseph Smith also produced the *"Inspired Version,"* which is now found in notes in the edition of the Scriptures published by the LDS Church. However, as the KJV is not the translation of choice of many evangelicals who would be reading this work (the *New International Version* being the currently most popular translation), I will be using an intermediate translation, one that stands between the KJV and NIV, the *New American Standard Bible, Updated Edition* (1995, Lockman Foundation). The added advantage is that the author is a critical consultant on this translation, allowing for more familiarity with the translation itself.

4. For a critique of the LDS position on the translation and transmission of the Bible, see my book, *Letters to a Mormon Elder* (Minneapolis: Bethany House Publishers, 1993), 21–44.

5. Bruce R. McConkie, *Mormon Doctrine*, 2nd ed., rev. (Salt Lake City: Bookcraft, 1966), 284–285, LDSCL.

6. Ezra Taft Benson, *Teachings of Ezra Taft Benson* (Salt Lake City: Bookcraft, 1988), 4, LDSCL. On page 101 of the same book, we read this strong statement:

> The first vision of the Prophet Joseph Smith is bedrock theology to the Church. The adversary knows this and has attacked Joseph Smith's credibility from the day he announced the visitation of the Father and the Son. You should always bear testimony to the truth of the First Vision. Joseph Smith did see the Father and the Son. They conversed with him as he said they did. Any leader who, without reservation, cannot declare his testimony that God and Jesus Christ appeared to Joseph Smith can never be a true leader, a true shepherd. If we do not accept this truth— if we have not received a witness about this great revelation—we cannot inspire faith in those whom we lead.

7. One of Mormonism's leading scholars, James Talmage (and a General Authority), said the following in the General Conference of April 1920:

> This Church, therefore, from its beginning, has been unique, for the organization of the Church was forecasted in this declaration that at the time of Joseph Smith's first vision there was no Church of Jesus Christ upon the earth; and I do not see why people should take issue with us for making that statement (CR1920Apr:103).

8. I noted a number of the historical problems with Mormonism in *Letters to a Mormon Elder*, 88–106. For a fuller treatment of this issue, see H. Michael Marquardt and Wesley P. Walters, *Inventing Mormonism* (Salt Lake City: Smith Research Associates, 1994), 1–41, and Jerald and Sandra Tanner, *Mormonism: Shadow or Reality?* (Salt Lake City: Utah Lighthouse Ministry, 1982), 143–162.

9. Joseph Fielding Smith, ed., *Teachings of the Prophet Joseph Smith* (Salt Lake City: Deseret Book Press, 1938), 370, LDSCL.

10. These include G. B. Arbaugh, *Revelation in Mormonism* (Chicago: University of Chicago Press, 1932); Boyd Kirkland, "Elohim and Jehovah in Mormonism and the Bible," *Dialogue: A Journal of Mormon Thought*, 19 (1986): 77–93; and Van Hale, "The Doctrinal Impact of the King Follet Discourse," *BYU Studies*, 18 (1978): no. 2, 213ff, LDSCL.

11. A concept that likewise developed over time in Smith's theology, it being absent from the time period encompassing the founding of the Church itself.

12. For example, Joseph Fielding Smith, *Answers to Gospel Questions* (Salt Lake City: Deseret Book, 1957–1963), 3:155, LDSCL.

13. In fact, Joseph Smith often altered previous revelations to "fit" later concepts. Note, for example, the wholesale insertion of material into what is now known as Section 27 of the *Doctrine and Covenants*. Over 400 words have been added or deleted from this one revelation, without any notification to the reader of the editing that was done by Smith himself.

14. This is the description given by the LDS scriptures themselves.

15. See Charles M. Larson, *By His Own Hand Upon Papyrus* (Grand Rapids: Institute for Religious Research, 1992) for a recent examination of the *Book of Abraham*. See also Jerald and Sandra Tanner, *Mormonism: Shadow or Reality?* 294–369, and *Letters to a Mormon Elder*, 157–168.

16. Hyrum M. Smith and Janne M. Sjodahl, *The Doctrine and Covenants Commentary Containing Revelations Given to Joseph Smith Jr., the Prophet, With an Introduction and Historical and Exegetical Notes*, rev. ed. (Salt Lake City: Deseret Book Company, 1954), 458, note, "Some take exception to the glorious doctrine here taught, that those who are called forth in the first resurrection are destined to become gods. There is no valid reason for objection." They then quote from Brigham Young (*Journal of Discourses*, 3:93), where Young said,

> Jesus is the elder Brother, and all the brethren shall come in for a share with Him; for an equal share according to their works and calling, and they shall be crowned with Him. Do you read of any such thing as the Savior praying that the Saints may be one with Him, as He and the Father are one? The Bible is full of such doctrine, and there is no harm in it, as long as it agrees with the New Testament. . . . The Lord created you and me for the purpose of becoming gods. . . . How many will become thus privileged? Those who honor the Father and the Son; those who receive the Holy Ghost, and magnify their calling; and are found pure and holy; they shall be crowned in the presence of the Father and the Son.

17. Interestingly, BYU scholar Stephen Robinson notes concerning this passage, "We believe this not because it is the clear teaching of the Bible but because it was the personal experience of the prophet Joseph Smith in his first vision and because the information is further clarified for us in modern revelation." Blomberg and Robinson, *How Wide the Divide?*, 78.

18. The story of how this portion of LDS scripture came into existence is most interesting. The reader is referred to Lyndon W. Cook, *The Revelations of the Prophet Joseph Smith* (Provo, Utah.: Seventy's Mission Bookstore, 1981), 293–295 for information. It should be noted that at this time the official LDS scriptures included Section 101, which read in part, "Inasmuch as this church of Christ has been reproached with the crimes of fornication and polygamy, we declare that we believe, that one man should have one wife; and one woman, but one husband, except in case of death, when either is at liberty to marry again." Section 132 was not published until 1852 and did not become a part of the *Doctrine and Covenants* until 1876. When it was added to the canon, Section 101 was removed.

19. One might consider well what is recorded in the introduction to the fifth volume of the *Documentary History of the Church*, 32–33, LDSCL:

On the morning of the 12th of July, 1843; Joseph and Hyrum Smith came into the office in the upper story of the brick store, on the bank of the Mississippi river. They were talking on the subject of plural marriage. Hyrum said to Joseph, "If you will write the revelation on celestial marriage, I will take it and read it to Emma, and I believe I can convince her of its truth, and you will hereafter have peace." Joseph smiled and remarked, "You do not know Emma as well as I do." Hyrum repeated his opinion, and further remarked, "The doctrine is so plain, I can convince any reasonable man or woman of its truth, purity and heavenly origin," or words to that effect. Joseph then said, "Well, I will write the revelation and we will see." He then requested me to get paper and prepare to write. Hyrum very urgently requested Joseph to write the revelation by means of the Urim and Thummim, but Joseph in reply said he did not need to, for he knew the revelation perfectly from beginning to end.

Joseph and Hyrum then sat down and Joseph commenced to dictate the revelation on celestial marriage, and I wrote it, sentence by sentence, as he dictated. After the whole was written, Joseph asked me to read it through, slowly and carefully, which I did, and he pronounced it correct. He then remarked that there was much more that he could write on the same subject, but what was written was sufficient for the present.

Hyrum then took the revelation to read to Emma. Joseph remained with me in the office until Hyrum returned. When he came back, Joseph asked him how he had succeeded. Hyrum replied that he had never received a more severe talking to in his life, that Emma was very bitter and full of resentment and anger.

Joseph quietly remarked, "I told you you did not know Emma as well as I did." Joseph then put the revelation in his pocket, and they both left the office.

The revelation was read to several of the authorities during the day. Toward evening Bishop Newel K. Whitney asked Joseph if he had any objections to his taking a copy of the revelation; Joseph replied that he had not, and handed it to him. It was carefully copied the following day by Joseph C. Kingsbury. Two or three days after the revelation was written, Joseph related to me and several others that Emma had so teased, and urgently entreated him for the privilege of destroying it, that he became so weary of her teasing, and to get rid of her annoyance, he told her she might destroy it and she had done so, but he had consented to her wish in this matter to pacify her, realizing that he knew the revelation perfectly, and could rewrite it at any time if necessary.

The copy made by Joseph C. Kingsbury is a true and correct copy of the original in every respect. The copy was carefully preserved by Bishop Whitney, and but few knew of its existence until the temporary location of the Camps of Israel at Winter Quarters, on the Missouri River, in 1846. (signed) WM. CLAYTON. Salt Lake City, Feb. 16th, 1874.

20. Quoted from the official web site of the Church of Jesus Christ of Latter-day Saints (http://www.lds.org/policy/family.html). On the same web page we find the following (http://www.lds.org/Global_Media_Guide/Core_Beliefs_and_Doctrines.html):

Godhead

A paramount doctrine of The Church of Jesus Christ of Latter-day Saints is a belief in God the Father, his Son, Jesus Christ, and the Holy Ghost. The three

make up the Godhead. They are one in purpose but separate in being.
21. See chapter 6.

Chapter 5

1. This being the statement that God is an exalted man. Blomberg and Robinson, *How Wide the Divide?*, 85.
2. James R. Clark, *Messages of the First Presidency of The Church of Jesus Christ of Latter-day Saints* [1833–1951], 6 vols. (Salt Lake City: Bookcraft, 1965–1975), 1:209, LDSCL, notes not only the tremendous importance of this sermon but sheds valuable light upon it as well:

   > The King Follett Sermon to the General Conference of the Church in April and the one following in this compilation given at a meeting in the Grove, east of the Temple in Nauvoo, Illinois, June 16, 1844, constitute the final summary of Joseph Smith before his death of the "Mormon" doctrine of God. Because both of these sermons as they stand in the DHC are not stenographic reports, the editor of the DHC felt it wise to make some explanatory remarks concerning certain statements in the sermons. These footnotes we have also included in the documents as we publish them here. The "Mormon" doctrine of the Godhead began with the First Vision of Joseph Smith in 1820 when God the Father, and His Son, Jesus Christ, appeared to Joseph Smith. From that time until 1844 Joseph Smith's direct contacts with heavenly messengers and beings seems never to have ceased. Much of what he sets forth in these two famous sermons he quite likely learned from his personal contacts with Deity and His messengers. He also says in the June 16, 1844 sermon that he learned some of the concepts of God found in the sermon "by translating the papyrus which is now in my house." The reference here is to the papyrus rolls of Abraham found in Egypt in 1821 and which Joseph Smith obtained in 1835, a partial translation of which appears in the *Book of Abraham* in *The Pearl of Great Price*. The sermons also give evidence of Joseph Smith's acquaintance with other ancient scriptures and of his study of Hebrew with a Jewish Rabbi in 1835–1836. Perhaps only one other doctrinal exposition of the Godhead in official LDS literature will stand alongside these two sermons and that is the Doctrinal Exposition by The First Presidency and the Twelve Apostles entitled *The Father and the Son*, issued June 30, 1916.

3. Joseph Fielding Smith, ed., *Teachings of the Prophet Joseph Smith*, 342, LDSCL. All following citations of the King Follett Discourse likewise come from this source.
4. Ibid., 345. Italics in the printed edition.
5. Many Christian philosophers have pointed out the obvious flaw in such a concept: If every God was once a man, then, what about the first God? If the law is inviolable, did not this God have to be a man before becoming a God? Some LDS have said that there was never a "first," but that the regression is eternal. Such an argument is irrational on many grounds. The simplest means of demonstrating this is to point out that the number of exalted beings is increasing as time passes. If the number increases with the passing of time, and cannot decrease (Gods don't cease to be Gods), then as we go back in time the number *decreases*. Eventually, one must arrive at the first God who began the process. It is fairly simple

to document that this idea has been found in LDS writings. Mormon Apostle Orson Pratt noted in his book *The Seer*, 132 (September 1853):

> We were begotten by our Father in Heaven; the person of our Father in Heaven was begotten by a still more ancient Father and so on, from generation to generation, from one heavenly world to another still more ancient, until our minds are wearied and lost in the multiplicity of generations and successive worlds, and as a last resort, we wonder in our minds how far back the genealogy extends, and how the first world was formed, and the first father was begotten. But why does man seek for a *first*, when revelation informs him that God's works are without beginning? Do you still seek for a *first* link where the chain is endless? Can you conceive of a *first* year in endless duration? . . . The Fullness of Truth, dwelling in an endless succession of past generations, would produce an endless succession of personal Gods, each possessing equal wisdom, power, and glory with all the rest. In worshipping any one of these Gods we worship the whole, and in worshipping the whole, we still worship but one God; for it is the same God who dwells in them all; the personages are only His different dwelling places.

It seems to me that Pratt here goes well into the realm of "speculation," though again the Mormon is left to deal with the difficulty of an apostle teaching on religious truth and yet, in so doing, not providing authoritative counsel and doctrine.

6. Ibid., 345–346. Italics in printed edition.
7. Thus, when LDS writers refer to God as "eternal," they are normally referring to God's existence *en toto*, that is, on the same level as saying, as they do, that *man* is "eternal."
8. K. Codell Carter, writing on the subject of "Godhood" in the *Encyclopedia of Mormonism* (New York: Macmillan Publishing, 1992), "Latter-day Saints believe that God achieved his exalted rank by progressing much as man must progress and that God is a perfected and exalted man." He then cites from the King Follett Discourse as evidence of this belief.
9. One will search in vain for such a passage in Scripture, even in the *Joseph Smith Translation*. It seems to be a confused conflation of a number of passages in John, none of which, in context, provide any support for the interpretation provided by Smith.
10. Most Mormons dislike the term polytheism due to its connections with "paganism" and the like. However, the term is most appropriate, especially in this context, where the phrase "plurality of gods" hardly does justice to the concepts here enunciated. We also note the fascinating use of the phrase "Christian polytheist" by BYU professor Eugene England in a fairly recent issue of *BYU Studies*, 29:3 (Summer 1989): 33:

> He begins his discussion with a quotation from 1 Corinthians 8:5–6: "There be gods many and lords many. But to us there is but one God the Father." Despite the context of this scripture—a discussion by Paul of belief in idols—Brigham Young, B. H. Roberts, Joseph Fielding Smith, and many others have used it as a brief explanation of how it is possible to be both a Christian polytheist (technically a henotheist) and a monotheist: how we can talk sometimes in an adventuresome mode about multiple orders of godhood, and how we can consider the advanced

spheres that exist in the infinities, and yet at the same time, without contradiction, we can talk in a worshipful mode about our one God and his perfect knowledge and supreme redemptive power in the sphere of our world.

Likewise, Donl Peterson and Charles Tate, *The Pearl of Great Price: Revelations From God*, Religious Studies Center Monograph Series (Provo, Utah: Religious Studies Center, Brigham Young University, 1989), 102, interestingly note:

> Mormonism is simultaneously monotheistic, tritheistic, and polytheistic. There is but one God, yet there is a Godhead of three, and beyond them, "gods many, and lords many" (1 Cor. 8:5). But regardless of the multiplicity of personages bearing divine titles, they are one in that priesthood which governs throughout the eternities.

11. Ibid., 348. Italics in printed edition.

12. See the review of Smith's effort by Sean Hahn, *Joseph Smith the Translator* (http://www.aomin.org/jsmith.html).

13. At this point Smith goes into a discussion of how the German translation is more accurate than the English because it has "Jacob" rather than "James" at places. Seemingly, Smith did not know German well enough to realize that "Jacobus" in German is the equivalent of "James" in English.

14. A quick glance at almost any recognized lexical source for the Hebrew language will show that Smith is in error. The term can be used in many ways, but in the Qal form it is used only of God's activity, and hence carries great theological import. Thomas E. McComiskey, in the *Theological Wordbook of the Old Testament* (Chicago: Moody Press, 1980), 1:127, notes that *bara* "differs from *yasar* 'to fashion' in that the latter primarily emphasizes the shaping of an object, while *bara* emphasizes the initiation of the object." Later in his article he writes,

> The limitation of this word to divine activity indicates that the area of meaning delineated by the root falls outside the sphere of human ability. Since the word never occurs with the object of the material, and since the primary emphasis of the word is on the newness of the created object, the word lends itself well to the concept of creation *ex nihilo*, although that concept is not necessarily inherent within the meaning of the word.

Hence, Smith's assertion that *bara* means "to organize" is highly misleading at best, and downright erroneous at worst.

15. B. H. Roberts noted that he felt the proper term here must be "coeternal" not "coequal." See the note, 353, LDSCL.

16. *Teachings of the Prophet Joseph Smith*, 369.

17. The KJV translation is, in fact, inferior at this point, as the better translation is "to His God and Father" (*NASB*). This passage contains an example of what is known as Granville Sharp's Rule. For a discussion of this rule of Greek grammar, see *The King James Only Controversy* (Minneapolis: Bethany House Publishers, 1995), 267–270.

18. *Teachings of the Prophet Joseph Smith*, 370.

19. In passing we should note a basic error in Smith's exegesis: As modern translations such as the *NASB* bring out, Paul is making reference to heathen or pagan gods: "For even if there are so-called gods whether in heaven or on earth, as indeed there are many gods and many lords. . . ." The Greek participle, λεγόμενοι, fully warrants the translation "so-called." These are deities that are *called*

deities but are, in fact, not. The entire context of the passage supports this understanding, for Paul argues that there is only one true God (v. 4) and then says that *Christians* know that there is only one God (v. 6) but not all men have this knowledge (v. 7). To place oneself with those who do *not* have this knowledge is to join the ranks of the heathen.

20. At this point Smith again addresses Genesis 1:1 and his assertion that this passage teaches a plurality of gods. He says,

> I will show from the Hebrew Bible that I am correct, and the first word shows a plurality of Gods; and I want the apostates and learned men to come here and prove to the contrary, if they can. An unlearned boy must give you a little Hebrew. *Berosheit baurau Eloheim ait aushamayeen vehau auraits,* rendered by King James' translators, "In the beginning God created the heaven and the earth." I want to analyze the word *Berosheit.* Rosh, the head; *Sheit,* a grammatical termination; the *Baith* was not originally put there when the inspired man wrote it, but it has been since added by an old Jew. *Baurau* signifies to bring forth; *Eloheim* is from the word *Eloi,* God, in the singular number; and by adding the word *heim,* it renders it Gods. It read first, "In the beginning the head of the Gods brought forth the Gods," or, as others have translated it, "The head of the Gods called the Gods together." I want to show a little learning as well as other fools.

The kindest thing that can be said of Smith's interpretation is that he could have used a few more years of instruction in Hebrew. Elohim is plural indeed; but it is most often used with a singular verb, and hence properly translated as a singular. *Bara* in Genesis 1:1 is singular, and hence is properly translated, "God created," not, "the Gods created."

21. *Teachings of the Prophet Joseph Smith,* 372.

22. Daniel H. Ludlow, ed., *The Encyclopedia of Mormonism,* 4 vols. (New York: Macmillan Publishing, 1992), Appendix 4, LDSCL. The pronouncement is signed by the members of the First Presidency, Joseph F. Smith, John R. Winder, and Anthon H. Lund.

23. The current LDS Hymnal contains a selection, number 292, titled *O My Father.* It is a popular tune, as it also appears in the LDS publication *Gospel Principles* (p. 326). The third line also makes mention of the heavenly Mother. It reads in part,

> *In the heav'ns are parents single?*
> *No, the thought makes reason stare!*
> *Truth is reason; truth eternal*
> *Tells me I've a mother there.*

The next line goes on to say,

> *When I lay this mortal by,*
> *Father, Mother, may I meet you*
> *in your royal courts on high?*

24. *The Encyclopedia of Mormonism,* Appendix 4, LDSCL.

25. For those unfamiliar with the LDS Endowment ceremonies, we note that actors on a stage are portraying (that is, in the old style—in the vast majority of temples today, movies present these scenes) various events, such as Creation, the Fall, etc. Temple patrons are viewing these films seated, dressed in their Temple garments. At certain points they stand to make various signs and symbols repre-

senting various oaths being taken, which fit into the dialogue taking place before them on the stage or movie screen.

26. Cited in Jerald and Sandra Tanner, *Evolution of the Mormon Temple Ceremony: 1842–1990* (Salt Lake City: Utah Lighthouse Ministry, 1990), 65.

27. For a full discussion of Michael, Adam, and the Adam-God doctrine, *see* Jerald and Sandra Tanner, *Mormonism: Shadow or Reality?*, 173ff.

28. Ibid., 79–80.

29. Westminster Confession of Faith, cited from *BibleWorks 3.5*, Hermeneutika Software, electronic version, copyright © 1991 by M. S. Bushell.

Chapter 6

1. *Search These Commandments* (Salt Lake City: The Church of Jesus Christ of Latter-day Saints, 1984). It carries the copyright of the Corporation of the President of the Church of Jesus Christ of Latter-day Saints.

2. Compare, however, Isaiah 48:11.

3. *Doctrines of the Gospel* (Salt Lake City: The Church of Jesus Christ of Latter-day Saints, 1986), 7–8.

4. The person familiar with LDS theology will find it interesting that in the intervening material there is a citation of Bruce R. McConkie's Fireside Talk at BYU titled *Our Relationship With the Lord*. This talk is well known, for in it McConkie counseled against seeking a personal relationship with the Lord Jesus Christ. The impossible position the LDS are placed in by their theology of God is well illustrated in McConkie's attempts to explain who it is that Mormons worship and how Jesus is not to be worshiped as the Father is. This leads to a direct violation of the commandment to worship Jehovah alone.

5. CR1898Apr:19, LDSCL.

6. CR1901Oct:91, LDSCL.

7. CR1902Oct:81, LDSCL.

8. CR1910Apr:78, LDSCL.
   Note the same emphasis in Orson F. Whitney, CR1920Oct:36:

   > The gospel is the plan of eternal progression, and perfection is its goal. Apart from our ancestors who figured in the former dispensations, neither we nor they can attain perfection. But by unity, which brings power, and by faith, which makes all things possible, the glorious end can be achieved.

   The same speaker presented the same emphasis seven years later from the pulpit at Conference (CR1927Oct:147):

   > Answering now the question; How are the principles of the gospel made available and effectual for man's salvation and exaltation? It is through the Fall and the Redemption. "Adam fell that men might be"— that a race of Spirits might tabernacle in the flesh, and thus become souls, capable of endless increase, of eternal progression and exaltation. But the fall brought death—eternal death, which had to be overcome before these spirits, these souls, God's sons and daughters, could fulfill their heaven-decreed destiny and go on to perfection.

9. CR1918Oct:87, LDSCL.

10. Joseph F. Merrill, CR1937Oct:73, LDSCL. So likewise the same speaker returned

to this topic in 1945 (CR1945Apr:113) and said,

> Yes, the Church teaches the fact that each of us is a child of God, both in the spirit and in the flesh. Since in the realm of life, like begets like, we normally must possess, even though in ultra-microscopic quantities, the attributes of God our Father. And a characteristic teaching of the Church is that "as God now is man may become"—a statement in poetic language of our magnificent doctrine of eternal progression. Man is in very deed the acme of creation.

11. CR1941Oct:66, LDSCL.
12. CR1941Apr:104, LDSCL.
13. CR1945Apr:73, LDSCL.
14. CR1948Oct:15, LDSCL.
15. Another example is found in the words of Apostle Delbert Stapley, CR1961Apr:66:

> In the important doctrinal discourse known as the "King Follett Sermon" the Prophet Joseph Smith, referring to those who "shall be heirs of God and joint-heirs with Jesus Christ," described joint-heirship as inheriting the same power, the same glory, and the same exaltation, until an individual ascends to the station of Godhood and rises to the throne of eternal power, sharing the rewards with all the faithful who have preceded him.

16. CR1951Apr:37, LDSCL.
17. CR1952Apr:24, LDSCL.
18. CR1956Apr:106, LDSCL.
19. CR1958Apr:50–51, LDSCL.
20. CR1964Oct:29, LDSCL.
21. CR1964Oct:49–50, LDSCL.
22. CR1967Oct:122, LDSCL.
23. "Conference Issues 1970–1987," *The Church News* (Salt Lake City: Deseret News Publishing Company), 9.
24. Ibid., October 1994, 15.

Chapter 7

1. Lorenzo Snow, *Teachings of Lorenzo Snow*, compiled by Clyde J. Williams (Salt Lake City: Bookcraft, 1984), viii.
2. Orson Pratt, *Journal of Discourses*, ed. George D. Watt, et al. (Liverpool: F. D. Richards, et al., 1854–1886), 2:345, LDSCL.
3. Orson Pratt, *The Seer*, n.p., n.d., 23.
4. Parley P. Pratt, *Key to the Science of Theology*, 10th ed. (Salt Lake City: Deseret Book, 1948), 33, 37, LDSCL.
5. George Q. Cannon, *Gospel Truth: Discourses and Writings of President George Q. Cannon, First Counselor to Presidents John Taylor, Wilford Woodruff, and Lorenzo Snow* (1880–1901), compiled by Jerreld L. Newquist (Salt Lake City: Zion's Book Store, 1957), 1:9, LDSCL.
6. Ibid., 1:131, LDSCL.
7. Ibid., 1:129, LDSCL.
8. Ibid.

9. Ibid., 1:131, LDSCL.

10. Wilford Woodruff, *Journal of Discourses*, 6:120, LDSCL.

11. Bruce R. McConkie, *Mormon Doctrine* (Salt Lake City: Bookcraft, 1966), 239, LDSCL.

12. B. H. Roberts, *The Seventy's Course in Theology, Fourth Year* (Salt Lake City: *Deseret News*, 1911), 70, LDSCL.

13. Ibid., 70–71.

14. B. H. Roberts, *The Seventy's Course in Theology, Third Year* (Salt Lake City: *Deseret News*, 1911), 193, LDSCL.

15. B. H. Roberts, *The Mormon Doctrine of Deity: The Roberts-Van Der Donckt Discussion to Which Is Added a Discourse, Jesus Christ: The Revelation of God by B. H. Roberts, Also A Collection of Authoritative Mormon Utterances on the Being and Nature of God* (Salt Lake City: *Deseret News*, 1903), 130, LDSCL.

16. James E. Talmage, *Articles of Faith*, 12th ed., rev. (Salt Lake City: The Church of Jesus Christ of Latter-day Saints, 1978), 470, LDSCL.

17. James E. Talmage, *The Vitality of Mormonism* (Boston: The Gorham Press, 1919), 245, LDSCL.

18. John A. Widtsoe, *A Rational Theology As Taught by The Church of Jesus Christ of Latter-day Saints* (Salt Lake City: Deseret Book Company, 1965), 66, LDSCL.

19. Ibid., 66–67, LDSCL.

20. *Ensign*, June 1985, 16.

21. An example of this that also explains why he is hardly the favorite of many who teach at BYU is found in a letter he wrote to Professor Eugene England on February 19, 1981. This famous letter, in which McConkie admitted that Brigham Young contradicted himself on the matter of the "Adam-God doctrine," also contained the following enlightening paragraph:

> If it is true, as I am advised, that you speak on this subject of the progression of God at firesides and elsewhere, you should cease to do so. If you give other people copies of the material you sent me, with the quotations it contains, you should cease to do so. It is not in your province to set in order the Church or to determine what its doctrines shall be. It is axiomatic among us to know that God has given apostles and prophets "for the edifying of the body of Christ," and that their ministry is to see that "we henceforth be no more children, tossed to and fro, and carried about with every wind of doctrine, by the slight of men, and cunning craftiness, whereby they lie in wait to deceive" (Eph. 4:11–16). This means, among other things, that it is my province to teach to the Church what the doctrine is. You do not have a divine commission to correct me or any of the Brethren. The Lord does not operate that way. If I lead the Church astray, that is my responsibility, but the fact still remains that I am the one appointed with all the rest involved so to do. The appointment is not given to the faculty at Brigham Young University or to any of the members of the Church. The Lord's house is a house of order and those who hold the keys are appointed to proclaim the doctrines (p. 8).

22. Bruce R. McConkie, *Mormon Doctrine*, 511, LDSCL.

23. Ibid., 576–577.

24. Indeed, McConkie said the same thing in other contexts. The seeming answer to the contradiction is that there are different levels of "worship."

25. A popular expression of this is found in *Two Letters to a Baptist Minister*:

We solemnly plead guilty to believing in many Gods. If this is a crime it is time for a new translation of the Holy Scriptures. Does not the good book say "and God said, let us make man in our own image?" What are you going to do with the words "us" and "our'" in this Scripture? Does this not prove a plurality of Gods? (Ben E. Rich, ed., *Scrapbook of Mormon Literature*, 2 vols. (Chicago: Henry C. Etten & Co., 1913), 2:128, LDSCL.

26. Ibid., 238–239.
27. Ibid., 465–466.
28. Daniel H Ludlow, ed., *The Encyclopedia of Mormonism*, 4 vols. (New York: Macmillan Publishing, 1992).
29. Ibid., vol. 2, "God the Father," LDSCL.
30. Ibid, vol. 1, "Doctrine," LDSCL.
31. Ibid.
32. Ibid.
33. This article can be obtained at the following web site: http://www.sfgate.com/cgi-bin/chronicle/article.cgi?file=SC36289.DTL&directory=/chronicle/archive/1997/04/13.
34. A transcript of the report can be found at the following web site: http://www.pbs.org/newshour/bb/religion/july-dec97/mormons_7-18.html.
35. The article can be found at the following web site: http://www.pathfinder.com/@@4IOIsQYA8e4ehlWz/time/magazine/1997/dom/970804/religion.kingdom_come_.html

Chapter 8

1. English Bible translators normally indicate the Tetragrammaton, יהוה, *YHWH, Yahweh*, through the use of the small-caps version, LORD. This is significant in Mormonism, for as we have seen, the LDS Church says Elohim (God the Father) is one God, while Jehovah (the LORD) is a second God, actually begotten by the first. "Jehovah" is a very bad mispronunciation of "Yahweh" that continues in English solely due to tradition and usage, nothing more. There is absolutely no basis in the Bible whatsoever for the distinction found in modern LDS theology between Elohim and Jehovah; in fact, many passages, such as Deuteronomy 4:35, say, "Yahweh, He is Elohim; there is no other besides Him (singular)" (see also 4:39; 1 Kings 18:39; Psalm 100:3). The Bible applies passages about Yahweh to the Father (Isaiah 53:6, for example, as well as Matthew 22:44; Psalm 110:1, etc.), the Son (John 12:39–41; Isaiah 6:1; Hebrews 1:10–12; Psalm 102:25–27, etc.), and the Spirit (who is consistently called the Spirit of Yahweh, as in Isaiah 11:2).

2. With reference to the doctrine of the Trinity, it should be noted that the name Yahweh is used of the Father, the Son, and the Spirit. Hence, the divine name is used of the one *Being* of God that is shared fully by three *Persons*, providing another testimony to the Trinity in the biblical text itself. See the discussion in my work on that subject, *The Forgotten Trinity* (Minneapolis: Bethany House Publishers, 1998).

3. The reader will note that in Mormonism there is a greater God than Yahweh, and that is Elohim, who is likewise worshiped. The result of this can only be a violation of the commandment, repeated often in Scripture, to worship Yahweh alone.

4. Interestingly, some LDS apologists like to utilize liberalism and extreme types of form-criticism to get around the united testimony of the Old Testament. I look at the Hebrew text with the same respect shown by Jesus of Nazareth, and personally find His views to be far more reliable than the current trend in culture or "scholarship." This is not to say I buy into the anti-intellectualism of a wide spectrum of the Christian church, for I do not. But I also believe that a large portion of "religious scholarship" is far more concerned about being accepted in our culture than it is about being honest with God's truth. For an example of believing scholarship in this area, see Walter Kaiser Jr., *Toward an Old Testament Theology* (Grand Rapids, Mich.: Acadamie Books, Zondervan Publishing House, 1978).

5. The LXX rendering is not only an excellent translation of the Hebrew but is also significant for the study of Jesus' deity in the New Testament. I believe Jesus purposefully draws from this very passage in John 13:19 to identify himself as the "I AM," using the Greek phrase ἐγώ εἰμί (*ego eimi*). Compare Greek text at John 13:19.

6. The "multiple eternities" argument is addressed in chapter 11, p. 179.

7. Some Mormons have been confused by this terminology, and, desperately searching for evidences of polytheism in the Old Testament, have insisted that there are two gods mentioned here—one, the King of Israel, and the other, the Redeemer, the LORD of hosts. However, the text does not allow such an interpretation. The Hebrew is plain in saying that the one God, the LORD, is in view, who is described by two phrases, "the King of Israel" and Israel's "Redeemer."

8. The KJV rendering, "God," is simply a dynamic interpretive translation of the Hebrew term צוּר (*zor*), "Rock," possibly influenced by the LXX's rendering of the passage.

9. The Hebrew of the text is directly contradictory to LDS theology, for it reads, "וּמִבַּלְעָדַי אֵין אֱלֹהִים," which is literally translated, "Aside from Me (singular) there is no God (Elohim)." Since this is Yahweh speaking, we have a direct statement that there is no Elohim other than Yahweh. Yet, in Mormon theology, Elohim is the Father of Yahweh in a spiritual preexistence.

10. The NASB translation is literal and brings out the emphasis found in the Greek text itself: ἐδουλεύσατε τοῖς φύσει μὴ οὖσιν θεοῖς·, that is, the Galatians had served those "which by nature are not being gods." There is only one God *by nature*, and men well know this. (Romans 1:18–23)

11. Dr. Blomberg, in his dialogue with Dr. Robinson in *How Wide the Divide?* rightly noted that evangelicals (I would have said simply Christians) "are determined to preserve the distinction between the Creator and the creation, particularly in light of Paul's teaching in Romans 1:18–32 that the heart of idolatry and rebellion against God is to worship the creature rather than the Creator" (p. 97). When responding to this issue, Robinson quite plainly confessed, "This may be the heart of the disagreement between us, for Latter-day Saints maintain that God's work is to *remove* the distinctions and barriers between us and to make us what God is" (p. 81). Craig L. Blomberg and Stephen E. Robinson, *How Wide the Divide?* (Downers Grove, Ill.: InterVarsity Press, 1997).

12. Some LDS apologists refer to the incarnation of Christ as evidence of the reality that God can, indeed, be a man. Yet this passage, and many others, show the error of this use of the Incarnation. It has been well said that the Gospel is not that men can become gods, but that God became a man in Christ Jesus. That is, the Incarnation is, like God himself, *unique*. God, as to His being, is eternal and

unchanging. The Incarnation did not change God's *being*, nor did it mean that God was once a man.

13. The *Book of Abraham* in *The Pearl of Great Price* gives as the location of God's dwelling a star named "Kolob."

14. The KJV translation, "God is a spirit," misses the point of the anarthrous use of "spirit" here. "God is spirit" = πνεῦμα ὁ θεός, where the position of the predicate nominative (the verb being assumed) tells us something *about* God, that is, it is descriptive.

15. It is relevant, then, to point out the conflict between the claim in *D & C* 130:22, that God the Father has a body of flesh and bones as tangible as any man's, and the definition provided by the Lord Jesus:

> "See My hands and My feet, that it is I Myself; touch Me and see, for a spirit does not have flesh and bones as you see that I have" (Luke 24:39).

16. "I fill" = אֲנִי מָלֵא. This does not say "My influence fills," but *I* fill.

17. "Contain you" = יְכַלְכְּלוּ, using the second person masculine suffix, "you." The text does not say, "Your influence."

18. Invisible: ἀοράτῳ, normally rendered "not capable of being seen." "The only God" = μόνῳ θεῷ, a plain statement of monotheism in the New Testament.

19. The Greek refers to an inability to be seen: ὃν εἶδεν οὐδεὶς ἀνθρώπων οὐδὲ ἰδεῖν δύναται.

20. Wayne Grudem, *Systematic Theology: An Introduction to Biblical Theology* (Grand Rapids: Zondervan, 1994), 187.

21. Remember again that in Mormonism, the "main" God of the Godhead is Elohim, not Jehovah, yet Jehovah says you shall not worship any other God!

22. This includes the various anthropomorphisms in the Bible, phrases that speak of God's eyes, ears, hands, and the like. The vast majority of these are self-evidently metaphorical, such as cases in which God "bares His arm" and destroys nations or where the "blast of His nostrils" parted the Red Sea. Most modern LDS apologists who are scholarly in their outlook do not attempt to press these phrases, recognizing that this forces them to deal with God being a consuming fire (Exodus 24:17; Hebrews 12:29) or a very large bird with wings (Exodus 19:4; Psalm 17:8).

23. Hebrew: הַפְּכְכָם

24. Willem A. VanGemeren, "Psalms" in *The Expositor's Bible Commentary*, Frank E. Gaebelein, ed. (Grand Rapids, Mich.: Zondervan, 1991), 377.

25. Indeed, though it takes us a little beyond our limitations in this study, the very meaning of "holiness" is connected with this idea of "completely other." God is utterly unlike anything else, and hence is holy.

26. Hebrew: וּמֵעוֹלָם עַד־עוֹלָם; *me olam ad olam.* There is no stronger way to express ongoing, limitless existence than this. Often LDS apologists will attempt to say that the Hebrew language does not strictly have a word for "eternity," and on a linguistic basis, they are right. However, it does not follow that one cannot express the *concept* through a *combination* of words. *Olam* may, in some contexts, not mean "eternal" in an absolute sense. But meaning is always determined by context, and here the context leaves us with no doubt. The psalmist is contrasting the created nature of the world with the uncreated and hence *eternal* nature of the Creator, Yahweh. As Franz Delitzsch put it,

> The Lord was God before the world was—that is the first assertion of verse 2; His divine existence reaches out of the unlimited past into the

unlimited future—this is the second. . . . This is also seen from . . . verse 4, the supra-temporality of God or the omnipresence of God in time . . . that God as the Almighty (אֵל), in the midst of this change of generations, which is His work, remains Himself eternally the same. This ever the same, absolute existence has its ground herein, that time, although God fills it up with His working, is no limitation to Him. . . . Thus it is to God with a thousand years: they do not last long to Him; they do not affect Him; as the close of them, as at the beginning, He is the Absolute One (אֵל). Time is as nothing to Him, the Eternal One. (C. F. Keil and F. Delitzsch, *Commentary on the Old Testament: Psalms* [Grand Rapids, Mich.: Eerdmans, 1982], 50–52).

27. The Septuagint (LXX) has a striking rendering, ἀπὸ τοῦ αἰῶνος ἕως τοῦ αἰῶνος σὺ εἶ, "from the age until the age you are." Also, it is significant that the LXX provides a contrast between the world, which comes into existence at a point in time, and the timeless God, who simply "is" (aorist tense verb vs. present).

28. Dr. Blomberg noted in *How Wide the Divide?* that God's immutability is under question in "evangelical" circles. He wrote,

> Evangelicals, at the same time, are increasingly expressing dissatisfaction with their classical formulations of doctrines such as the immutability, impassibility and simplicity of God. Spurred on in part by parallel developments in other modern theologies, various evangelical theologians are now speaking of God's openness, God's suffering, God's ability to change his mind, God's choice to remain ignorant of certain future events so as to allow his creatures genuine freedom, growth in God's Being that inevitably comes by interaction with those creatures, and the like. Some evangelicals, of course, object for various reasons to all such suggestions, and, as in Mormonism, stereotypes held at the grassroots level are the last to be changed. In what ways both groups will continue to develop remains to be seen (p. 109).

I question the identification of someone as truly "evangelical" who would promote the idea that God is not immutable. I do not include such concepts as "process theology" in the realm of evangelical belief. Norman Geisler has well styled such movements as "neotheism" in his book *Creating God in the Image of Man?* (Minneapolis: Bethany House Publishers, 1997). I have likewise criticized this movement in my book *God's Sovereign Grace* (Southbridge, Mass.: Crowne Publications, 1991), 123–152. Mormonism may well continue to "develop," but it is not development in evangelicalism to show a willingness to compromise or abandon the plain teaching of Scripture regarding the perfection of God's being due to "developments" in other areas of "theology." Theology separated from Scripture is nothing more than man's musings in the darkness.

29. Christian teachers have pointed out for two thousand years that the many passages that speak of God "repenting" or the like must be understood from *our* perspective as time-bound creatures, not from *God's* perspective, as the Eternal One. The ongoing work of God in time does not change—but our experience of it does, and for this reason at times it *seems* God has "changed" in some way in His actions in the world. For example, when Moses is called to intercede as the leader of the people of Israel, and God relents of His stated intention to destroy the people, this does not present a contradiction in Scripture. Instead, God's actions train and grow Moses as a leader, which was God's intention all along. Many

other examples could be noted. For an exceptional discussion of this issue, see John Calvin, *Institutes of the Christian Religion*, Book 1, Chapter 17.

30. Hebrew: לֹא אִישׁ אֵל, literally, "Not a man (is) God." Someone might say, "But this is only in the sense that He does not lie or go back on His word." Quite true—but the reason He does not lie and go back on His word is because He is fundamentally and ontologically *different* than the creature, man.

31. Hebrew: אֵל אָנֹכִי וְלֹא־אִישׁ, literally, "God I am, and not *ish*, man."

32. *See* Francis J. Beckwith and Stephen E. Parrish, *The Mormon Concept of God: A Philosophical Analysis* (Lewiston, N.Y.: E. Mellen Press, 1991).

33. Hebrew for "abomination" is תּוֹעֵבָה.

34. Jeremiah 10:11 is the only verse in Jeremiah's prophecy that is written in Aramaic rather than Hebrew. As a result, many feel it is a gloss or interpolation. However, a much more logical reason exists. Charles Feinberg notes, "It should, however, be remembered that Aramaic was the lingua franca of the day; so the pagan idolators would be able to read the judgment of God on their idolatry." And in a textual note, he also says,

> No one has ever explained why an interpolator would introduce it here. It was a proverbial saying; so it was given in the language of the people (so Streane). The best explanation appears to be that it is in Aramaic so that the exiles could use these very words as a reply to solicitations by the Chaldeans to join in their idol worship (Charles L. Feinberg, "Jeremiah" in *The Expositor's Bible Commentary*, 6:449–450).

35. Hebrew: לְבַדִּי.

36. Hebrew: וְיֹצֵר רוּחַ־אָדָם בְּקִרְבּוֹ, literally rendered by the NASB.

37. Westminster Shorter Catechism, cited from *BibleWorks 3.5*, Hermeneutika Software, electronic version, copyright © 1991 by M. S. Bushell.

38. Craig L. Blomberg and Stephen E. Robinson, *How Wide the Divide?* (Downers Grove, Ill.: InterVarsity Press, 1997), 80.

39. I also note that the term "image" is used in the New Testament many times when it cannot possibly refer to "physical qualities" as Robinson here asserts. For example, in Romans 8:29 the elect are said to be conformed to the "image" of Christ. Does this mean that as we are sanctified, we start to look more and more like a Jewish male? Or do we "look like Christ" in a *metaphorical* sense, in that we act like Him, think like Him, love like Him, etc.?

40. Wayne Grudem, *Systematic Theology: An Introduction to Biblical Doctrine* (Grand Rapids, Mich.: Zondervan, 1994), 442–443.

41. The current edition of the LDS scriptures does not note this change. However, it appears in the edition published by the RLDS Church titled *Joseph Smith's "New Translation" of the Bible* (Independence, Mo.: Herald Publishing House, 1970), 29. That this reading was known to early LDS leaders is proven by its appearance in John Taylor's *An Examination Into and an Elucidation of the Great Principle of the Mediation and Atonement of Our Lord and Savior Jesus Christ* (Salt Lake City: *Deseret News*, 1882), chap. 11, LDSCL. Taylor specifically quotes it as follows: "The Father accepted the offer of His well-beloved Son and proceeded to carry out the decision of the Council, and, as we are informed in the Bible (*Inspired Translation*), God said to His Only Begotten, 'Let us make man in our image, after our likeness, and it was so.' " This matches the rendering in the RLDS source word-for-word.

42. We acknowledge that Smith would not have yet developed the idea of the cor-

poreality of God the Father at the point where he worked on the text of Genesis. This only shows the problems inherent with a prophet who changes his theology over time.

Chapter 9

1. We should note that this passage is not teaching that the Father is the Son. The doctrine of the Trinity expressly denies the identification of the Father and the Son as one *person*. The verb used in this passage is plural; hence, it can literally be translated "I and the Father, *we* are one." LDS often assume that Christians are modalists, who believe the Father and the Son are one *person*, when this is untrue. The issue is always one *Being* shared by three *persons*.
2. In fact, the common LDS usage of the passage is directly contradicted by a leading LDS authority, James Talmage, in his book *Jesus the Christ*, 15th ed., rev. (Salt Lake City: The Church of Jesus Christ of Latter-day Saints, 1977), 501, LDSCL. Note Talmage's words:

    > Divinely Appointed Judges Called "Gods."—In Psalm 82:6, judges invested by divine appointment are called "gods." To this scripture the Savior referred in His reply to the Jews in Solomon's porch. Judges so authorized officiated as the representatives of God and are honored by the exalted title "gods." Compare the similar appellation applied to Moses (Ex. 4:16; 7:1). Jesus Christ possessed divine authorization, not through the word of God transmitted to Him by man, but as an inherent attribute. The inconsistency of calling human judges "gods," and of ascribing blasphemy to the Christ who called Himself the Son of God, would have been apparent to the Jews but for their sin darkened minds.

3. In light of the fact that Stephen was "filled with the Holy Spirit," we might well consider the fact that when we speak in a way that is pleasing to God, we may well offend many of those around us. God's truth is often offensive to those who embrace falsehood.
4. Exodus 15:6, 12; Deuteronomy 33:2; Job 40:14; Psalm 16:8, 11; 17:7; 18:35; 20:6; 21:8; 44:3; 45:4, 9; 48:10; 60:5; 63:8; 73:23; 77:10; 78:54; 80:15, 17; 89:13; 98:1; 108:6; 109:6, 31; 110:1; 118:15–16; 138:7; Proverbs 3:16; Ecclesiastes 10:2; Isaiah 41:10; 48:13; Habakkuk 2:16; 3:4; and in the New Testament, Matthew 26:64, where the phrase is "the right hand of power."
5. Craig L. Blomberg and Stephen E. Robinson, *How Wide the Divide?* (Downers Grove, Ill.: InterVarsity Press, 1997).
6. Ibid., 80.
7. Ibid., 81.
8. For in-depth discussion of the relevant passages, such as John 1:1; Colossians 1:15–18; etc., see my work on the subject, *The Forgotten Trinity* (Minneapolis: Bethany House, 1998).

Chapter 10

1. I fully believe in the perseverance of true, saving faith. I simply cannot have infallible knowledge that any one of my brothers and sisters has it. God has not given me that ability. I can *grow* in my confidence over time, but the final test of whether faith is true or not is its perseverance.

Chapter 11

1. Excluding the written "debate" of sorts between the Catholic Van der Donckt and B. H. Roberts, which took place early in this century.

2. Indeed, one major criticism of the work by both parties would be a rather heavy dose of what one might call a "postmodern" tendency to level out all issues of truth. In the joint conclusion to the book a question is asked in the following form: "Is 'justification by faith' or 'justification by faith *alone*' the more appropriate summary of the Bible's teaching on that topic?" "More appropriate"? The Reformers would gasp at such a view of the issue. It is not a matter of "more appropriate," it is a matter of "true or false." That which is "more appropriate" will lead to eternal life, that which is "less appropriate" to eternal damnation. Somehow the term "appropriate" just doesn't *seem appropriate* at such a juncture.

3. The reader will grant me one indulgence, however, at this point, as one particular assertion of this book strikes very close to home for me in light of my work in textual criticism and Bible translation (as seen in my book *The King James Only Controversy*). *How Wide the Divide?* provides a joint statement regarding the topic of Scripture. At one point we read, "We judge that changes or corrections in successive copies and editions of the LDS scriptures are not sufficient reason to judge those scriptures inauthentic, since the biblical texts themselves were subjected to a similar process" (p. 75). It must be said that the processes inherent in the transmission of the biblical text over time were *fundamentally* different from the purposeful process of editing that took place in the text of the *Book of Mormon* and especially the *Doctrine and Covenants*. It should be remembered that not only were entire sections of the *D & C* removed over time but massive changes, involving hundreds of words, took place within a few years of the giving of various of the revelations. The largest textual variant in all the New Testament (Mark 16:9–20) pales into insignificance beside the *purposeful* and often *doctrinal* editing of the Mormon scriptures.

4. Craig L. Blomberg and Stephen E. Robinson, *How Wide the Divide?* (Downers Grove, Ill.: InterVarsity Press, 1997), 77.

5. Ibid., 162–163.

6. Ibid., 163.

7. Ibid., 86.

8. Indeed, this writer is not aware of a single occurrence of the phrase "exalted by grace" in any sermon or writing of a General Authority. Instead, Joseph Smith taught, "Knowledge saves a man, and in the world of spirits a man cannot be exalted but by knowledge" (*Teachings of the Prophet Joseph Smith*, 357). Exaltation is consistently made a matter of works, obedience, and worthiness in LDS theology. As George Q. Cannon said, "And I obeyed the doctrine of patriarchal marriage, upon the same principle, because I knew that it was a principle of salvation and of exaltation, and that if I would be exalted in the presence of God I must obey the law" (*Journal of Discourses* 24:147). Robinson's emphasis on grace may well be commendable in a relative sense, but it is *not* what the Church has taught from its inception.

9. CR1938Oct:42, LDSCL.

10. CR1949Apr:90, LDSCL.

11. *Family Home Evenings* (Salt Lake City: The Church of Jesus Christ of Latter-day Saints, 1972), 125–126.

12. Daniel H. Ludlow, ed., *The Encyclopedia of Mormonism*, 4 vols. (New York: Mac-

millan Publishing, 1992), Appendix 4, LDSCL.

13. Stephen E. Robinson, *Are Mormons Christians?* (Salt Lake City: Bookcraft, 1991), 66, 68.
14. *How Wide the Divide?*, 90.
15. See the excellent discussion of God's eternal existence in Wayne Grudem, *Systematic Theology: An Introduction to Biblical Doctrine* (Grand Rapids, Mich.: Zondervan, 1994), 160–175, and James P. Boyce, *Abstract of Systematic Theology*, reprint, (Escondido, Calif.: Den Dulk Christian Foundation, 1887), 65–85.
16. *How Wide the Divide?*, 92.
17. Ibid., 88.
18. Cited in *Search These Commandments* (Salt Lake City: The Church of Jesus Christ of Latter-day Saints, 1984), 153.
19. This dissertation is available for download via the Internet from: http://www.umi.com/hp/support/dexplorer/.
20. David Lamont Paulsen, "Comparative Coherency of Mormon (Finitistic) and Classical Theism," Doctoral Dissertation, University of Michigan, 1975, 74–75.
21. Ibid., 76.
22. Ibid., 79.
23. Ibid.
24. *How Wide the Divide?*, 132.
25. Eugene England, BYU Studies, vol. 29, no. 3, 33.
26. *How Wide the Divide?*, 195.

Chapter 12

1. Daniel C. Peterson and Stephen D. Ricks, *Offenders for a Word: How Anti-Mormons Play Word Games to Attack the Latter-day Saints* (Salt Lake City: Aspen Books, 1992).
2. Ibid., 129–131.
3. Ibid., 129.
4. Craig L. Blomberg and Stephen E. Robinson, *How Wide the Divide?* (Downers Grove, Ill.: InterVarsity Press, 1997), 135–136.
5. Brigham Young, *Journal of Discourses*, ed. George D. Watt, 26 vols. (Liverpool: F. D. Richards, et al., 1854–1886), 11:122, LDSCL.
6. Ibid., 8:115, LDSCL.
7. Ibid., 1:50–51, LDSCL.
8. Ibid., 4:218, LDSCL.
9. This is a concept that developed after Joseph Smith's life, as Smith referred to the Father as "Jehovah." Mormon theology regarding the names Elohim and Jehovah is quite muddled, as the Bible uses the two terms of the one true God. See the relevant chapter in *Letters to a Mormon Elder* (Minneapolis: Bethany House Publishers, 1993), 67–75.
10. In biblical terminology, the two terms are very closely related, and both refer to the unique relationship of Father and Son. "Firstborn" refers to preeminence and authority, while "only-begotten" is better rendered "unique," and likewise speaks to the special relationship between Father and Son. These terms are closely examined in my work on the Trinity, *The Forgotten Trinity*, (Minneapolis: Bethany House Publishers, 1998).
11. Brigham Young, *Journal of Discourses* 1:238, LDSCL.
12. Ibid., 11:268, LDSCL.

13. Heber C. Kimball, *Journal of Discourses* 8:211, LDSCL.

14. Orson Pratt, *The Seer*, 158.

15. James Talmage, CR1915Apr:121, LDSCL.

16. James Talmage, *Jesus the Christ*, 15th ed., rev. (Salt Lake City: The Church of Jesus Christ of Latter-day Saints, 1977), 21–22, LDSCL.

17. Ibid., 81. Heber J. Grant cited this same passage in the *Millennial Star* (January 5, 1922): 2, LDSCL, and said:

> We believe absolutely that Jesus Christ is the Son of God, begotten of God, the first-born in the spirit and the only-begotten in the flesh; that He is the Son of God just as much as you and I are the sons of our fathers.

18. Talmage, *Jesus the Christ*, 418–419, LDSCL.

19. Bruce R. McConkie, *Mormon Doctrine*, 2nd ed., rev. (Salt Lake City: Bookcraft, 1966), 546–547, LDSCL.

20. Ibid., 742, LDSCL.

21. Bruce R. McConkie, *The Promised Messiah* (Salt Lake City: Deseret Book, 1978), 467–469, LDSCL.

22. Ibid., 473.

23. Bruce R. McConkie, *The Mortal Messiah* (Salt Lake City: Deseret Book, 1979–1982), 1:319.

24. Bruce R. McConkie, *Doctrinal New Testament Commentary, Colossians–Revelation* (Salt Lake City: Bookcraft, 1973), 138, 141, LDSCL.

25. This pronouncement is found in many sources, including Talmage's *Jesus the Christ*. I am quoting from Appendix 4 of the *Encyclopedia of Mormonism*, Daniel H. Ludlow, ed. (New York: Macmillan Publishing, 1992), LDSCL.

26. Cited in Rulon T. Burton, *We Believe: Doctrines and Principles of the Church of Jesus Christ of Latter-day Saints* (Salt Lake City: Tabernacle Books, 1994), "God," LDSCL.

27. Ibid.

28. CR1967Oct:142, LDSCL.

29. CR1962Apr:108, LDSCL.

30. Joseph Fielding Smith, *Doctrines of Salvation*, Bruce R. McConkie, ed. (Salt Lake City: Bookcraft, 1954–1956), 1:18, LDSCL.

31. Ezra Taft Benson, *Teachings of Ezra Taft Benson* (Salt Lake City: Bookcraft, 1988), 7.

32. *Family Home Evenings* (Salt Lake City: The Church of Jesus Christ of Latter-day Saints, 1972), 125–126.

33. *Messages for Exaltation: Eternal Insights from the Book of Mormon* (Salt Lake City: Deseret Sunday School Union, 1967), 199. The title page reads, "For the Sunday Schools of the Church of Jesus Christ of Latter-day Saints, Gospel Doctrine Class."

34. Ibid., 378–379.

35. *Encyclopedia of Mormonism*, "Jesus Christ," LDSCL.

36. Ibid.

37. Ibid.

38. Letter written February 19, 1981.

Appendix

1. The article appears on pages 7 through 10.

2. Daniel Peterson and Stephen Ricks, *Offenders for a Word: How Anti-Mormons Play*

Word Games to Attack the Latter-day Saints (Salt Lake City: Aspen Books, 1992), 75–95.

3. Stephen Robinson, *Are Mormons Christians?* (Salt Lake City: Bookcraft, 1991), 60–65.

4. Craig L. Blomberg and Stephen E. Robinson, *How Wide the Divide?* (Downers Grove, Ill.: InterVarsity Press, 1997), 80–81, 208–209.

5. Robinson, 60, citing Irenaeus, *Against Heresies*, 4:38.

6. Joseph Fielding Smith, ed., *Teachings of the Prophet Joseph Smith* (Salt Lake City: Deseret Book Press, 1938), 345, LDSCL.

7. G. L. Prestige, *God in Patristic Thought* (London: SPCK, 1952), 74–75.

8. Ibid., 3.

9. *Teachings of the Prophet Joseph Smith*, 354.

10. Prestige, 3.

11. Prestige, 4–5.

12. J. N. D. Kelly, *Early Christian Doctrines* (San Francisco: Harper & Row, 1978), 83.

13. Irenaeus, *Against Heresies* 3:11;1, Sage Library CD-ROM, 882. Note that this quotation precedes the quotation given by Robinson.

14. Ibid., 3:4:2, Sage Library CD-ROM, 862–863.

15. Ibid., 4:38:4, Sage Library CD-ROM, 1077.

16. Ibid.

17. Ibid.

18. Ibid.

19. Ibid., 4:38:1, Sage Library CD-ROM, 1074.

20. See Stephen Robinson's statement on this in chapter 11.

21. Irenaeus, *Against Heresies* 4:38;2, Sage Library CD-ROM, 1075.

22. Ibid., 4:38:3, Sage Library CD-ROM, 1076.

23. Ibid., 4:38:4, Sage Library CD-ROM, 1076–1077.

24. *Ensign* (March 1988): 11.

25. Jaroslav Pelikan, *The Christian Tradition: A History of the Development of Doctrine*, vols. 1 & 2 (Chicago: The University of Chicago Press, 1971, 1974).

26. Ibid., 2:248.

27. Ibid., 2:267–268.

28. Ignatius, *Magnesians*, 8:1, Sage Library CD-ROM, 131.

29. Justin Martyr, *Dialogue with Trypho*, 124, Sage Library CD-ROM, 534.

30. Ibid., 5, Sage Library CD-ROM, 382–383.

31. Ibid., 11, Sage Library CD-ROM, 388.

32. Aristides of Athens, *Apology*, 1, Sage Library CD-ROM, 458–459.

33. Ibid., 4, Sage Library CD-ROM, 461.

34. Tatian, *Address to the Greeks*, 4, Sage Library CD-ROM, 132.

35. Ibid., 5, Sage Library CD-ROM, 133.

36. Athenagoras, *A Plea for the Christians*, 4, Sage Library CD-ROM, 260.

37. Ibid., 10, Sage Library CD-ROM, 265.

38. Irenaeus, *Against Heresies*, 1:22:1, Sage Library CD-ROM, 714.

39. Ibid., 2:34:2, Sage Library CD-ROM, 852.

40. Tertullian, *Apology*, 17, Sage Library CD-ROM, 57.

41. Tertullian, *Prescription Against Heretics*, 13, Sage Library CD-ROM, 465–466.

42. Tertullian, *Against Hermogenes*, 4, Sage Library CD-ROM, 882.

43. Tertullian, *Against Marcion*, 1:3, Sage Library CD-ROM, 511.

44. Novatian, *Concerning the Trinity*, 31, Sage Library CD-ROM, 1350.

45. Cyril of Jerusalem, *Catechetical Lectures*, 6:11, Sage Library CD-ROM, 170.
46. Ibid., 4:4–5, Sage Library CD-ROM, 144–145.
47. Hilary, *On the Trinity*, 2:6, Sage Library CD-ROM, 247.
48. Epiphanius, *Against All Heresies*, 70:5, in William Jurgens, *The Faith of the Early Fathers* (Collegeville, Minn.: Liturgical Press, 1979), 2:75.
49. Gregory Nazianus, *Second Oration on Easter*, 3, Sage Library CD-ROM, 817.
50. Augustine, *The True Religion*, 25:46, in William Jurgens, *The Faith of the Early Fathers*, 3:40.
51. Many LDS sources cite the doctoral dissertation of Keith Edward Norman (1980, Duke University) titled *Deification: The Content of Athanasian Soteriology*. Yet just a few selected citations from Norman support the thesis I have presented regarding the nature of divinization, and the concern of the early Fathers to safeguard the uniqueness of God:

"Adam, the first man, is thus the 'prototype of our divinization' " (p. 81); "Man was created in order to contemplate his Maker. The ideal picture of the archetypal Adam is that of one who (quoting) continuously contemplates by his purity the image of the Father, God the Word, in whose image he was made, and is filled with admiration when he grasps his providence toward the universe. He is superior to sensual things and all bodily impressions, and by the power of his mind clings to the divine and intelligible realities in heaven" (pp. 86–87); "In commenting on the Saviour's injunction to be perfect and merciful as God is (Matthew 5:48; Luke 6:36), he [Athanasius] is careful to caution that this appropriation of divine patterns does not mean that we become such as the Father is in essence, but in 'beneficent acts' (εὐεργεσίας)" (p. 113); "the *imago Dei* is not focused on man's physical being" (p. 140); "The explicit exhortation by Jesus to "be perfect" as the Father is, from Matthew 5:48, is linked by Athanasius to the parallel expression in Luke 6:36, to be merciful in the manner of God. This is not developed in the direction of Greek metaphysics; in fact, the anti-Arian context requires him to disavow any such essential ontological likeness. Rather, he correctly identifies the ethical content of the passage, and exhorts us to imitate God's beneficent acts, so that through us God may be glorified, rather than for us to seek the reward from men" (p. 158); "For Athanasius it was 'an admitted truth about God' that he is self-sufficient and complete in himself.

Furthermore, God is immaterial as well as incorporeal, invisible and untouchable, and has power over all the universe, being transcendent to it. This transcendence is especially emphasized in his doctrine of creation. In contrast to the divine Word, 'Men are composed of parts and created from nothing;' *their* word is composite and perishable" (p. 174); "Athanasius is careful to avoid applying human terminology to God as much as possible, and reproaches the Arians for speaking σωματικῶς about him. . . . By distinguishing clearly between the Divine and the human, Athanasius can accuse the Arians of Greek idolatry, since they speak of a divine being who is not equal to the Father. For Athanasius, 'there is nothing between God and creature which can be called divine' " (p. 175); "Although we can imitate godly virtues, 'we cannot become like God in essence,' he [Athanasius] insists, and he stresses the ontological disparity between man and God even when citing the standard proof texts for deification" (p. 179); "As regards nature, or οὐσία, the principle of Athanasian ontology is that 'we are creatures and other than God.' . . . As a corollary to the doctrine of creation *ex nihilo*, man cannot be divine by essence, but is something 'wholly other.' . . . But this theology throws into question the terminology of Athanasian soteriology, since 'the concept of a transcendental, absolutely omnipotent god, implying the utterly subordinate and creaturely character of the world created by him out of nothing' precluded any achievement of self-deification or mystical 'possession of god,' which might make room for pantheism. In fact, it is just such willfulness, which aimed to become 'equal to God' (on the basis of the unity invoked in John 17) which draws forth from Athanasius a curse upon the Arians as children of the devil for their 'unreasoning audacity' and reckless self-deceit" (pp. 183–184); "From the standpoint of Athanasius' ontology, the inescapable conclusion from the foregoing is that θεοποίησις is a contradiction in terms. Only the Son is God by nature, and if he deifies his followers by virtue of that Godhood, they cannot be essentially divine; they remain beings created 'out of nothing' and thus always subject, at least in principle, to change and corruption. It is in this context that Athanasius stressed our deification by "adoption" into sonship" (p. 190); "While the Son is ἀληθινὸς θεός, ὁμοούσιος with the Father, 'other beings to whom he said, 'I said ye are gods,' had this grace from the Father, only by participation. . . . ' It is the operation of grace which distinguishes us, the recipients, as sons, from the only-begotten Son by nature, the dispenser of that grace" (p. 197).

In conclusion, Norman notes, "[Athanasius'] constant emphasis on participation, or deification by grace as opposed to nature, safeguards against both polytheism on the one hand and pantheism on the other. The deified Christian is never equal to God in essence, and remains subordinate by nature, nor is one identified with God so as to lose his individual consciousness or activity. The difference, for Athanasius, between Christ and the Christian, is that what the Savior possesses (φύσει καὶ ἀληθείᾳ), the saved attains (θέσει καὶ χάριτι)," p. 206.

52. Athanasius, *Against the Heathen*, 6, Sage Library CD-ROM, 215.
53. Ibid., 3:45:4, Sage Library CD-ROM, 266.
54. Ibid., 3:47:2, Sage Library CD-ROM, 269.
55. Ibid., 3:39, Sage Library CD-ROM, 258–259.
56. Athanasius, *Against the Arians*, 3:39, Sage Library CD-ROM, 1022.
57. Athanasius, *On the Incarnation*, 54, Sage Library CD-ROM, 342.
58. Athanasius, *Four Discourses Against the Arians*, 3:17, Sage Library CD-ROM, 1005–1006.
59. Athanasius, *Defense of the Nicene Definition*, 3:10–11, Sage Library CD-ROM, 518.
60. Athanasius, *Ad Afros*, 7, Sage Library CD-ROM, 1176.

INDEX